# SOCIOLOGY

# THE BASICS

A lively, accessible and comprehensive introduction to the diverse ways of thinking about social life, *Sociology: The Basics* examines:

- The scope, history and purpose of sociology
- Ways of understanding 'the social'
- The state of the world we live in today
- Suffering and social inequalities
- Key tools for researching and thinking about the social
- The impact of new technologies.

The reader is encouraged to think critically about the structures, meanings, histories and cultures found in the rapidly changing world we live in. With tasks to stimulate the sociological mind and suggestions for further reading both within the text and on an accompanying web-page (http://www.routledge.com/books/details/9780415472067/), this book is essential reading for all those studying sociology, and those with an interest in how the modern world works.

**Ken Plummer** is Emeritus Professor of Sociology at the University of Essex, UK, and is internationally known for his research on sexualities and narrative. He is author of the best selling *Sociology: A Global Introduction* (with John Macionis, 5th edition, 2011).

# The Basics

# SOCIOLOGY
# **THE BASICS**

**Ken Plummer**

Routledge
Taylor & Francis Group

LONDON AND NEW YORK

First published in 2010
by Routledge

This edition published in 2010
by Routledge
2 Park Square, Milton Park, Abingdon, Oxon OX14 4RN

Simultaneously published in the USA and Canada
by Routledge
270 Madison Avenue, New York, NY 10016

*Routledge is an imprint of the Taylor & Francis Group, an informa business*

© 2010 Ken Plummer

Typeset in Aldus and Scala Sans by
HWA Text and Data Management, London

*British Library Cataloguing in Publication Data*
A catalogue record for this book is available from the British Library

*Library of Congress Cataloging-in-Publication Data*
Plummer, Kenneth.
  Sociology : the basics / Ken Plummer.
      p. cm. – (The basics)
  Includes bibliographical references and index.
  [etc.]
  1. Sociology. I. Title.
  HM585.P58 2010
  301–dc22                            2010001790

ISBN10: 0-415-47205-9 (hbk)
ISBN10: 0-415-47206-7 (pbk)
ISBN10: 0-203-84772-5 (ebk)

ISBN13: 978-0-415-47205-0 (hbk)
ISBN13: 978-0-415-47206-7 (pbk)
ISBN13: 978-0-203-84772-5 (ebk)

For all my students who taught me much

# CONTENTS

# ILLUSTRATIONS

## Figures

## Tables

# SOCIAL HAUNTINGS

So these are the hauntings of social things.
Attuning to people and drenched with their presence,
We do things together. We move with the other –
The living, the dead, the soon to arrive.
Sociality becoming the air that we breathe.
Our life's social worlds, so stuffed with the possible.
Proliferating multiples and things on the move.
Yet, here we all dwell in the rituals we make;
The pounding of patterns to engulf and entrap us.
These worlds not of our making that haunt till we die.
The tiniest things and the grandest of horrors.
Inhumanities of people and generations at war;
Gendered classed races, sexy nations disabled;
Excluding, exploiting, dehumanising the world.
The stratified hauntings of pain we endure.
Standing amazed at this chaos and complexity
We celebrate, critique and cry in our shame.
Our utopian dreamings of empowering lives.
Each generation more justice, a flourishing for all?
Sociology: the endless challenge for a better world.

# PREFACE

# WELCOME TO THE SOCIAL MAZE

Two roads diverged in a wood, and I took the one less travelled by
Robert Frost, 'The Road Not Taken', 1916

Welcome to the social maze. At the heart of this maze is a new way of thinking and imagining social life. We will start on eight journeys to a possible grasping of these new ways for thinking about human social worlds. Never mind if you do not arrive at the centre of the maze, I hope you will enjoy some of the journeys. On the first exploration, in Chapter 1, I want you to get a glimpse of what we are looking for – the domain of the social – and I give lots of examples. I will encourage you to become an 'outsider' and suggest that sociology can look at anything – anything that engages you (from sport to science to sex). The second journey will examine just what we mean by the social and how we can think about it. It will look at some of the images we create to think about social things. Chapter 3 will move us into the hurly-burly of teeming human life as it emerges across the world in the twenty-first century and looks at a few changes taking place in it. How can we possibly find ways of grasping this complexity? Our next puzzle (Chapter 4) will be to consider how sociology, the discipline designed to look at the social, developed in the Western world to deal with just this problem. Chapters 5 and 6 will then start to struggle with laying out some road maps for doing sociology – for thinking about theory and methods. I cannot give precise satnavs but will aim, from a vast literature on all this, to distil a few wisdoms that will help you orientate yourself to what sociologists try to do. The seventh pathway looks at a topic which haunts most of the other pathways – the human sufferings and inequalities we find along our way. It is just one key area of sociological investigation but one which most sociologists would agree is central. On my final journey (Chapter 8), I ask why we should bother with all this anyway. I ask: Why? What's the point of it all? What role does sociology have to play in the modern world? Each chapter is a pathway that can stand on its own and any one alone just might take you to the holy grail of sociology. ...

Like all books in this series, I am only looking at the basics of sociology. A short introductory book can hardly do justice to a complex and inexhaustible subject. I have had to be very selective for a reader who I assume knows nothing about the subject. My hope is that the little I can say in a short space will tempt you to expand your ways of thinking about the social and explore further the workings of the social in the world we live. Each chapter will end with some advice on going further (and each chapter will also provide boxes to help your thinking). There is a website (http://www.routledge.com/books/details/9780415472067/) organised by pages of the book giving you sources and leads to follow things up further. I do recommend you look at it. Finally, even a little book like this accrues a great many debts. Here I would just like to thank a small group for their support during the period in which I wrote this book. They are: Benedict Rogge, Daniel Nehring, Peter Nardi, Rob Stones, Harvey Molotch and Everard Longland. Of course, all of life's many companions shape all things that we do and I am grateful to have had some good companions on my life travels. So here I will also thank these too. Even though many have been long absent in my life, they have all left their mark.

Ken Plummer
Wivenhoe, January 2010

# IN A WORLD I NEVER MADE

Men make their own history, but they do not make it as they please;
they do not make it under self-selected circumstances, but under
circumstances existing already, given and transmitted from the
past. The tradition of all dead generations weighs like a nightmare
on the brains of the living.
Karl Marx, *The Eighteenth Brumaire of Louis Bonaparte*, 2000 [1851]

Bewitched, bothered and bewildered am I.
Richard Rodgers and Lorenz Hart, *Pal Joey*, 1940

At birth, we are – each one of us – hurled into a social world we
never ever made. We will have absolutely no say about which
country we are born into, who our parents and siblings may be,
what language we will initially speak, or what religion or education
we will be given. We will have no say about whether we are born
in Afghanistan, Algeria, Australia, Argentina – or one of several
hundred other countries in the world. We will have no say whether
we are born into nations – or families – considered super-rich or
in abject poverty. We will have no say whether our initial family is
Christian, Buddhist, Jewish, Muslim or any one of several thousand
other smaller religions found across the world. What is significant

here is that we are born into a world that pre-exists us and will continue after us. We are thrown into a social world that was quite simply not one we had any say in making. And it is this very world which sociologists study. Every day we confront social facts and social currents which 'come to each one of us from outside and ... sweep us along in spite of ourselves'.[1] We look at worlds we cannot wish away – worlds that await us and shape us, independently of whatever we may wish.

But then, very soon, most of us learn to find our own feet in this 'thrown into world'. Most significantly, we start to become aware of other people in this world (usually initially our dear – or not so dear – mothers, fathers and siblings): we start to become attuned to them. We learn how to please them and others; and indeed how to annoy them. We slowly start to imagine the worlds that they live in and how they may respond to us. Like it or not, we become increasingly socialised to act towards them, to develop a primitive empathy or sympathy towards others. If we do not – if we fail to learn this empathy – then we will not be able to communicate, we will not be able to routinely go about daily social life in any kind of satisfactory way. Sociology is also charged with studying this daily life of adjustment – how the billions of people who dwell on planet earth get through the day living with each other. How we adapt and conform, rebel and innovate, ritualise and withdraw. We look at the complicated relations between our bodies, our feelings and our ways of behaving with others in the living of everyday life so that social worlds can proceed in a fairly intelligible and orderly fashion most of the time. It will of course also be subject to serious conflict and breakdown, and sociology looks at this too.

What is fascinating about this everyday world is that we – that little child thrown into a strange but given world at birth – actually also make parts of it ourselves. It turns out that from the moment we are thrown into this constraining world at birth till the moment we die and it comes to a dramatic end, we are given an active energy

---

1  This is a reference to the sociologist Émile Durkheim. (Durkheim, 1982, pp. 52–3). There are no further footnotes or references in this book as they are hereafter provided page by page, often with links, on the web site that accompanies this book. See http://www.routledge. com/books/details/9780415472067/.

to keep going – to move through the world with a tremendous creative ability to act in it and on it. We little human animals are the creators of social life all the time: we are active agents who make social worlds. Socialised into it, we then make it work for us. And sociology studies this too: sociologists ask how people come to assemble their social lives and social worlds in radically different ways in different times and places. Whilst some of us can develop ways of being the active agents of their lives, many others have much less access to such skills. While no one is determined, we are not capable or knowledgeable actors in the world to the same degree. And here is a key problem for sociologists (we will return often to it).

## SOCIOLOGY AS CRITIQUE AND WONDER

The physicist looks at the skies and stands in amazement at the universe. The musician listens to Mozart, Beethoven or Stravinsky – or Abba – and stands in amazement at the magnificent works that little human beings can produce on earth. The sportsperson finds their adrenalin gushing at the thought of running or going to a football stadium. And the sociologist gets up every day and stands in wonder at the little social worlds – and indeed human societies – that we have created for ourselves: their meaning, order, conflict, chaos and change. For the sociologist, social life is sometimes sensed as something quite inspiring, and sometimes as something quite horrendous which brings about disenchantment, anger and despair. Sociologists stand in awe and dreading, rage and delight at the humanly produced social world with all its joys and its sufferings. We critique it and we critically celebrate it. Standing in amazement at the complex patterns of human social life, we examine both the good things worth fostering and bad things to strive to remove. Sociology becomes the systematic, sceptical study of all things social.

### THE DARK SIDE OF SOCIETY – THE MISERIES AND SUFFERINGS OF HUMAN SOCIAL LIFE

So here is the bad news. On a bad day I can hardly get out of my bed. The weight of the world and its suffering bears down upon me: the human misery, as it has confronted the billions before me. Luckily, I am not a depressive so I have my ways of getting up and springing into action. But lying there some mornings, I see the long historical march of humanity's inhumanities, the horrors of the world and the sufferings of humankind: and I squirm. How can it be, that for so long and with such seeming stupidity and blindness, human beings have continued ceaselessly to make human social worlds in which so very many suffer – that are so manifestly inhuman? Here is a world full of wars and tyranny, poverty and inequality, genocides and violence. Here is the horrendous treatment of other peoples different from us and the vast neglect and denial of the sufferings of others. All this seems to have been history's lot: they are just a few of the routine topics for sociology.

Sociologists just cannot stop seeing this suffering. Everywhere it seems societies cast 'others' into the roles of enemies and monsters – creating hierarchies of 'the good' to value and 'the bad' to dehumanise. It was after all human beings that designed slavery for much of history – a system that still exists (upwards of 27 million are in forced labour, child labour and sexual slavery today). It was human beings that set up the mass slaughtering of witchcraft trials and religious Inquisitions (deaths caused by the Spanish Inquisition starting in the late fifteenth century vary from 3 million – considered absurdly high – to 3,000 – which over a three hundred year period seems absurdly low!). It was also human activity – apparently supported by gods – which created the 'caste' system of social stratification (see Chapter 7), as Ayrian-speaking people moved into India around 1500 BCE; and a group of people called the untouchables, falling outside of regular human life, were left with all the dirty jobs. It is all a history of kings, rulers and popery dominating in splendour over the vast immiserated masses. There has been no period free from wars – over land, status, wealth and religion – and by all accounts the twentieth century was the bloodiest century of all: with its genocides, world wars, revolutionary mass slaughters, its 'fascisms' and its 'communisms'. There is controversy over how to count the number of actual 'mega-deaths' – but somewhere between 180 million and 200 million is a number often cited. That is to say that probably one in ten of the population of the world of 1900 were slaughtered through war or genocide in the twentieth century. And the widespread problems of poverty, hunger and disease throughout time have only been marginally diminished in the current time. To all this must now be added the growing awareness of global warming and a potential ecological catastrophe before too long. We humans do not seem to have made a very good job of living together peacefully, happily and productively. All this is the stuff of great literature, poetry and film making – and sociology.

Sociology, then, generates concern at the billions of wasted and damaged lives engulfed by 'man's inhumanity to man'. Sociologists are interested in the social conditions which can produce human social suffering. They are concerned with the ways in which private and individual sufferings have major social and structural origins. Personal problems are public issues. Given this, many say that sociology is the dismal science – a dark, bleak, pessimistic discipline. Don't hang around with sociologists, they say, because the trade of sociologists makes them pretty gloomy people.

## ALWAYS LOOK ON THE BRIGHT SIDE OF LIFE: THE JOYS AND POTENTIALS OF HUMAN SOCIAL LIFE

Indeed, all this may have been enough to make you put this book down. But hold on. Is it really all such bad news? Critical we are. But at the same time, we cannot stop seeing how – most of the time – people in societies also go about their daily rounds working with each other, caring for each other, loving each other and much of the time in ease and cooperation.

A few years ago, as I lay in my modern hospital bed shortly after ten hours of major life-saving surgery, I pondered just how all this had come to be. My life-threatening illness – chronic liver cirrhosis – had killed millions of people throughout history; but over the past fifty years or so, the invention of transplant surgery through modern science had come to save thousands of lives. A life threatening illness had been tamed. But it was so much more than this. Here I was in a modern hospital – a hugely expensive bureaucracy employing thousands of workers in thousands of different ways in a massive division of labour in order to save my life and the lives of thousands of others. All around me I could see social acts of great learned skill and scientific knowledge, myriad social acts of

humane and loving care, multiple social acts of practical activity –
cleaning the floors, pushing trolleys with patients, providing food,
keeping the plumbing going, welcoming the outpatients, organising
beds, orchestrating a million little daily routines. This was no small
human *and social* endeavour. How had this come to be? As I lay there
I celebrated the wonder of human social organisation and the way
it had fashioned this whole experience. I pondered – in a flash – the
history of hospitals, the training of doctors and nurses from all over
the world, the social meanings of caring for others, the generosity
and altruism of many people, the skills of surgeons passed on
from generation to generation, the daily organisation of timetables
and roles – for nurses, doctors, porters, ambulance drivers, social
workers, pharmacists, phlebotomists, physiotherapists, transplant
co-ordinators, volunteers, administrators, ward managers and the
rest. I pondered indeed my own social timetable on the ward and
my daily encounters with a myriad of health professions, a string
of rituals from x-ray to medication. And I thought: this is what
sociologists want to understand. Just how did this all come together?
Just how does this work? And all of this so I – and all the others –
could live?

Yet this is just one of hundreds of stories I could tell of my
sociological amazement over many years. There are the marvels of
a post-modern world, of massive human creativity and imagination.
Of science, medicine, art, music: the clothes we fashion, the food we
create, the music we delight in, the knowledge we have accumulated
over the millennia – the museums and libraries, the technologies
that get people on to the moon and allow them to speak to people
all over the world. It goes on and on. Sociologists also look in sheer
wonder at human social world making, at the ways in which we
solve problems, do daily life, and often treat each other with care,
respect, kindness and love. And all in a sort of orderly way. We look
at the social organisation of everyday living – and the fortunate and
fulfilled lives, even the privileged lives that some lead. And we ask
about the social conditions under which the good, humane and
happy social life can be lived?

## THE GOOD NEWS AND THE BAD NEWS

Sociologists then are Janus-faced. In one direction we look for the problems and suffering and are highly critical. In the other direction, we look for the joys and humanity of the social world, and are (cautious and critically) celebratory. This has been a long time problem in the thinking about society. It is found for instance quite strikingly in the enlightenment philosopher Voltaire's famous satire *Candide* (1759). Here the hero follows his teacher Dr Pangloss's philosophy that 'everything is for the best in the best of all possible worlds' (the Panglossian philosophy), only to encounter everywhere he travels the horrors of rape, bestiality, exploitation, murder, war and catastrophe. Concluding, he is led to say that this is not the best of all possible worlds, but we do make our own lives. We had better, he says, cultivate our own gardens. And here we may find some happiness in the world.

### THINK ON: TRAVELLING IN THE AIR

I am waiting for a plane at a major international airport, and I stand in awe at what this is all about. How did it come to be that millions of *homo sapiens* can now travel daily across the globe in the air? This was not really possible even a hundred years ago? And I ponder the sheer complexity of this social action? From millions of little individual lives decisions are made to get from A to B (say Buenos Aires to Cairo, but anywhere). Phone calls are made, web sites are searched and tour operators are brought in. A massive worldwide system of booking involving thousands of business operations is brought into play. This is human endeavour at a manifestly global level. Bookings are made. Arrivals and departures are fixed. And airport terminals reached – here are huge complex enterprises where it would seem possible for so much to go wrong: queuing, ticketing, baggaging, passporting, security, boardings, take off, landings. In 2006, there were some 4.4 billion passengers across the world. At Heathrow, London, alone some 68 million people moved through it. (Atlanta is the world's busiest with 85 million passengers per year). Here are amazingly complex timetables in place – in major international airports, planes take off and land every few seconds! And these places – spaces – are now built as huge cathedrals of consumption, as places where you do not just want to fly, but somehow need to buy a wide bunch of expensive commodities. I have often pondered why nearly all major airports have a fascinating bar where caviar, smoked salmon, sea food and champagne is served (it is the last thing I fancy before going up into the air: is it status food for the wealthy?). But there must be a demand for this. Airports are fascinating objects of study: they are communities, shopping malls and places of work. They show massive divisions of labour, multiple complex social encounters, the social organisation of spaces. There are sign systems that need to be understood, practical activities to be done, architecture to be tacitly understood. It is a world of markets, communication, conflicts, change and above all social order. And with it, there is a whole 'underworld' of airports that we know little about but which we sometimes read about. And we haven't even got up into the air yet.

Once we take off, a whole series of other wonders come into play. Who could have imagined 200 years ago that we would invent large metal cans to house some 600 people which can then fly in the air across space at nearly 1000 kilometres an hour. And even more than that: in these cans we would be served hot meals (vegetarian low cholesterol fusion Thai would be my meal of choice), play computer games and a have the choice of some 200 DVDs to watch, along with seemingly endless music to listen to from a variety of playlists? (Heaven forbid that we should be bored in our eight-hour trip across thousands of miles). A whole world of autopilots, airport mechanics, ground staff and of course flight attendants come into play. And finally I ponder what this means to the millions of individual lives and pathways criss-crossing round the world to meet business appointments and loved ones? To watch the faces at the arrival gates tells a lot. The ending of the Richard Curtis film *Love Actually* (2003) shows the arrival gate of Heathrow and the screen slowly opens up to show hundreds of expectant faces meeting and greeting each other from their travels. Here indeed is a social structure at work – thousands of people doing things together in patterned ways – making social order at airports, making society work.

But hold on you rightly say: there is also very bad news here too. Most of the world's population have never been near a plane or an airport – suggesting a massive inequality of the world. And much can go wrong, technology is running amok, the environment is being damaged and planes can crash. After all, there were four planes hijacked and no survivors in the attacks by al-Qaeda on the Twin Towers of the World Trade Center and the Pentagon on September 11, 2001. Some 3,000 victims (and 19 terrorist hijackers) were killed and this has set up a train of horrific events that are shaping the course of the twenty first century.

For more on all this, see John Urry, *Mobilities* (2007) Chapter 7 'Flying Around'.

One more example must suffice and it is a much more general one. Although sociologists see and write about terrible things in the world, I have long been impressed – in literature and life – at the myriad little ways in which people construct their own little social worlds and go about their everyday lives, wherever they can, not being too nasty or disruptive to other people, and very often being kind to their neighbours and friends. Yes, we know there is conflict, there are bad neighbours, and according to some sociologists, the decline of community. But there are also the ubiquitous little worlds of human care, kindness and sensitivity to others. If you look at much great literature, you will certainly find tragedy and drama, hatred and jealousy. But you will also frequently find a celebration of ordinary people going about their ordinary lives. George Elliot's nineteenth-century novel *Middlemarch* is a marvellous example. Generally considered to be one of the world's greatest novels, it tells the story of industrialisation and change coming to a small nineteenth-century community, with all the class and gender divisions you would expect to find. But it also tells the story of everyday heroism, of people getting on with their lives, sometimes looking after others, sometimes doing altruistic acts – and all the little personal foibles this generates. This is the social organisation of everyday life, it is everywhere and it is truly astounding. Sociologists thus also study the little acts of everyday life, how people care for each other – and indeed love each other. There is then a sociology of everyday life, a sociology of care – as well as a sociology of play and a sociology of love.

## A SOCIOLOGY OF EVERY DAMNED THING

So in the end, it seems, sociology can study anything and everything – both the big things and the little things. Traditionally it is studied through a series of key institutions such as religion, education and the economy. Look at any school or college textbook on sociology (a good way to get the sense of the taken for granted in a field of study) and you will find chapters on social things like the family, the government and the workplace. But sociology actually studies a lot more: its range is the whole of social life. Since everything that human beings do involves social things, everything and anything can be analysed sociologically.

This certainly means it clearly studies all the *big* issues of social life – terrorism, environmental catastrophe, the new information technologies, the drug trade and migration. But it also means that sociologists can be interested in absolutely anything at all, including all the little things of everyday life. So here is a quick alphabet of a few topics. There is a sociology of Australia, a sociology of the body, a sociology of consumption, a sociology of drugs and deviance. There are sociologies of education, of food and football, of global things, of horror films. Sociologists study Ireland and Italy, Jamaica and Johannesburg. They investigate the sociology of knowledge, love, music and norms. They study oriental despotism, patriarchy, queer politics, rape, suicide, transgender, the upper classes and urban life, voting behaviour, welfare, X-treme sports, youth and zero-tolerance policies. There can indeed be a sociological approach to any damn thing you can think of – even the most unlikely sounding subjects. If it involves people coming together socially, then it can be studied sociologically. Wherever there are social things, sociologists can study them. This means that sometimes sociology is mocked as a rather wild and silly discipline – because it can study the most seemingly ridiculous things, and seem to be trivial in the extremes. I hope to show you that this itself is a very silly view. Sociologists study all that is social in human life and that means everything.

## SO IS SOCIOLOGY SILLY? THE THREE 'T'S.

Let me give three of these seemingly 'silly' examples quickly. I will call them the three T's: the sociology of tomatoes, the sociology of toilets and the sociology of telephones – the 'tomatoes, toilets and telephones' problem! Now you may laugh: and at first sight some might say this is typical and just what gives sociology a bad name. A sociology of tomatoes, or a sociology of toilets indeed? Think on. Here are their concerns.

What does *a sociology of tomatoes* look like? I have one colleague who has – for many years now – specialised in the sociology of tomatoes. He is a professor and he runs a research centre at a major university. He is a very serious man, and if you get him talking about tomatoes he will not stop. Why? He can trace the history of tomatoes – from the earliest Aztec salsa through to the famous Heinz Ketchup bottle and on to the latest fashionable pizza and bloody Mary cocktail. He can show how the tomato has been continually transformed in the ways it has been produced, exchanged and consumed. He looks at its role in recent capitalist societies and shows how 'it' was an early pioneer in mass production and a contemporary contributor to the creation of global cuisines. And these days it has become even more interesting as the variety or tomatoes found in our supermarkets become simultaneously more and more standardised and yet of a much wider range than people could have ever bought before. How can we get such standardisation and yet such diversity at the same time – and often just round the corner? How has capitalism organised the tomato? How the world has changed. Just go to the tomatoes and have a look next time you are in a supermarket. What is the chain of people that got the tomatoes there? Why are they in this form? Who is buying them and who is making money out of them? And before you know it, you are discussing the historical nature of the global economic system under capitalism. And we haven't even started to discuss genetic modification and the environmental issues.

OK, but toilets? What can a *sociology of toilets* possibly be about? Well, I have another colleague, Harvey Molotch, a dear friend as it happens, and a world leader in 'urban sociology', who in recent years has taken to studying what he calls 'stuff'. He looks at all the social things we use daily – from toasters to chairs and asks questions about their social history (where did they come from), their social appearance (why do they come to look like they do) and how they are they used in everyday life. Our worlds are cluttered with objects – you could make a quick list of the things surrounding you right now, from computers to pens to books to mobile phones and so on. These are all social objects and they all have a sociology. Well a few years back, he got interested in toilets (and jokingly, he and his colleagues call it 'shit studies'). Now surely I can't be serious: a sociology of toilets? Shit studies? Again, think on.

Toilets raise a major spectrum of issues. Over the past century, they have become basic to our modern world (which reader does not use one?). And yet the flush toilet (WC) is recognised globally as an icon of modernity – an emblem of wealth. For an estimated 40 per cent of the world's population lives without one. Over two and a half billion people urinate and defecate in open spaces – in fields, mud, forests, bushes. Think alone of the smell and sights: but also of the environmental degradation. And the consequences for health? The lack of sanitation breeds diseases. When we socially reorganise sanitation, we change the smells, sights and health of a society. So a sociology of toilets raises the big issues of *health and modernity*: how did changes in sanitation in the nineteenth century prove to be a decisive factor in changing health and morbidity levels? And of *social inequalities* today – who in the world get the 'decent' toilets, even luxury bathrooms; and how do the poor so often dwell in such appalling sanitary conditions today ?

But now move to the more mundane level of everyday life. Spend a week observing your behaviour and those of others in toilets: look for the tacit and overt social rules that organise your behaviour, and also the little social rituals you have developed. These things have been studied by sociologists to suggest ways in which our everyday lives are regulated by fine systems of rules and rituals, many of which we hardly notice. Think about the long queues often found for women's toilets; think generally about the gender differences – men rarely talk in toilets, women often do. Think about the adjustment of dress and the comportment of body. Maybe watch Paromita Vohra's documentary film *Q2P* (see this book's website for details; this documentary can also be found on YouTube). Set in Mumbai, it looks at who has to queue to pee and shows how gender and class inequalities are revealed through toilets. Sometimes, too, sociologists look into the so called deviant patterns – where rules are broken. In one remarkable classic and controversial sociological study *Tea Room Trade*, the sociologist Laud Humphreys (1930–1988) showed how toilets could be used by heterosexual men for homosexual pickups with routine users remaining unaware of the homosexual activities that were taking place.

Finally, consider *a sociology of telephones*? Probably no means of communication has revolutionised the daily lives of ordinary people more than the telephone. Invented around 1876, it diffused gradually from a few thousand elite users to a widespread way of communicating across the social classes and the world. By 2007, there were over three billion mobile phone subscriptions, and in low-income societies where most could not even think of using landlines, hundreds of millions of people now have their own mobile numbers. For most of human history, communication had been face-to-face. Now human interactions started to be more and more mediated by technologies – shifting who we could speak to, when we could speak to them and indeed where we could speak to them. In the short space of about ten years, the mobile phone revolutionised everyday life – putting people in perpetual contact and making it possible to communicate with anybody, anywhere, anytime, anyplace. Centuries of past social worlds were radically broken down as time and space was re-ordered. And here is the rise of a new mobile youth culture – anticipating a future world. The young lead here and it is hard to imagine them giving up their mobile phones in a future world. They will probably just become more and more refined. Phones are also speeding up the changes in language. Languages – a key area of interest for sociologists – are always changing, but 'mobiles' have stepped up this process of change as texting becomes commonplace. There is a lot to be said on phones, and indeed sociologists have written many books on it.

## SUMMARY

Sociology is the systematic, sceptical and critical study of the social. It investigates the human construction of social worlds. It can study anything from the big issues (like war and poverty) to the smaller things (like tomatoes, toilets and telephones) and can be both critical and celebratory. We are born into a world we never made, but one in which we then act and change. Sociologists adopt an outsider stance. Once encountered, the world will never be seen in quite the same way again.

### THINK ON: PERPETUAL PUZZLEMENT – THE SOCIOLOGIST AS STRANGER AND OUTSIDER

The sociologist is often seen as a kind of outsider. Entering the human social worlds of others, it should be clear that all sociological thinking has – at least momentarily – to feel challenged by the differences of others. *People – in other countries, groups and times – are different from you.* But in order to truly see this, there needs to be a temporary abandonment of your own taken for granted view of the world and a call for empathy to the world view of others. You need to suspend your own world and for a while hold back on all judgments. At this most basic level, there are some sociologists who conduct 'breaching experiments' making strange our everyday life experiences. They invite students for example to question everything that is said to them: to ask and probe every convention of the daily round. A friend says 'how are you'? They ask back: 'what do you mean by that'? They go to shop and barter over the price of goods (in many cultures, this is the norm; but it is not so in the UK or North America). They move their face right up to the face of the person they are speaking to, even almost rubbing noses. They sit with friends and question everything that is said. A bit like 'candid camera' these little experiments in breaking the routine soon show how much our society depends on trust, kindness and understanding each other.

This leads us to one of sociology's key problems: the need to challenge *ethnocentrism* and the closely linked issue of egocentrism. These are stances that put our own 'taken for granted' ways of thinking at the centre of the social world, as if we are always right and know *the* truth. Ethnocentrism assumes that our culture (our *ethno* – way of life) is at the centre of the world; whereas egocentrism assumes that the world revolves around us. We need to purge ourselves from their influence. Sociology demands as a pre-requisite that we get rid of this self-centred view of the world and that we – as the contemporary and influential sociologist Zygmunt Bauman puts it – *defamiliarise ourselves with the familiar*. It stresses the need to always see the differences (and value) of other lives and cultures; and indeed the value of the differences of other standpoints. At its strongest, it absolutely forbids us to pronounce on other's worlds and instead to take them seriously on their own terms. It makes us humble in the face of the world's differences.

To take the simplest example of this in everyday life: you are going on a holiday to a country you do not know. You are the stranger. Now you can of course just go to another culture and trample on it: assume your own culture is best and not bother with what you find there. You would become one of those ignorant, crass holidaymakers that are an embarrassment to everyone! You would speak only in your own language; not bother to learn any of the new customs expected of everyone; and take little interest in what is going on that makes that culture historically different – its politics, its religion, its family life. Worst of all, you will probably extol the virtues of your own country – when you face different foods, different ways of queuing, different modes of talking to each other. You will be, in short, a narrow-minded, uncouth holidaymaker abroad.

But if you are at all sensitive, then travelling can be very difficult. You often come to feel a complete fool, as you stumble against a language you cannot speak and customs, mores and folkways you do not understand. I know that I sometimes feel like a very young child when I cannot even say, 'Excuse me', or 'where is this or that?' in the host language. Or simply when I want to ask for a cup of coffee and cannot express myself. What a bumbling, incompetent fool I am? How can they – why should they – bother with me? People are usually kind and they try to help. But without a basic knowledge of a culture's language it is hard to move around easily in it. And it goes much further than that. The meanings of cultures lie deep: the meaning of the garden in Japan, the bullfight in Spain, the veil in Iran. (Kate Fox's *Watching the English* (2005) is a field study of the English which gets at the taken for granted oddities of English culture).

Here is the social as outsider not insider: of people who do not belong, who dwell on the margins, who are deviants, strangers and outsiders. The social is defined not just by who belongs, but by who does not. Often it is best studied and analysed *not* through the eyes of the people who belong and are in it – but rather through the eyes of those outside. It is only the outsider who can see what is truly taken for granted. Hence sociology takes seriously the voices and eyes of immigrants, the strangers in town, the outsiders and the marginal. Sociology looks at the 'invisible man', the alienated young, the disenfranchised, the gothic and the queer.

## EXPLORING FURTHER

MORE THINKING

Think of a few areas of social life that interest you – dance, dress, dogs, democracy, drugs or drink for example – and start to build a diary or blog on which you build up a sociological analysis of it. By the end of reading this book, you should be starting to think sociologically and will have produced your first own small-scale sociological study. Perhaps start by linking the closing discussion of ethnocentrism and egocentrism and inspecting your own assumptions. Ponder whether you can suspend belief in them – at least for a while? As you read each chapter of this book, build up a few more observations, a little collection of relevant links and maybe some key words. Note that words in **bold** throughout the text are gathered together in a glossary at the end of the book and are key words to understand.

FURTHER READING

Textbooks are often a good way to sense the range of topics covered and get a feel for a discipline. There are many texts: possibly try Anthony Giddens, *Sociology* (currently in its sixth edition, 2009); John Fulcher and John Scott, *Sociology* (currently in its third edition, 2007) or my own, John Macionis and Ken Plummer, *Sociology: A Global Introduction* (in its fifth edition, 2011). Useful collections of readings can be found in Ken Plummer and Daniel Nehring, *Sociology: The Readings* (2011). The classic introductions to sociology are: Peter Berger, *Invitation to Sociology* (1966), Norbert Elias, *What is Sociology?* (1978) and Zygmunt Bauman, *Thinking Sociologically* (second edition with Tim May, 2001). Lively, more recent additions to these introductions include Ben Agger's *The Virtual Self* (2004), Richard Jenkins' *Foundations of Sociology* (2002) and Charles Lemert's *Social Things* (4th edition, 2008). Berger's book turned me on to sociology in the 1960s, and Lemert's book is the 'classic' of today. On tomatoes, telephones and tomatoes, see Mark Harvey, *Exploring the Tomato* (2002); Manuel Castells, *The Rise of the Network Society* (1996) and Harvey Molotch and Laura Noren, *Toilet* (2010).

2

# THINKING THE SOCIAL

Society is not a mere sum of individuals. Rather, the system formed by their association represents a specific reality which has its own characteristic ... The group thinks, feels, and acts quite differently from the way in which its members would were they isolated
Émile Durkheim, *The Rules of Sociological Method*, 1895

No one is alone.
Stephen Sondheim, *Into the Woods*, 1986

So what is this thing called 'the social' which sociologists study? This is the place to start. Many people prefer to view human life as biological, individual, economic or religious; but for sociologists, the starting point is always with the social. This is an idea with several meanings – indeed when I first came to study it forty odd years ago as an exuberant young man, I naively knew three others words that connected strongly to it: *social* partying, *social* work, and *social*ism. At that time, I liked all three and thought it had to be a good subject to study! But I soon learnt it was oh so much more than that.

## WHAT IS THE SOCIAL?

What I hope to get clear is that sociology studies a distinctive reality of life. The ideas of both 'social' and 'society' derive from the Latin *socius*, which originally meant friend or companion. This suggests both an active companionship and friendship. Ideas of the 'social' were developed in the nineteenth century to mean, more and more, a cluster of human associations and communities that mediate human experience; family, village, parish, town, voluntary association and class. They often indicated associations of people coming together for friendly purposes (as in the friendly societies, self help and trade unions). Since then, the idea of 'society' has grown to become a central idea for sociologists – highlighted, even constructed, by them, as they made it their object of study. The social comes to capture the idea of people functioning together in associations outside of the workings of the state (what is now often called 'civic society').

### SOCIAL FACTS/ DOING THINGS TOGETHER

Simply put, these days 'the social' has two meanings: it can depict a reality that comes to exist independently on its own (*sui generis*), or as a reality of interactions and communications between people. The view that the social has a life of its own was famously claimed by the much celebrated founding French sociologist Émile Durkheim (1858–1917). For him, society stood uniquely as a collective reality over and above any individual. In a way it works like a crowd: society comes to have a life of its own and we get coerced to behave in certain ways through it. Sociologists hence study this social as a fact external to individuals which constrains us. (These are often famously called **'social facts'**).[1]

By contrast, another influential early sociologist, Georg Simmel (1858–1918), had a different view seeing the social as embedded in relations and interactions. He claimed that 'society is merely … a constellation of individuals who are the actual realities'. For him, communicating with others in the same species became a distinctive **social form** of life (the human species could have been unsocial).

---

1   Words in bold can be found in the glossary at the end of the book, and developed more on the web site.

The social is human interaction and it is the study of this interaction which is at the heart of sociology.

More recently, a leading contemporary sociologist, Howard S. Becker (1928–) suggested that sociology means studying people 'doing things together'. The social is a relationship and we ask about the ways in which we connect to each other: how do we live with each other, and how might we survive without others (sometimes called 'the Robinson Crusoe problem' after the famous novel by Daniel Defoe)? We ask how a society is possible and how human beings can come to live together. As another leading early sociologist Max Weber (1864–1920) (see website) asked: how do we come to 'take into account the behaviour of others?' Social beings cannot survive and meet their needs other than through social co-operation and association. In this sense the social lives in our imaginations as we come to live through the minds of the others (a process which sociologists sometimes call role taking and the **inter-subjective**). How then might this happen?

## ACQUIRING THE SOCIAL: SOCIALISATION AND THE SELF

A newly born baby, full of bodily desires, is a very human animal – but it is not a very social one. As every good parent across the world knows, it takes a while to train a baby and to help to make it properly social. This process – early or primary **socialisation** – is done very differently across different cultures and across histories: children are raised by wet nurses, nannies, in communes and large families, by single parents, residential homes and so on. There is much diversity in child-rearing habits, and much research which charts how children come to construct their language, their sense of self and their social habits – for good or bad. What seems clear is that if they are left on their own, without the formative impacts of other people, then they will simply not develop. Many studies of feral children left living in isolation and then discovered later show that they simply cannot then function as social beings. (Instances can be found on the web site *Feral Children*).

One of the commonest controversies raised in social science is that of the so called 'nature–nurture' debate: do we become who we are because of our biology (genes and the like); or do we become who we are because of our upbringing and wider environmental factors? After a century and a half of endless dispute, this now seems to be a false debate (even though many prolong it). *Both* environment *and* genes play significant roles in the shaping of human lives. It is true that different researchers and disciplines will inevitably emphasise different aspects; but most will now agree that the interaction between the two is a crucial matter. *There are always evolutionary pushes and specific biological and genetic influences at the same time as there are always also specific historical and cultural shapers.* In this book about sociology, it is these social shapers that take pride of place and they are often overlooked.

## AWARENESS OF OTHERS: THE SELF AND INTERACTION

One core idea here is that of the developing human **self** – an idea profoundly shaped by the ideas of the psychologist William James (1842–1910), the sociologist Charles Horton Cooley (1864–1929), the philosopher George Herbert Mead (1863–1931) and the sociologists now commonly known as **symbolic interactionists**. There is a very long intellectual tradition of examining the self – its character, its sources, its changes and the role it plays in creating social orders and making our human natures coherent. The self asks who we are in social action, and serves to create a necessary bridge between the truly unique person and the more general social being. Having some sense of self and self awareness helps us to evolve more as coherent, even flourishing, social people.

This self suggests that the ways we communicate socially – through and with other people across life – lies at the core of our beings. But we have to learn it from our earliest childhood experience. It starts when the baby begins to realise there is something beyond its own world of instinctual gratification, as it comes to recognise and identify with the faces and hands around it (on which it depends). Bit by bit it moves from a pulsating little bundle of egocentric desires towards the recognition of others and ultimately a much wider social world. The early stages of this self may simply happen when the child responds mechanically to others; but gradually the child comes to identify with parents and ultimately to broaden and create a wider sense of others – friends, communities, societies. Mead talks about this as moving through various phases – imitation, playing the roles of others, acquiring a sense of others to play games, and ultimately a much wider sense of community: the generalised others. In Mead's work, we have a key early account of the core dynamics of how we become social. We can use the analogy of learning a sport or a game of chess – think how they require taking the role of others to play adequately: all our interactions in social life are like this. Failure to take the roles of others adequately is a major source of social breakdown.

The idea of self suggests an inner being (often called an 'I') who is engaged in a constant dialogue with an outer world of expectations (sometimes called the 'Me'). This is a process in which we are ceaselessly having a conversation with ourselves and others, and through which we are struggling to understand who we are and to make sense of our lives and worlds. This conversation depends on the prior existence of the social and communication bonds. To do this, we are always connecting, even balancing, our inner resources given to us in our bodies and emotions (partly genetic) with those we find all around us in other people – near and far – whose significance helps give meaning to our lives. We are never alone with a self. Who we are is always being reflected back to us – like a mirror image – by other people, and we come to dwell in the mind of others. We weave mirror-like webs of communications – flows of **semiotics** (symbols, signs) – where others are always shaping our next moves. In this sense then socialisation continues from birth to death and is a life-long process. (Sociologists often refer to this as adult socialisation and secondary socialisation). What matters here is that we come to live in the thoughts of imagined others even when we are unaware of this, and our social lives are constantly being shaped by this. The self is reflective and reflexive and tries to make sense of social life in a perpetual conversation with itself.

These others can be initially seen as a kind of continuum which spans the following:

| Individuals | Self/ interaction | Groups/ organisations | Society/ state | World/ global |
|---|---|---|---|---|
| *Micro* | | *Meso* | | *Macro* |

*Figure 2.1*  A continuum of the social

Sociology studies all this. We can approach these social others from the smallest units (micro) of individuals and selves to the largest (macro) of society and world, through a range of middling units of groups and organisations (often called the meso). This gives us three different kinds of sociology. Micro-sociology looks at social actions, face to face interactions and contexts – examining how people make sense of the worlds they live in. Macro-sociology looks at whole societies, often comparing features of social structures (or stable patterns) and key social institutions (or organised habits) like the economy or education. Meso-sociology looks at the patterns that connect them – the interactions in organisations like work places, schools or hospitals.

Any aspect of life can be analysed through these levels. Take for instance the issue of crime. Looking at the *micro level*, a key concern is the way in which much crime is learned conduct – we pick up 'deviant' patterns of behaviour from the groups we hang around with or through being with in situations which offer opportunities for crimes. Situations, stresses, and social group learning become key tools for understanding law breaking and other 'deviances'. Sociologists are not especially interested in crimes as purely individual – as biological (bad seeds, criminal types, criminal genes) or as personality types (psychopaths, sick people, and dangerous people). Rather, their interest lies in group learning and the ways in which deviant selves are acquired. They also focus on the *interactional*, how does a crime actually take place in a situation. How does a gang member pull a knife in a particular situation? How do delinquents see society and each other? What kind of situation allows some people to think it is OK to fraud on their taxes? What surrounds acts of theft, rape, homicide, drunken driving, drug taking, terrorism that facilitates their happenings? How do people come to see themselves in this situation and what stories and language might they bring to it they help it move the way it does.

Moving on to the *meso level*, sociologists take an interest in the ways in which police, courts and prisons function as huge bureaucracies – and the ways in which people get processed through them. At the wider, *macro* or *structural level*, the focus turns to the way in which crime is bound up the normal conditions of social life. There is a definite pattern to it and it is found in all societies. Patterns can soon be detected: look at criminal statistics and you will soon sense that crimes are not random: overwhelmingly they are usually committed by young men – and often from lower class and ethnic backgrounds. How is this so – or is it even true? Maybe the statistics measure something else – the making of statistics as social acts themselves? We can also ask questions about the institutions of law, policing, prisons and the like which are organised and structured in varying ways across time and history; and we can ask how they play a role in shaping crime – maybe preventing it, maybe structuring crime itself? At an even wider level we have the global. Here we look at the different rates of crime across societies – why is crime very low in traditional Muslim countries, or in Japan, and in the Western world, in Switzerland – and why does it soar in others? How does it take on increasingly global form like trafficking, smuggling, money laundering, and the drug trade?

Sociology then examines all things social – the wide range of connections that people make with each other. It encourages a way of thinking that sees that the air we breathe as social: 'the social' is everywhere. We are always linked to others, so the wider whole is always greater than the part. Typically, *we search for underlying patterns in these relations, examine the meanings that people give to their lives in cultures, and see all of this as flowing in a constant and perpetual stream of social actions.* There is no such thing as an isolated individual: in John Donne's famous poem 'No man is an island'. Even the most seemingly natural things – like our individualities, our bodies, our feelings, our senses – change enormously under different social situations. This is probably *not* how most people routinely see their daily world.

The largest unit of the social is often seen to be '**society**'. All societies – old or new, big or small – have to organise resources to live – food, shelter, clothing, things, 'capital'. They have to keep some level of order with each other – if everybody just did their own thing, chaos and breakdown would probably ensue. Certainly, conflicts need to be managed. Further because human animals, above all other animals, have developed elaborate languages and ways of talking, they need to organise both their beliefs and their ways of communicating with each other. And finally, they have to pass this on and reproduce their society from one generation to the next or they might die off. In short, all societies need (a) economies,

(b) political and legal systems – governance, (c) cultures, beliefs and communication, as well as (d) mechanisms of socialisation. These are the building blocks of all social organisation. Such concerns will keep reappearing throughout this book.

## THE BODY AS SOCIAL

Let's consider a very telling example: *the human body*. It is telling because as we look at fleshy individuals – that seemingly most individual of things – sociologists find them drenched in social relations. Our 'social bodies' display how people 'do things together' – always, everywhere bodies are profoundly 'social'. Our bodies, our feelings and our senses – change enormously under different social situations. We see the world differently, experience the body differently, even walk differently in different societies. *Bodies change under the rule of the social*.

The body is a good example because common sense leads us to think of it as being overwhelmingly biological and natural. And it is of course: biologists (and many psychologists) rightly focus primarily on the biological workings of our brains, our inherited genes, our hormones. They need to look at the evolution, structures and functions of our biological body. The taken-for-granted assumption is that of the 'natural body'. There surely is no case in sociology to reject biology in any way and indeed a lot of sociologists work closely with biologists, sometimes doing 'sociobiology', sometimes looking at the social life of animals, sometimes critically examining the role of 'nature' and the natural in social life, and often these days linking to important environmental issues. But despite all this, sociologists look at the body and biology as something that must also always be seen as something profoundly social for human beings. So in what ways are bodies social?

The simple response is that we do things to our bodies because other people matter. We relate our bodies to others. As we connect to others, so social expectations are built up for how we should move our bodies and adorn them. Ultimately our bodily conducts can come to take on a life of their own – coercing the way we act. At the simplest level consider how we adorn and display our bodies through our clothes, hair styles, tattoos and body piercings. What

## THINK ON: THE SOCIAL BODY

Consider the many ways in which the body is social. For example:

1   We purify and clean our bodies through a range of activities – bathing and hairdressing, cosmetics and hygiene. Different societies expect different regimes of cleanliness. And there are often very strong differences of class and gender in these practices – we are back to the sociology of toilets here!

2   We repair and maintain our bodies – through medical work (nursing, surgery, environmental health) and body modification (tattoos, plastic surgery, transgender surgery). Again there are major differences here in class and gender, and many millions of people in the industrial world are employed to work on our bodies through major health (body) organisations.

3   We discipline and regulate our bodies – dieting, exercise, training and taking them to the gym. Here sociologists study fitness regimes, medical regimes and educational regimes of all kinds. They are busy studying the gym, the health spa and Weightwatchers.

4   We represent our bodies in different ways – think of the ways the body is portrayed in art, film, writing, fashion and advertising.

5   We develop the world of our senses – think how they are shaped by social circumstances. What we can *eat and taste* varies greatly across cultures (snakes, snails and semen) – along with contrasting ways we eat (with hands, sticks, plates). Likewise, how people *hear* (the new Ipod sounds blocks out the sounds of the birds in the woods), *see* (the new world of rapid YouTube images is different from watching the slow sunset), and *touch* differs across groups and societies ('touchy' cultures and 'hands off' cultures).

There is indeed a developing *sociology of the senses* which focuses on each of our senses.

6  We commodify our bodies: our bodies are turned into commodities for sale. From the sale of whole people into slavery through to the sale of body parts and on to 'sex work'. Everything from skin, bone and blood to organs and genetic materials of 'the other' are now up for sale, and there is a massive international market of global trafficking (which is almost invariably in one direction: from the poorest to the richest).

7  We transform and extend our bodies. In some ways, humans are cyborg creatures – the part animal and part machine creatures. We do not leave our 'natural bodies' alone. Instead, we extend them *outwards* through tools, machines, clocks, computers; the computer keyboard is joined in cybernetic system with the screen to our bodies, the neurosurgeon hands are guided by fibre optic microscopy during an operation, and the body of the game player in the local video arcade connects their body with a machine for play. Likewise we extend our body *inwards* with a vast array of prosthetic devices – from contact lenses and artificial limbs to full blown transgender surgery or transplant surgery.

8  We also present and perform our bodies – in drama and in interviews, and in all kinds of body rituals.

9  We do sex: we turn our bodies into objects of pleasures and desires, and given them multiple different meanings for doing this. From reproduction to violence, we use our bodies sexually for social purposes.

For a lively and wide-ranging collection of discussions on all this, see Miriam Fraser and Monica Greco, *The Body: A Reader* (2004).

a fuss many of us make! We *have* to dress in certain ways and not others. It is not biology that drives us to wear fashion but culture. Indeed, we identify people through their modes of dress and the fashions and styles that tie them to their cultures and generations. Youth in 2010 do not dress like youth did in 1950; the Mahi tribe do not dress like Victorian patriarchs. We obviously do things with our bodies that have social implications. But the ways we do this – sometimes called 'body projects' – extend way beyond this simple example. There is now a well developed *sociology of the body*, and the box provides some examples for you to think about.

In short, across history and across cultures we put our bodies to social uses of all kinds. It is never just or simply a biological force which determines our behaviour. Groups and different cultures make sense of their bodies in different ways. The body has different histories – we quite literally live our bodies in different ways at different times. A slave body is not the body of a modern super-rich; a black woman's body drenched in abject poverty is not the same as the multi-billionairess pop star Madonna sexing her wealthy way through the world and adopting African children.

In a telling and influential study, the much celebrated German-English sociologist Norbert Elias (1897–1990) made important contributions to the study of both sociology and social change. A refugee from Hitler's Germany, his studies of *The Civilizing Process* (originally published in Germany in 1939: a critical year in the denial of humanity in European history) suggested how from the Middle Ages onwards in most of Europe, people came to exert greater self-control over their behaviour and their bodies. Through a series of studies of ways of eating, sleeping, dressing, spitting, having sex, defecating and dying, he charts the changing ways of life.

Thus, medieval life was unpredictable, highly emotional, often chaotic and indulgent, and there were few codes around bodily functions. Bodies were volatile, endangered, short-lived, surrounded by disease, death, violence and a putrid stench; they encountered torture, killings. But Elias claims that court society slowly started to change all this, by bringing about etiquette for body management, locations for defecation and for sleeping. Restraint appeared in codes such as those managing table manners. The state developed side by side with a 'civilised' system of self-control. This ' civilised society' has self-discipline, self-control, higher levels of shame and embarrassment. People are taught to hide natural functions – like defecating and urinating; we become less emotional; we come to see ourselves and our bodies as distinctively separate. (And the sociological followers of Elias – of which there are many – have suggested that more recently there has been further changes on the body. It has now become informalised – i.e. we have made many things very casual in our approach to the body.) Changes in our bodies then walk in parallel with changes in society.

## MAKING SENSE OF THE SOCIAL: METAPHORS OF THE SOCIAL WE LIVE BY

The work of Elias moves from detailed description of social life to a wider understanding of **social structure** and process. All sociology will sooner or later bring you to the issue of sociological **theory** whose core task is to deliberate upon how best to understand and even explain these wider workings of the social – of how we are coerced by social facts and do things together. There are many introductions to sociological theory, and this short book does not aim to duplicate them in any way. What I want to do here though is give you a feel for just a few of the imageries (the tropes) that might help us make these wider connections to the social (Table 2:1 suggests some more).

Generally, behind every major social theory, there is an imagery (a trope, a metaphor) or way of seeing the social world. These suggest ways of explaining just how the social works – they are ways to open your eyes for seeing the social world in new ways. Each imagery provides one way of seeing – and *every way of seeing is also always a way of not seeing*. The limits of our language are often the limits of our visions. They are not mutually exclusive and they are often mixed up; but here I just flag a few to help you become sensitive to them. If you spend a few hours looking around the world through some of the different languages here, you may find yourself starting to 'think sociologically'.

### THE SOCIAL AS A BOND: CONNECTING TO EACH OTHER

The social immediately suggests our solidarities and interconnect-edness, the ties we make to others. We ask who bonds with whom,

*Table 2.1*  Metaphors of the social that we live by: opening images

| | *Think of the social as if it was* | *Theories and words to look out for (note: they are not mutually exclusive and hence any one theory can hold multiple images):* |
|---|---|---|
| 1 | Connections, bondings; solidarity; togetherness. | **Functionalism**; community studies; network theory; **anomie** |
| 2 | Structures; patterns; organisation; like organism, or machine or system | **Functionalism**; evolutionary theory; cybernetics |
| 3 | War; power; struggle; conflict. | Conflict theory; Marxism; **feminism**; race theory; queer theory; post-colonialism; critical theory |
| 4 | Drama | Role theory; dramaturgy; identity theory |
| 5 | Language; discourse and the social construction of meanings | **Hermeneutic** sociology; **symbolic interaction**; interpretative sociology; **discourse theory**; phenomenological sociology; **social constructionism**; **narrative** sociology; **dialogic** theory |
| 6 | Conversation | **Ethnomethodology**; conversational analysis |
| 7 | Exchange; rationality and market place | Often central in economic theory; but in sociology becomes only one of many possibilities, see Peter Blau's *Exchange and Power in Social Life*. |
| 8 | Rituals; games | Games theory; interaction; ritual chains |
| 9 | Fragments; labyrinths; matrixes; movements; complexities | **Postmodernism**; complexity theory; mobilities |
| 10 | World interconnectedness | **Globalisation**; World Systems theory |

A short introduction cannot introduce you to the full range of sociological theories, but this table glimpses a few through their imageries. For more, at an introductory level, see Daniel Rigney's *The Metaphorical Society: An Invitation to Social Theory* (2001). For a quick guide to theoretical terms, see John Scott's *Sociology: The Key Concepts* (2006) – especially the appendix: glossary of theoretical approaches. A more advanced text is Donald N.Levine's *Visions of the Sociological Tradition* (1995).

how, where and when? And what indeed are the implications of not bonding? There is a strong historical connection here to what has been philosophically called 'social contract theory': the pact between the members of a society to help make it work. This social bond is found most at work in families, communities, gangs, friendships and civic groups of all kinds (choirs, teams, religious groups, sporting associations, workplace unions) and sociologists try to explain the ties, the connections, the belongings and companionships which humans create with each other. Often it has an economic base – common workplace, common consumption. Always it suggests some kind of normative bond i.e. people share economic situations and **norms**. A great deal of sociology looks at these bonds in different kinds of groups and organisations and how we do things together.

One concern of sociologists working with this imagery has been with the so-called decline of community, with **anomie** and the breakdown of the social bonds in the modern world. Robert D. Putnam's influential work *Bowling Alone* (2000) follows this pattern. He suggests that since the 1960s, people in the US have withdrawn from civic life: there has been a breakdown of the social bond and with this a breakdown of trust. The title of the book suggests it all: when once people went out bowling together and belonged together, now they have become lonely bowlers. Here we see the decline of community, the breakdown of the family, a broken society. At the same time, there are others who say this is not true: what is actually happening is a reworking of the bonds. Families now are not like families of the past: they still bond but now in different ways – families are smaller, more intense and the bonds may be tighter. Think of the mobile phone. Far from breaking relationships it now often makes families link up 24 hours a day. Internet and mobile phone communications have fostered new 'networks', wider global connections, and a widening of our bonds. Likewise, while the old locally based (and often craft-based) communities may have collapsed and declined, new communities have appeared everywhere – shaped by social movements, interests, and of course internet networking. We still need the bonds even as they change their shape.

The idea of **social capital** highlights how life is organised through social connections: having social capital means you are well connected. It suggests not just that bonds are created through others but these bonds serve as valuable assets in life. They do not just provide cohesion and togetherness but also enable people to gain mutual advantages from each other. The term 'capital' has traditionally been an economic term, but the emphasis on the 'social' highlights the fact that resources also accrue to people through their networks and mutual acquaintances. People look after their own from womb to tomb: good connections advance some people more than others. Privileged people maintain and advance their privileges through connections with other privileged people; different kinds of bonds give very different kinds of returns. So, for example, going to Oxbridge or the Ivy League universities can set up connections and links for life. Social bonds may simply secure advantages of some groups over others, generating and amplifying social inequalities (see also Chapter 7). A good introduction to all this – and the work of its key proponents Pierre Bourdieu, James Coleman and Robert Putnam is John Field's short account in *Social Capital* (2008).

## THE SOCIAL AS STRUCTURE, FUNCTION AND INSTITUTION: THE METAPHORS OF THE BODY

Another set of images of the social (with a long history) are derived from seeing the social holistically – as a functioning structure. Here we ask questions about a society's parts and how they **function**: the social is studied through its major institutions and the roles these play in solving problems and helping make a society work. Table 2:2 suggests the most basic way in which this works.

Most famed for this argument in the nineteenth century was the eccentric, founding British sociologist Herbert Spencer (1820–1903). Heavily influenced by the work of Charles Darwin, he saw societies evolving like animal bodies. Just as bodies have identifiable structures (hearts, brains, skin, legs, livers) so societies have identifiable structures – economies, political systems, legal systems, families, religions. Just as bodies have structures with clear functions (hearts pump the blood, brains co-ordinate activities and provide intelligence, livers cleanse the body) so societies have identifiable

*Table 2.2*    Problems in living and their institutions

| Problems in social life: key concerns | Structures, institutions, practices |
|---|---|
| Getting basic resources – food, shelter | The Economic (including work and consumption) |
| Getting organised – achieving goals | The Polity |
| Keeping things orderly | The Law – and socialisation |
| Reproducing the society | The Family, kinship, intimacies |
| Fostering good relations | Civic life, citizenship, welfare |
| Developing communications | Language and media |
| Acquiring and developing knowledge | Science and education |
| Cultivating a spiritual side to life | Religion |
| Others | *Note: This is* not *meant as an exhaustive list* |

functional structures – economies help us organise resources and adapt to the environment, politics helps societies achieve goals, communities help socialise and integrate the diverse components, and law regulates and controls a society. And more: just as a body evolves over time from the simplest organism to the most complex through a process of differentiation and adaptation, so societies have developed over a long period of time and becomes increasingly differentiated and adaptable. The work of the mid-twentieth-century giant of sociological theory, Talcott Parsons (1902–1979), helped further develop such ideas which we will look a little at in Chapter 4.

THE SOCIAL AS CONFLICT OF INTEREST: POWER, WAR AND STRUGGLE

Unlike the images of the social bond or functioning organism or machine, many see the social less benignly: as a war of endless political conflicts between different group interests. Here we ask about human struggles and conflicts in social relations. Indeed, the history of societies can easily be seen as the history of one damn war after another. From the wars of the Romans and the Greeks to the wars around the world today (there are currently over forty trouble spots in the world from Afghanistan to Zimbabwe), it is not hard to see conflicts and turmoil as the stuff – the very dynamic – of so much of the social. In contrast to the image of bonding, our focus now moves to our differences. Society now is seen as a war between conflicting interests.

Some have focused on the general interest of society and the nature of power and conflict. Niccolò Machiavelli (1469–1527) wrote *The Prince* in 1513 as a guide book of rules and war strategies for the Medici prince whose favour he courted; whilst Thomas Hobbes (1588–1679) was immersed in debates over civil wars and revolutions when he wrote *The Leviathan* in 1651. Both were early influential political thinkers who saw human beings in need of strong governments. Left on their own, Machiavelli claimed people would be 'ungrateful, fickle, lying, hypocritical, fearful and grasping'. Without strong governments, Hobbes claimed – left in a natural state – lives would be 'solitary, poor, nasty, brutish and short'. Both saw the need for strong government. Even if people's own interests were squashed, for the social to function well there had to be a strong ruler. Such debates came to an extreme head in the subsequent conflicts in the French and Russian Revolutions; and set the contexts for much of the debate today about democracy.

The sociologist most identified with this image of society is Karl Marx (1818–1883). Of all the social thinkers you will fleetingly encounter in this short book, he has had the greatest world influence: for much of the twentieth century his ideas shaped life in at least a third of the world (and especially Russia and China). Marx focused on the material needs of people and their labour, and suggested that the history of all societies was the history of class struggle. People fell into conflict as they came to recognise the denial of their human interests and their exploitation in classes. But it is broader than this. As well as class conflicts, many have highlighted the long battle between the sexes and the abuse of women, of the cruel conflicts between the races, and of course the bloody wars and violence between the nations. We need to understand who dominates and how power and autonomy is taken from many people (see Table 2.3). Some, like Simmel, have even suggested that conflict is endemic in all human interaction and can be found everywhere in everyday

*Table 2.3*   Conflict is everywhere in society (these ideas are explored more in Chapters 5 and 7).

| Key interests in conflict and their power struggles | Forms of stratification |
| --- | --- |
| Economic | Class, caste, slavery, global inequality |
| Ethnicity | Race, racialisation, racism |
| Gender | Patriarchy, gender order, sexism. |
| Age | Generations and division |
| States and nations | Colonisation, genocide and wars |
| Sexuality | Heterosexism, homophobia |
| Health | Sickness and disablement |

life. Others even suggest that conflict may well be a necessity for societies to work. Conflict, then, has long been of great interest to sociologists and provided much of its imagery.

### THE SOCIAL EXPLAINED AS EVERYDAY DRAMA: ACTING TOGETHER

When sociologists want to focus on the doings of the social – how social life is lived daily – the most common images evoked are those of drama. Social life is a theatre: we are seen to play social roles as we glide across our lives – we become actors, playing parts, using props, rehearsing the parts we have to play, sometimes embracing our roles and sometimes 'distancing' ourselves from them. **Identities** become masks, as ultimately, we ask questions about the disparities between the real and its presented appearance. Its key sociological thinker has been Erving Goffman (1922–1982), the most influential 'micro-sociologist' of the twentieth century. As we have seen, micro-sociology is less concerned with large-scale **social structures** such as the state and the economy, and examines instead the close up, small scale, face-to-face social life in which people encounter each other. In a stream of books published mainly in the 1960s, Goffman showed us how societies may be seen as partially constituted through these face to face encounters in which people manage the impressions they give to each other. In his first book, intriguingly called *The Presentation of Self in Everyday Life* (1956), he observed the lives of people on a Hebrides Island and documents the myriad ways in which people play roles and present themselves in different ways (front stage and back stage) as they move across different social situations, working hard to manage the impressions they give off of themselves. The book becomes a kind of manual of the skills we all employ in our daily lives. In his later book *Asylums* (1961) – a sociological best seller – he went on to examine the underlife of people living in hospitals, concentration camps, prisons and what he calls 'total institutions' where people are cut off from the routines of normal everyday life. Again his focus is on the drama of life – in this case with how the self gets mortified in these extreme situations, and how people rework a sense of who they are (Goffman has much to say: a useful guide to his work is Greg Smith's *Erving Goffman* (2007)).

There is, however, nothing new about this drama image. That people hide behind masks and veils is present in Greek drama. It is present through all the rites and ceremonies of many tribal societies. It is there in masquerades and carnivals that form part of religious ceremonies enacted to contact with spirits and ancestors. Shakespeare frequently uses the stage as a metaphor for life: 'All the world's a stage, And all the men and women merely players. They have their exits and their entrances; and one man in his time plays many parts'. (Jacques in *As You Like It*, II, vii). Or even more dramatically: 'Life's but a walking shadow, a poor player, that struts and frets his hour upon the stage and then is heard no more; it is a tale told by an idiot, full of sound and fury, signifying nothing.' (*Macbeth,* V, v).Much of this is also captured in the twentieth century play by the Italian playwright Luigi Pirandello: *Six Characters in Search of an Author* (1921).

## THE SOCIAL EXPLAINED AS LANGUAGE: THE DISCOURSES OF THE SOCIAL

Closely linked to the drama image is another which also borrows heavily from the humanities and from theories of communications. This is the idea that society is structured like a language, and can be analysed as a **discourse**. Here the social is regulated through a series of finely balanced rules – in much the same way as our speech and talk is. At the most general level, the social is seen as a discourse and a key thinker here has been the French philosopher of ideas Michel Foucault (1926–1984). His ideas are complicated but very influential. In a much quoted passage from an key early book, *The Order of Things* (1969: xv), he describes a discourse about classifying and defining things from a Chinese encyclopedia. Here is a classification of animals: they are

(a) Belonging to the Emperor, (b) embalmed, (c) tame (d) suckling pigs, (e) sirens (f) fabulous (g) stray dogs, (h) included in the present classification, (i) frenzied (j) innumerable, (k) drawn with a fine camel hair brush, (l) et cetera, (m) having just broken the water pitcher, (n) that from a long way off look like flies.

Now I am pretty sure that this classification will make no sense to you; but this is the point. Societies depend upon classifications like these – languages, discourses – that help them make sense of themselves to themselves. *But they are usually unintelligible to those outside*. They are not – as we often like to think – supremely rational, God-given or natural. They are, rather, unmistakably tied up with the specific historical context. Foucault wants to us to look at these vast systems of ideas, thoughts, knowledge and the institutions that

*Table 2.4*  A basic guide to Foucault's key writings

| Examine the discourses of | To show power relations inside institutions like | Key book |
| --- | --- | --- |
| Criminology | Prisons, courts, law, policing, surveillance | *Discipline and Punish* (1975) |
| Health | Hospitals | *The Birth of the Clinic* (1963) |
| Mental illness and psychiatry | Asylums, classification systems, welfare | *Madness and Civilization* (1961) |
| Sexology, psychology, social science | Therapy, prison, governmental interventions, law | *The History of Sexuality* (1976) |
| The humanities, literature and history | Academic life, universities | *The Archaeology of Knowledge* (1969) |
| Religion, politics, education | Government, schools | Found in many of his interviews and essays |

they work though. And he claims that when you do look at them, you will always find that it is power which organises them. Power is everywhere in language. Table 2.4 indicates the range of his work.

## THE SOCIAL AS THE SEARCH FOR MEANING: HUMAN CULTURES

Human sociality is marked by its complex symbols: we are the meaning-making, symbol-manipulating animal that creates **culture**, history, memory, identity and conversation. We pass our meanings on from generation to generation. Of course all animals communicate, but they do not – as far as we can tell – develop such intricate signs and linguistic systems. What other animals have so many gods, explore the scientific universe, write the histories of their lives and times, develop art and music, or write Shakespearean tragedies? Human social life is cultural life.

Let's be clear. It is not that other animals are disengaged from meaning – all animals have versions of communication and even languages. But as far as we can tell, most living creatures are guided by instincts, a biological programming over which they have little control. A few animals – notably chimpanzees and related primates – have the capacity for limited culture: researchers have observed them using tools and teaching simple skills to their offspring. But only humans build complex systems of meaning making: spinning complex cultures, fostering religious, philosophical, scientific (even sociological) ideas about themselves and their societies. Only humans weave complex **narratives** about the nature of their own identities and personhood. Only humans cultivate linguistic skills for telling and memorialising history, their 'dead' and other times – indeed transmit histories and ideas to each other over long periods of time. We are the symbolic, narrating animal and sociology has long taken this to heart. If sociology wants to understand the humanly social, then, it is charged with inspecting closely the nature, content and consequences of the ways in which human activities create little social worlds of human meanings.

I return to this often in this book, but for the moment consider a quote. Raymond Williams (1921–1988) was a UK cultural sociologist who helped greatly clarify the meanings of culture when he wrote (1989: 4):

Culture is ordinary: that is the first fact. Every human society has its own shape, its own purposes, its own meanings. Every human society expresses these, in institutions, and in arts and learning. The making of a society is the finding of common meanings and directions, and its growth is an active debate and amendment under the pressures of experience, contact, and discovery, writing themselves into the land. The growing society is there, yet it is also made and remade in every individual mind. The making of a mind is, first, the slow learning of shapes, purposes, and meanings, so that work, observation and communication are possible. Then, second, but equal in importance, is the testing of these in experience, the making of new observations, comparisons, and meanings. A culture has two aspects: the known meanings and directions, which its members are trained to; the new observations and meanings, which are offered and tested. These are the ordinary processes of human societies and human minds, and we see through them the nature of a culture: that it is always both traditional and creative; that it is both the most ordinary common meanings and the finest individual meanings. We use the word culture in these two senses: to mean a whole way of life – the common meanings; to mean the arts and learning – the special processes of discovery and creative effort. Some writers reserve the word for one or other of these senses; I insist on both, and on the significance of their conjunction. The questions I ask about our culture are questions about deep personal meanings. Culture is ordinary, in every society and in every mind.

This world of meanings manifests itself in many ways, but one striking way is in its search for spirituality. Religious or spiritual experience can provide both extreme and commonplace examples of these meaningful worlds or cultures. In Haitian Voodoo, Gede spirits come to possess the bodies of the living. In India, Hindu worshippers find Bhadra Kali. Pentecostal churches round the world come to 'speak in tongues'. In Appalachia, the handling of poisonous snakes produces religious experiences. In Hong Kong, people worship their ancestors. Religions build special languages, wonderful symbols, elaborate rituals and fascinating stories about their people and their gods which are often wondrous to behold. Many millions of Jews believe in the story of Moses who parted the seas and – standing on the top of a mountain – was sent 'the ten commandments' through thunder, lightning and the sound of a trumpet. Likewise, many millions of Muslims believe that a human, Mohammad, was visited by an angel, Gabriel, who flew him on a horse to Jerusalem where he met Moses, Jesus and Abraham – and there climbed a ladder into the seven levels of heaven. And many millions of Christians have daily rituals to celebrate a saviour who was conceived by an unmarried and unpregnated woman and who was killed (crucified) but then arose from the dead – and lives on. Virgin births, the rising dead, heavens and hell. In addition, multiple new religions come and go only lasting a few generations or so. There is an ever expanding list of new religions – of Scientologists, Swedenborgians, Pentecostals, Moonies – and across the world, people search for meaning in a multiplicity of religions. And this search for meaning in human life – and the growing strength of many new religions as one route into this – is a key topic for sociologists.

## THINK ON: NEW METAPHORS OF SOCIAL LIFE – SOCIAL LOGOS AND THE BRANDING OF SOCIETY

An early image of the modern world was to see it as a gigantic machine – vividly portrayed in Fritz Lang's classic science fiction silent film *Metropolis* (1927) and in Charlie Chaplin's *Modern Times* (1936) (both downloadable on the YouTube). It was also found in major literary writings such as Kafka, Dickens and others. We have gone on looking for images to capture society – and recent metaphors have often taken a lead from logos and brand names. As consumption and shopping has grown under global capitalism, so world brands such as Coca-Cola, McDonald's, American Express, Nike, Disney, Wal-Mart, Apple and Google have come to symbolise a much wider social organisation. Social scientists now write about Wal-Mart, Coca-Cola, Google or the Nike shoe as if they provide a key to understanding how a society works. Understand Google, and you have a key to the way information works. Understand Wal-Mart and you understand the workings of modern capitalism. Sociologists now write about *The Disneyization of Society* and *Coca-Globalization*.

George Ritzer's best selling sociological work *The McDonaldization of Society* is a prime example. First published in 1993 (with a fifth edition in 2007), it has spawned many debates. Ritzer developed Max Weber's ideas of rationality and bureaucracy and takes the fast food company McDonald's as a point of entry for thinking not just about fast food in itself, but as a metaphor for the ways in which much consumer behaviour is organised. For Ritzer, society is becoming McDonaldised and there are four key features of this. Everywhere across the world – not just in McDonald's, but in university courses, religious groups, in sports – you will find the same themes: efficiency, calculablity, predictablity and uniformity, and control through automation. The world is starting to act like a giant McDonald's. We have McUniversities, McMedia, McReligions, and even McChildren.

## SUMMARY

The social can be seen both as an external fact (like a crowd) that coerces us to behave in certain ways or as our relationships with others – as doing things together. Key images for thinking about the social are raised – socialisation, the social as a bond, as conflict, as drama, as discourse, as culture, as machine, as logo. All of these (and there are many more) are starting points for sociological theory.

## EXPLORING FURTHER

### MORE THINKING

Clarify the different meanings of the word 'social' – think of your own uses of the term in daily language and make connections to the opening sections of this chapter. Think now of the topic that interests you sociologically (see Chapter 1 p. 17) and ask what is social about it? Think about the nature of metaphor and what is meant by 'metaphors of the social we live by'. Take some of the images raised in this chapter and think about the language it uses – try and apply it to the world around you, and to the things that interest you. Do these images help you see the world differently? And how might different ways of seeing also be ways of not seeing.

FURTHER READING

This chapter is only the lightest of introductions to what is often called social theory. There very many good books that provide full and interesting accounts of this. Shaun Best's *A Beginner's Guide to Social Theory* (2002) is a good start and guides you through by theory in a lively way; Rob Stones' *Key Sociological Thinkers* (2008) looks at some of the more celebrated sociological thinkers, past and present; and Steven Seidman's *Contested Knowledge* (2008) gives particular prominence to recent theories. On the body, Bryan S. Turner's *The Body and Society* (2008) is the classic that initiated this as major field of enquiry.

You might like to follow up some of the metaphors. On changing social bonds, see Robert Bellah *et al., Habits of the Heart* (2007). On drama in everyday life, the classic is still Erving Goffman *The Presentation of Self in Everyday Life* (1956). Readings on conflicts are found at the end of Chapter 7. The classic example (and easiest to read) of Foucault and discourse is his study of the changing nature of prisons and control in *Discipline and Punish* (1991). On the logo and branding of society, the classic is George Ritzer, *The McDonalidization of Society* (2008)

# TEEMING SOCIAL LIFE

In the history of mankind, the amount of time civilization has existed is minute ... it is very much an immature and ongoing experiment, the success of which is by no means proven.

Colin Turnbull, *The Human Cycle*, 1984

The times they are a-changin'

Bob Dylan, Title of his third LP, 1964

Our world has some seven billion people living in about two hundred countries across seven continents. Understanding the social means examining this global human social complexity as it teems across planet earth. This is a main task of sociology, and it is no small order. So let's start at the beginning and look for a few signs to help with this.

## COSMOS AND EVOLUTION: ON ARRIVING IN THE WORLD WE LIVE IN

Understanding the world we live in requires that we know a little of our past; and this is a very humbling history. As every school child is taught, Planet Earth is some 4.5 billion years old in a universe some

15 billion years old; and it is but one member of billions of galaxies (from Hubble Space Telescope data in 1999, it was estimated that there were 125 billion galaxies in the universe, and more recently with a new camera, it has observed some 3,000 visible galaxies: a lot, then). No life of any kind at all appeared for a long time on Planet Earth, and it was billions of years before dinosaurs ruled the earth – and then disappeared. Sixty-five million years ago primates emerged, followed by the great apes around 12 million years ago. Studying fossil records, it seems that cultural fundamentals like fire, tools, weapons, simple shelters, and basic clothing started to appear around two million years ago. There are signs that after the last great ice age, the earth's human population may have been around five million but by 500 BCE it had probably leapt to 100 million. Major civilisations of the past (including Egypt, Chinese, Arab and the Mesoamerican) only began 5,000 years ago. Major civilisations come and go, none last for long in the grand scheme of things. The major societies that developed from then were nomadic, agricultural, and feudal. But the industrial world as we know it began a mere 300 years ago. *It is with this tiny part of societal history that most of contemporary sociology is concerned.* So here we have world history in scarcely twenty lines. And of course millions will disagree with this story – 'creationists' for example still want people to believe the history of the earth is much simpler: made by God in a few days, or no more than a few thousand.

It is very humbling and important to remember the scale of all this when we are examining contemporary societies. When we make grand claims for today, we should always remember the much grander claims of our past. But sociology itself was born in this very recent moment. It was the product of this recent nineteenth-century change – of what is often called the 'Great Transformation': The Industrial Revolution, the French Revolution, the American Revolution – and the major shifts in living conditions as people moved from the land to the city, to factory life and capitalism, and migrating in large numbers around the world. Here, in this modern world, with its entrenchment of a new kind of urban poverty and class system, sociology was born. And now it tries to trace its emergence along diverse pathways into what we call **'multiple modernities'** (i.e. the different shapes that the modern world takes).

## DARWIN, EMERGENCE AND A PLANET OF THE APES

Sociology emerged in the time that the work of Charles Darwin (1809–1882) was gaining prominence. During the nineteenth century his key ideas of evolution and emergence were developing and have since come to be understood as a major explanation of human life. Ultimately, what sets primates apart from other teeming earth life is intelligence, based on the largest brains (relative to body size) of all living creatures. And just as Darwin was busy studying and comparing different kinds of plant and animal life across the world, so many of the earliest sociologists, historians and anthropologists were busy drawing out comparisons between different kinds of societies in the past and present. Some wanted a greater appreciation of their own past and looked at ancient Greek, Roman, and Eastern antiquities. Others moved out to non-European peoples, whose ways of life differed strikingly from those of European. Often they were exploring countries that Europe had invaded, colonised and Christianised. And with full blown **ethnocentrism**, they often saw these cultures as inferior to their own.

The history of societies in part can be seen as the evolution of food – no food, no society. In early societies, one key task involved roaming around the earth to find food sources (hunter-gatherers). Once food stocks were depleted, there was a need to move on. But once the idea of cultivating food was struck upon, societies could become more settled. Geographic differences in both local vegetation systems and animals were more or less available for 'domestication'. Water systems needed to be developed; plants needed to be grown in settled areas; animals reared. The rise of food production varied around the world. But where food production was developed and advanced, many other skills could be developed: writing, germ control, technology, political systems.

## SIGHTINGS OF THIS WORLD TODAY: CIRCA 2010

Let's leave this brief excursion into the past: it is the modern – and largely Western – world which has been of greatest interest to sociologists. This modern world is often divided into the 'long' nineteenth century (1789–1914) – from the French Revolution to the start of the first World War – and the 'short' twentieth century

(1914–1989), running through two World Wars, a cold war, the collapse of the Soviet Union, the fall of the Berlin Wall and the Tiananmen Square massacre in 1989. This latter period is often seen as a struggle between the liberal West and totalitarian regimes or as the struggle between capitalism and communism. Sociologists, historians and politicians debate these changes in enormous detail; but which ever account is preferred most will agree that the twentieth century was an unmistakably bloody century. Our big-brained animal is also pretty dumb. In his later years, the leading German philosopher and sociologist Jürgen Habermas (1929–) in his book *The Postnational Constellation* could remark:

> (this was) a century that 'invented' the gas chamber, total-war, state-sponsored genocide and extermination camps, brainwashing, state security apparatuses, and the panoptic surveillance of entire populations. The twentieth century 'generated' more victims, more dead soldiers, more murdered civilians, more displaced minorities, more torture, more dead from cold, from hunger, from maltreatments, more political prisoners and refugees, than could ever have been imagined. The phenomena of violence and barbarism mark the distinctive signature of the age.
>
> (Habermas, 2001, p. 45)

The twenty-first century, so far, is not faring much better. We still have wars, genocide, religious intolerance, pandemics, mass poverty. World conflicts are ubiquitous – especially in the divide between Arab cultures and Western ones in what has been crudely called 'the war on terror' starting with '9/11' and the Twin Towers. AIDS ravages much of the world but especially in Africa, a land of many countries, disastrous governments and much poverty. Global environmental warming is increasingly seen as a major world problem. The economic world tilts to China. So what – in a few pages – is the world we live in now actually like?

At the end of the 'noughties', there were roughly 200 major societies in the world and some seven billion people. Some societies cover expansive land mass and have teeming populations. The largest are China, Russia, the United States and India. At the other extreme, some of the smallest countries are mere islands. Some 40 countries have less than a million people, and the Vatican itself – located right in the middle of Rome – has a population of a scant 1,000. (Ironically, it may be the smallest in size and numbers but it exerts enormous influence on the world as the centre of the Catholic Church). Other small countries like Tuvalu, Nauru and Palau (only a few thousand) are not very well known – but places like Cyprus, Barbados and Iceland (slightly larger) are.

This contemporary world can be mapped in many ways, and these days you can have a lot of fun playing with world maps on the internet – starting with Google maps. In the recent past, societies have often been divided into the rich North and the poorer South, the more democratic West and the less democratic East. And for a good part of the twentieth century, people spoke of the three worlds: the first (industrial), the second (transitional) and the third world (relatively undeveloped and poor), later adding a fourth (new industrial countries – NICs) linked to the Pacific Rim and so called 'Asian Values'. With continuing rapid social change, such distinctions can no longer be so easily or clearly made. Sociology, oddly, has usually focused its attention on only a very, very small number of these countries (the so called 'West'), often giving a very skewed view of the global situation. Much of what I say in this book is limited to this, showing what has been the restricted nature of sociology in the past. Still, in the twenty-first century there are signs that sociology is becoming more global, as you will also see. So, here are a few features of this world we live in.

## THINK ON: SOCIAL THINKING BRINGS TOGETHER MANY DISCIPLINES

Sociology is at the heart of the social, but it is a massively collaborative effort. It needs to work closely with many other disciplines of study. Thus, sociologists need a *historian's* eye to sense where we are coming from – to know a little about the scale and range of human societies as they have existed across the centuries, or even the millennia. We need a *scientist's* eye to glimpse a little at where the human society sits in the vast scheme of the physical universe. We need an *anthropologist's* eye to see the ways in which societies can be so different yet so similar as they evolve their webs of meaning into contrasting cultures and symbols across the world. We need a critical *economist's* analysis to get to the heart of the working of modern global capitalism and contrasting economic systems. We need a dash of the *statistician's* skill to cut through some of the detail to help us grasp the scale of some of the social structures – and social problems – that we have to dwell with. We need a *philosopher's* mind to deal with some pretty profound issues around the meaning of knowledge (epistemology), the nature of human social life (ontology) and even the ultimate points of our existence (ethics).We need a bit of the *artist* to glimpse at the complexity and imaginations of unique human beings as they go about their myriad multiplicities of day to day doings. We need an *environmentalist's* passion to be aware of the ways in which our overcrowded planet is promoting some ways of life that will be non sustainable for future generations. All this and more. It's a tall order indeed, and indeed a sheer impossibility for any one discipline (or person!) to do. Sociology has to have its own divisions of labour – each to make contributions to this overall task. And bit by bit, and person by person, it can be put together.

POPULATION: WE LIVE ON AN OVERCROWDED PLANET

A striking feature of our world is that it is teeming with human life – 6.8 billion people at the last count (in November 2009; say that again slowly – 6,800,000,000 lives are busy living in the world – and ponder what that means). Of course, there are real differences across continents: China, India and Africa alone account for around 50 per cent of the world. China has, by far, the largest population (one and a half billion), India the second (well over a billion), with the USA, Indonesia and Brazil following. The population of Africa alone is expected to more than double by 2050 – to 2.3 billion. By contrast, Europe, North America, Japan and Australia have declining birth rates. And although the world growth rate has declined a little since the 1970s, it is still around 1.2 per cent a year, which actually means adding 70 million more people to the world's population each year – many more people than you would find in countries like the UK (with around 60 million).

Though there are major problems of measurement with such a count, one thing is sure: it is very large, and it has been growing dramatically over the past couple of centuries, as the striking Table 3.1 shows.

*Table 3: 1*    World populations

| 1750 | 791 millions |
|------|--------------|
| 1800 | 978 millions |
| 1900 | 1,650 millions (1.6 billion) |
| 1950 | 2,521 millions (2.5 billion) |
| 1999 | 5,978 millions (nearly 6 billion) |
| 2009 | 6,800 millions (getting on to 7 billion) |
| 2050 | 9,100 millions (prediction of 9 billion) |

For most of the world's history, our planet looks positively empty with just a few million people roaming around it. There were a million perhaps in the Paleolithic Age? Ten million in the Neolithic? Maybe a hundred million by the Bronze Age? But once industrialisation set in, we started hitting a billion. Now – just two hundred years on – it is tottering towards 7 billion (3 billion of which has happened in the last thirty years!). This is an astounding change and it suggests a major change in the nature of social life. Some say to greater prosperity; others to an overcrowded planet.

So, sociologically, this 'population explosion' cannot be ignored in debates about the state of the world. Important are issues of birth rates, death rates, age structures of the population and an overcrowded planet in a world environmental crisis. There are contrasting problems: of a rising birth rate in some parts of the world, and falling in others. For some the problem is too many people and not enough resources; for others the problem is too few people – falling birth rates and the greying of the population are creating new problems. Since the pioneering work of Thomas Malthus (1766–1834) on the exponential growth on population and the problems it would bring, there has been an ongoing debate about the social significance of demographic change.

## THE SHIFT FROM RURAL LIFE TO THE GLOBAL CITY: HALF THE WORLD NOW LIVE IN CITIES

Much of the world still lives in small communities, villages and isolated islands – but along with the rapidly growing population, there has been a massive shift to the city. Now more than half of the world's peoples are urbanised. The growth in just fifty years has been astonishing – from 732 *million* in cities in 1950 to 3.5 *billion* in 2005.

When cities first appeared – in the Middle East and elsewhere – they held only a small cluster of the world's population. By 1700, London – the largest city in Europe – had what seemed a staggering half a million. Now it stands at around seven and a half million (and some fourteen million as a metropolitan area). It is a major global city for finance – but only 25th on the scale of world cities. There are much bigger cities everywhere: by 2000, there were over 250 cities with populations greater than a million. Megacities have populations with greater than 8 million: Tokyo has some 35 million and New York some 18 million. Asia and Africa are the most rural continents today, but are set to double their urban populations to some 3.4 billion by 2030. Mumbai, Mexico City, São Paulo, Delhi, Shanghai, Jakarta are already well into double figures. Africa already has nearly 40 per cent of its populations living in cities – some 350 million city dwellers (more than in Canada and US combined).

Mike Davis, a popular and political sociologist, writes of the world now becoming a *Planet of Slums* – a world of shanty towns and *favelas* well depicted in films like Danny Boyle's Oscar-winning film *Slumdog Millionaire* (2008) or Fernando Meirelles and Kátia Lund's *City of God* (2002). Here the stories are told against backdrops of massive poverty, violence, and overcrowding of Mumbai and Rio de Janiero – stories which depict the daily struggle to survive.

Sociologists have long taken a keen interest in how cities develop new forms of social life, and often generate damaged lives.

## LABOUR AND THE ECONOMY: PERVASIVE CAPITALISM IN ALL ITS FORMS AND BREAKDOWNS

The modern world is essentially a capitalist world. **Capitalism** brings three key features: private individuals who own wealth-producing property (as opposed to **states** or rulers); money invested in order to make a profit; and free and open markets operating with minimal state intervention. We can find evidence of early capitalism with merchants making money through investing in goods throughout recent history – for example in Genoa and Venice in the twelfth century. But the arrival of a distinctively modern capitalism is usually linked to the rise of the industrial world, first in the cotton mills in England at the turn of the eighteenth century, and then throughout Europe and the United States. In this factory-based capitalism, workers sold their labour for (low) wages and in the process capitalist owners made profits.

The eighteenth-century thinker Adam Smith (1723–1790) – now featured on English bank notes – maintained (in *The Wealth of Nations*) that the market system is dominated by consumers who select goods and services that offer the greatest value. He developed ideas around what has come to be called market capitalism (and which is now identified politically with **neo-liberalism**). Producers compete with one another by providing the highest-quality goods and services at the lowest possible price. Thus, while entrepreneurs are motivated by personal gain, it is claimed that everyone benefits from more efficient production and ever-increasing value. In Smith's famous phrase, from narrow self-interest comes the 'greatest good for the greatest number of people'. This *laissez-faire* approach claimed that a free market and competitive economy would regulate itself by the 'invisible hand' of the laws of supply and demand. Government control of an economy would inevitably upset the complex market system, reducing producer motivation, diminishing the quantity and quality of goods produced, and short-changing consumers.

Early sociologists such as Marx and Weber (and later ones such as Polyani and Wallerstein) differed. The system was less of a rational market than a site of the 'battle of man against man ... to attain control over opportunities and advantages' (see Max Weber's *Economy and Society*, 1978: 93). One of Karl Marx's major contributions to social thinking was his scathing indictment of the workings of capital. For him, capitalism generated inequalities, exploitation and the poverty and pauperisation of workers as they found themselves disadvantaged in markets, forced to sell their labour power at less than its value (so that the owners can make more profits for themselves), and driven ultimately into conflicts with the owners of capital. Capitalism here is not the benevolent system of Adam Smith, but an inherently unstable and conflictual one – working in favour of the few and against the majority.

These models of capitalism are somewhat abstract and pure ideal capitalism is non-existent. Capitalism takes many forms, has been through many phases and keeps changing. In the early and middle nineteenth century *liberal capitalism* involved a free market with a supportive government and legal framework to help maintain it. But by the start of the twentieth century, mass assembly line production had emerged (often called *Fordism*), with ever increasing profits, investments and scale as work became more and more monotonous for the masses. After the Second World War, a pattern of *organised capitalism* emerged which involved an administered market and a more 'directive state'. There was, for example, in the UK between 1946 and 1979 much more 'state' intervention as governments often shaped economic policies. But during the 1970s and 1980s, a *neo-liberalism* was ushered in by Thatcher in the UK and Reagan in the United States. Here state intervention was decreased and the centrality of markets grew with more global and dispersed operations. In the UK it was marked by the end of nationalised industry, the decline in welfare state provisions, an increase in the service sector, a massive increase in consumption and a breakdown of a stable labour market with job security. The United States is usually seen as the purest form of capitalism – private markets are more extensive than in Europe – but even here the government does play a role in economic affairs. For example, the entire US military is government-operated; and in 2008–2009 the government had to intervene to prevent the collapse of businesses and banks in the 'bailout' of the financial crises.

For much of the twentieth century, industrial capitalism was in a 'cold war' with the East, especially China and the USSR (Russia), both of whom came to adopt and then 'drop' communist systems. After the crises of 1989 – the revolutions of Eastern Europe which heralded the end of the Soviet Union and the protests by Chinese students in Tiananmen Square – the triumph of capitalism has seemed assured for a while. Eastern Europe (including the German Democratic Republic, Czechoslovakia, Hungary, Poland, Romania and Bulgaria), moved towards market-led or capitalist system; and only North Korea, Laos, and Cuba maintain full communist regimes. (Some others, like China, espouse mixed doctrines). In 1992, the Soviet Union itself dissolved. Ten years later, three-quarters of state enterprises were partly or entirely under private ownership. So far the market reforms in Eastern Europe are very uneven. Some countries (Slovakia, the Czech Republic) are faring well; others (such as the Russian Federation itself) have brought out many of the weakest points of capitalism, with growing poverty and inequality, high competitiveness and social decline. Along the Pacific Rim, Japan, South Korea and Singapore, yet another blend of capitalism and socialism is found. During this century, China has also conspicuously opened itself to the market system – whilst still keeping central state control.

Right now we live in a global network capitalism where markets cross countries and crisis in one reverberates in all. With contemporary modern capitalism we increasingly find social instability, growing social inequalities and economic unpredictability across the world. In the 'credit crunch' and world wide economic crises of 2008 –2009, the banks had to be assisted to loans totalling trillions and trillions of dollars. And this has led some to believe indeed that this marked an end point for the capitalist system as it was. Governments across the world had to intervene in order to restore some kind of stability; and the neo-liberal dream bubble of total free enterprise was burst. In 2009, the whole system was seriously in question as it went into global melt down.

In the long run of world history, contemporary capitalism may come to be seen as a mere blip. Right now it is central to any thinking about the social world. We live in a profoundly – if wobbly – capitalist world.

THE ENVIRONMENT: CAN IT BE SUSTAINED?

In the grand scheme of things, civilisations – even the human species – will come and go. But whereas in the past the numbers on Planet Earth ('Gaia' as some leading environmentalists like James Lovelock call it) were very small and relatively little damage could be done to it by human activity, now – as populations expand (by three billion in the past thirty years), the planet comes under siege. At the start of the twenty-first century, sociology identifies how people's social activities are damaging the environment. We can see how people act collectively to overhunt and overfish, chop forests and create soil erosion, pollute water and air while building up toxic waste. It is social activity which helps generate climate change, global warming and an increase in weather related natural disasters. Indeed, these developments have led some sociologists to claim that the human world has never been more at risk: we need to investigate how our social relations are damaging the environment. A key book in discussing much of this has been *Risk Society* (1992) by the leading German sociologist Ulrich Beck which introduced the idea of the **risk society**. But others have now also claimed it is now the most significant issue in contemporary world politics.

THE RISE OF MODERN SCIENCE, THEORETICAL KNOWLEDGE AND
NEW TECHNOLOGIES

The world we live in is now shaped massively by science and research and the technologies that accompany them. Arabic-Islamic science was very advanced up until the thirteenth century, and there are histories of science in many other countries including China. But over the past four hundred years or so, modern science has developed in the West with accelerating speed: the enormous proliferation of scientific achievements along with its massive legitimation as the major source of knowledge (in law, medicine, education, etc.), means that for many science is indeed the defining feature of the modern world.

Thus, a quantum revolution has brought us a new understanding of outer space and energy – putting a man on the moon and dropping a bomb on Hiroshima to kill some 80,000 to 120,000. A biomolecular revolution has mapped out the human gene in the

Human Genome Project – and made possible cloning, designer babies, racial eugenics and the extension of human life. And the information (computer) revolution has generated a world of unparalleled communication possibilities through mobile phones and the internet – as well the potential for a cyborg, surveillance society. Modern science is omnipresent in the world we live in – some would say its central shaper. It is the task of sociologists to understand the social implications of these new developments.

## RATIONALISING SOCIAL LIFE: A WORLD OF BUREAUCRACY AND SURVEILLANCE

Modern societies are organisational societies which cultivate 'organisational people', who spend much of life in large scale hierarchical bureaucracies regulated by systems of rules, rationalities and responsibilities. Noticed and described famously by Max Weber in his idea of the Iron Cage at the turn of the nineteenth century (and well-illustrated in the novels of Franz Kafka), by the start of the twenty-first century it is has become an all pervasive mode of regulation that runs through government, religion, education, health, research, workplace, media, – nothing is untouched by it. It is the world of 'quality assurance', 'health and safety', 'audits', 'accountability', 'form filling, 'the audit culture', the 'surveillance society', and what George Ritzer has called *The McDonaldization of Society* (1993) which as we have seen (Chapter 2) suggests that the rules which govern the running of the McDonald's food chains have come to globally organise much of social life: we speak of the McDonaldization of education, religion, sport, health, social work and much else. Although it brings many problems, without it much of the world as we know it would not work: superstores would collapse, colleges would break down, medical records would not be available, and air travel would grind to a disastrous end! As usual, there are pluses and minuses, and it is the challenge for sociologists to analyse these changes.

GLOBAL RELIGIONS: GOD IS ALIVE AND WELL EVERYWHERE – IN A
SECULARISING WORLD

Science and rationality are not the only belief systems of the modern
world. Religion (and spirituality) plays a key role in all societies;
and there are thousands of idiosyncratic religions across the world,
with seven major ones, alongside huge numbers of non-believers.
Christianity has some two billion followers (mainly in Europe and
the Americas); Islam has another billion and a half followers (mainly
in Asian, African and the Arab states); Hinduism has around 900
million and Buddhists come in at about 6 per cent of humanity
– at 376 million. Judaism is relatively small with only 14 million
adherents world wide (six million – being in the United States).
Two other belief systems are not strictly religions. Much of China
has been shaped by Confucianism (ancestor worship) and latterly
communism – the anti-religion. There are also approximately one
billion people who are non-believers (in Europe around 40 million).

Sociologists have long been claiming that the world is becoming
more and more secularised – the gods are in decline as the world
becomes more rationalised. 'God is dead' was the famous remark
by Nietzsche and certainly atheism is on the rise as a major feature
of the modern world. But the world is also 'bubbling with religious
passions', to quote the leading sociologist of religion, Peter Berger,
himself a Catholic. In the United States for instance, well over 90 per
cent profess belief in God. Across the world we have seen the new
growth of mega-churches and electronic religion. In South Korea,
the Yoido Full Gospel Church has six daily services in a building
for 13,000 worshippers (with 30,000 more served by closed-circuit
television). And alongside this is the rise of many new religious
movements – maybe as many as 20,000 in Europe alone. Groups like
Hari Krishna, the Church of Scientology, the Unification Church
('The Moonies'), the Pentecostalist movements, and various
assorted New Age and Zen groups – all have risen in prominence.
And so too has been the rise of fundamentalism in all religions –
reasserting the traditions and authorities of the past, and leading to a
number of the world's major conflicts and trouble spots. Sociology
cannot grasp much about the modern world without grasping this
swirl of religious passion across the world.

## TERRITORIES AND THE GROWTH OF NATION-STATES

Most people living on the earth today live in nation-states. But this is a new phenomenon of recent history. It has far from typically been the case in the past, where land masses have been ruled diversely by tribal chiefs, kings, emperors and sultans – despots who ruled by force and theocracies held together by religion. Ethnic groups made claims to their territories and right up to the sixteenth century, people lived with these territorial limits set through land stewardship. Nation-states as we now know them only start to congeal during the nineteenth century. Starting with the Treaty of Westphalia (1648), criteria start to be set out to demarcate local domestic territories and recognise independent nations. Thereafter the old empires – the Russian Empire, the Austro-Hungarian Empire, the British Empire – started to collapse, and new nation-states started to appear. Nationalism is hence also a new and modern phenomenon. Modern nation-states subsequently became the core of the systems of catastrophic wars built around nationalism in the twentieth century.

A nation-state sounds like a contradiction. A **state** is a political organisation with effective rule, sovereignty, and governance over a limited geographic area – claiming a monopoly on authority, controlling armies and civil service, and believing it can use violence 'legitimately'. By contrast, a **nation** suggests a human and cultural community – connected often with religions, languages, ethnicities and a shared way of life. It is something to make sacrifice for, even lay one's life down for. It is often linked to nationalism, and usually generates strong identities. (I am German; I am Thai; I am a Maori). Often these are less real than **imagined communities** – an influential term developed by Benedict Anderson to suggest how nationalism is linked to the emergence of a 'print-capitalism' and the growing rejection of ideas of the monarchy and divine rule. (There has been much recent sociological research on the nation state and its workings by Michael Mann, Anthony Smith and Saskia Sassen; along with a concern about the democratisation or not of these states).

THE DEVELOPMENT OF MASS MOBILISATION, PROTEST AND
IDENTITY POLITICS.

Mass mobilisation and social movements began to take shape in Western countries during the later eighteenth century – symbolised massively by the French Revolution. During the nineteenth century a durable set of elements started to appear that moved through the world (through colonisation, migration, trade) whereby more and more groups and populations engaged in new forms of political actions. Charles Tilley (1929–2008) was a sociologist who spent much of his life showing the rise of social movements in parallel with the development of the ballot box. In his book *Social Movements 1768–2004*, he suggests that these new social movements (NSMs) combine three things. They develop public campaigns, getting organised to make collective claims on targeted audiences. They combine whole repertoires of political actions ranging from public meetings, processions, and rallies though to demonstrations, petitions and the creation of special purpose associations. And ultimately they display and present themselves to the public as good causes and worthy people. They are united, with large numbers of committed supporters.

Social movements have perhaps become the key feature of modern political life. What is interesting to note about them is that not only do they provide the momentum for political change, they also provide a sense of meaning in life. Very often people build their sense of who they are (their identities) from these very movements. Identity has become a basis for social action and change. The list of such organisational movements and identities is very long and very striking. Amongst them are the women's movement, gay, lesbian, bisexual and transgender (LGBT) movements, environmental movements, student movements, anti-globalisation movements, the right to life movement, the animal rights movement, the landless people's movement, the indigenous people's movements, the human rights and civil rights movements, the disability movement, the AIDS movement, and rights of all kinds. All these have been studied by sociologists and often made central to a grasp of contemporary political life.

## THINK ON: MAPPING THE STATE OF THE WORLD THROUGH THE INTERNET

Sociologists need always to keep in mind the bigger picture of the state of the world. These days this can be done through multiple websites which keep you up to date with facts, figures and comments. Here is a small selection to add to your 'favourites' list and which will help you keep up to date. Always be aware, though, that *all statistics bring problems*, and need thinking about critically. I provide only a key word for a starter search but links are provided on the book website.

- General data on all of the world's societies: search – *The World Bank; The CIA Factbook; United Nations; NationMaster; New Internationalist*
- Size of populations and their growth: search *United Nations World Population Reports (UNFPA)*
- Size of cities and rural areas: search *UNhabitat; state of the world*
- Basic economic development of the world's countries: search *United Nations; OECD*
- World poverty statistics: search *World Bank Poverty Net; Global Issues*
- The Human Development Index for each country in the world: search *UN Human Development Index*
- Environmental damage and degradation: search *World Watch; People Planet; UN Climate Change; World Environment Organization; DEFRA UK.*
- Human rights and abuse across the world: search *Amnesty International; Human Rights Watch*
- Genocides across the world: search *Genocide Watch*
- Migrations, refugees and displaced people across the world: search *United Nations High Commisioner for refugees (UNHCR)*
- Political freedom and democracy across the world: search *Freedom House*

- Diverse religions, their sizes and beliefs across the world: search *Adherents*
- Different languages across the world: search *Ethnologue*
- Different values across the world: *World Values Survey*
- Maps of the world: search *World Atlas; Google Maps; mapsoftheworld.com*

Why not start your own web page of favourites? This way you can regularly check up the state of the world and know what is going on.

## THE SHAPE OF THINGS TO COME: A HI-TECH, GLOBAL, POSTMODERN AND VERY UNEQUAL TWENTY-FIRST CENTURY?

Putting this all together, sociologists have regularly suggested that a new kind of society may have been emerging. In 1999, Anthony Giddens – one of the world's leading sociologists (certainly the UK's most prominent, and then director of the world-renowned London School of Economics) – gave a series of lectures on *Runaway World*, for the prestigious annual BBC Reith Lectures. He gave these lectures across the world – in Washington (on the family), in London (on democracy), in Hong Kong (on risk), and in Delhi (on tradition). You can find them all on the BBC's website under Reith Lectures, and in the short book *Runaway World* (2002). His central thesis suggested the modern world was fast running out of control and that we needed a sustained analysis in order to possibly get it back under control. He used the image of a huge juggernaut rolling rapidly out of control down a hill and remarked:

> We are the first generation to live in this society, whose contours we can as yet only dimly see. It is shaking up our existing ways of life, no matter where we happen to be. This is not – at least at the moment – a global order driven by collective human will. Instead, it is emerging in an anarchic, haphazard, fashion, carried along by a mixture of economic, technological and cultural imperatives. It is not settled or secure, but fraught with anxieties, as well as scarred by deep divisions.

> Many of us feel in the grip of forces over which we have no control.
> Can we re-impose our will upon them? I believe we can.
>
> (from Lecture 1)

A brief summary of some of the key changes which now preoccupy sociologists may indicate the scale and potential importance of what has been a keen concern of many sociologists over the past few decades. Often, they write apocalyptically – as if these changes herald *The End of History* (Francis Fukuyama) and *The End of the World as We Know it* (the title of one such book presented in 1999 by the Marxist historical sociologist, Immanuel Wallerstein). Certainly they have striking titles and arguments. They all want to understand this new emerging order. It has most commonly been called the *post-industrial society* (a term first used by the prominent US sociologist Daniel Bell in the 1960s to suggest a productive system based on service work and high technology). Others take this much further and speak of a *post-modern society* (Jean Baudrillard, Krishan Kumar) suggesting a break with the **Enlightenment** and **modernity** and the arrival of fragmentation, difference and **pluralism** Still others speak of a *late capitalism* and *late modernity* which usually suggest a continuation of the themes first analysed by Marx and which can still be seen at work in so-called modern societies. There are also analyses of *The Risk Society, The Reflexive Society* and *The Individualised Society* (all terms and books by the prominent German sociologist Ulrich Beck), of *Liquid Society* (Zygmunt Baumann's term), *Surveillance Society* (David Lyons), *The Information Age* and *The Network Society* (Manuel Castells), *The Global Age* (Martin Albrow), *The Exclusive Society* (Jock Young), the *Post-modern Society* (Baudrillard), and the *Post National Constellation* (Jürgen Harbermas). We hear of *Informalisation* (Cas Wouters), *The McDonaldization of Society* (George Ritzer), and *The Disneyization of Society* (Alan Bryman).

Whatever terms we use, it is generally agreed that somewhere back in the mid-twentieth century a new 'second great transformation' was emerging, one that continued with capitalism but found itself confronting new trends of **multiple modernities**. Modernising societies have refuted any general tend towards any common modernity. Rather, taken together, we see a new world emerging from plural pasts that are full of rapid change, uncertainty, risk, openness and individualism. There are many different emphases. Some see dark, pessimistic dystopias; others provide more optimistic, positive utopian images. Given there is so much analysis of this change with so many different themes picked up and developed, I can only highlight a few briefly here. Chapter 7 will consider the massive existence of inequality, but here I will focus on just three other (of many) key themes that every contemporary sociology has in some way to deal with.

### THE POSTMODERN, MULTICULTURAL AND HYBRIDIC: 'THERE IS NO ONE WAY OF LIFE AND NO ONE STORY OF ANYTHING'

A truly striking feature of the contemporary world is the growing awareness of the differences that we find within it – it is a buzzing world of some seven billion people in more than 200 **nations** with multiple languages and values struggling to make sense of different politics, religions, and ways of life. There is a cacophonous din of voices trying to be heard and the idea of **multiculturalism** helps capture this. It highlights the diversity both *between* different cultures like India or Zimbabwe whilst also recognising the massive differences of language, religion and life style *within* a country. Indonesia with more than 700 languages, Russia with over 150 cultures, and Canada has one of the highest levels of migrating groups. The complexities of these differences is only something we are beginning to take very seriously in this twenty first century. Societies are seen increasingly as **hybridic** – blending and mixing all these differences: there is no simple society or unified nation, political ideologues notwithstanding. This new world harbours many meanings but increasingly human social worlds are connected to **cosmopolitanism**, a kind of openness and tolerance to these differences (see Robert Holman's discussion of the many meanings of this term in his *Cosmopolitianisms*, 2009).

At the broadest level societies might now be seen as **postmodern**. *Postmodernism* was a major twentieth-century movement in architecture and the arts which recognised that linear coherence, unitary wholes or absolute truths were at an end (if indeed they had ever existed). We live increasingly in a fragmented world over-run with multiplicities and complexities, where all we can do, as the French philosopher Jean-François Lyotard (1924–1998) put it, is 'play with the pieces'. The term subsequently became a buzz world of the 1980s and helped shape the ways in which we now see different cultures as fragmented. The most serious challenge to all these positions, of course, comes from the development of **fundamentalisms** – views which assert there is only one way, and usually provide an authority (often religious) from a voice lodged somewhere in the past. It is here in this divide that we find much of the conflict of the contemporary world.

## THE MEDIA AND THE DIGITAL TECHNOLOGIES: 'WE LIVE IN SIMULATED WORLDS AND NETWORKS'

The new communication technologies started to arrive in the early nineteenth century and have radically changed the way the world now functions. The camera arrived in 1839, setting in train a new visual world of reproduction never possible before and leading to the ubiquity of recorded images – from camcorders to digital photography. The telephone arrived in 1876, bridging remarkable distances and heralding the mobile phone and a dramatic reordering of human communications. The phonograph arrived in 1877, anticipating the Walkman and the iPod a hundred years later: so now we can have music wherever we go – a far cry from the musics of the silent past. In the 1890s, film arrived leading to the twentieth century being called ' the century of the film and cinema' – where these new forms became an everyday experience for large numbers of people around the world. Radio and television start to appear in the 1920s and 1930s, and by the late 1950s became common place in most Western homes. And computing, digitalisation and the internet arrive in the last decades of the twentieth century to foster what has been called 'the information revolution'. Now we enter the age of the cyberspace, and the network. This new interactivity is profoundly shifting our communities, relations and structures of feeling.

In many ways the computer revolution has marked out a second 'grand transformation' – sweeping through social life and changing all in its wake: the **mediasation** and **digitalisation** of life as it has been called. We are currently only in its early days – scarcely two generations have moved through it, but the pace of change is stunning. No social institution has been untouched by it. Friendships and families now dwell on mobile phones and facebooks. Schools, hospitals, workplaces break down when the computer stops: we foster the 'e-revolution' in education and cyberhealth. Crime worlds shift into identity theft and computer hacking, whilst policing creates the new surveillance society. There is the cyberchurch, the online social movement, the digital democracy, the digital city, and of course the digital divide and the digital self. High technologies have now become routine across the world – vast numbers of people (around a third of the world at a recent count) now use the internet a lot of the time. And the impact on social life has been astounding. Sociologists now write books on *The Information Age* and *The Internet Galaxy* (titles by Manuel Castells), and *Cyberculture Theorists* (a book by David Bell).

### GLOBALISATION AND GLOCALISATION: '*THE WORLD IS ONE PLACE*'

Finally, we find that modern technologies and media communications now connect people across the remotest parts of the world. For most of history, it took months – years even – to trek from one country to another: now it is instantaneous. We can live globally in the here and now. There has been a massive speeding up and deepening of our world interconnections. This is **globalisation**: sociologists like to say there has been a compression of both time and space. Of course, there is nothing new about this idea – there have been voyages across the world for centuries. But what is striking now is the speed and pervasiveness of this change.

We can see globalisation at work everywhere. From the World Bank and the United Nations to Greenpeace and Disneyworld, from international marathons and global concerts to mass tourism and the internet, we can see more and more people moving in networks not bound to a fixed spatial community. People network across the globe, making the global their local and their local, the global. Many people are indeed becoming 'global citizens'. We can find these changes in every sphere of life (with controversies in each). We can find globalisation at work in economics (the flows of money and capital cross the world), politics (international organisations, digital social movements), new communications (everything from television satellites, digital media, personal computers, mobile phones, telephones, jet planes), and people (who move more easily round the world: sometimes positively, as in tourism and travel and chosen migration; and sometimes negatively – as refugees, human trafficking and displaced people). The world's problems are now seen much more as common world problems – problems no longer simply belong to any one country. Drugs markets spread across continents, cybercrimes push against the laws of any one country, international courts proclaim international justice. Terrorism has taken on new forms (as when suicide bombers are willing to fly into major buildings such as happened at the World Trade Center on 11 September 2001). And then there are major issues of environmental damage happening on a global scale. The global world becomes a risky place – a risk society. Modern societies have produced technological changes which have unforeseen consequences that we cannot easily predict. From the railway to the computer, from genetic engineering to nuclear weapons, the massive spread of networks of cars and planes, the development of genetically modified crops, the cloning of animals, the deforestation of the planet, 'designer children and surrogate mothering', all have consequences which may be far reaching and are at present unpredictable.

## THINK ON: READING ABOUT GLOBALISATON

Globalisation then is a much analysed process. In the 1980s and the 1990s, thousands of books were published about it: I count forty alone on my own book shelf including – to immediate hand – Pico Iyer's *The Global Soul* (2000), Richard Falk's *Predatory Globalization* (1999), Zygmunt Bauman's *Globalization: The Human Consequence* (1998), David Held's *Global Transformations* (1999), Jan Nederveen Pieterse's *Globalization and Culture* (2004), Ulrich Beck's *What is Globalization?* (2000), Martin Albrow's *The Global Age* (1996), Jon Binnie's *The Globalization of Sexuality* (2004), Mark Findlay's *The Globalisation of Crime* (1999), Christa Wichtereich's *The Globalized Woman* (1998) and George Ritzer's *The Globalization of Nothing* (2004). This is just a rag bag, certainly not the most influential or important, but enough to indicate it has been a key theme of recent sociology.

## THE STATE OF THE WORLD: DIAGNOSIS OF CHANGING TIMES

As always, sociology moves in changing times. At its best it can detect trends (in populations, in cities, in economies, in governments, in religions); but it is no fortune teller or futurologist and cannot predict where we are heading. The trends of the time are harbingers of mixed messages.

The bad news just gets worse and worse and provides my pessimistic sociological friends with a lot of ammunition. Poverty alone tells a tragic story. In 2005, at least 1.4 billion people still live on less than US $1.25 a day. Africa remains in a severe crisis, despite international aid. And over 3 billion (nearly half of humankind) live below the World Bank's US$2.50 a day poverty line. Some 50,000 people die each day from poverty-related causes – a third of all human deaths; and some 35,000 children die each day from preventable or easily treatable diseases. Over 20 per cent of the world's people (about 1.3 billion) lack the nutrition they need to work regularly, living in absolute poverty. And, of these, at least 800 million are at risk for their lives. To top it all, some 2.4 billion lack basic sanitation.

At the end of 2008, there were some 42 million internally displaced people – including some 15 million refugees. Some 27 million people across the world live in modern slavery. Maybe one in every three women has been beaten, coerced into sex or abused – usually by someone she knows; while as many as 5,000 women and girls are killed annually in so-called 'honour' killings (many of them for the dishonour of being raped!). Some 130 million girls and young women have undergone female genital mutilation. In 2007, some 72 million children worldwide were denied the right of education. There are some 100 million children who work on the streets and 'child labour' involves some 250 million working children. Child marriage is pervasive: in some countries over half of all girls are married by the time they reach age 18 (the figure is 74 per cent in the Democratic Republic of the Congo, 70 per cent in Niger, and around 50 per cent in Bangladesh and Afghanistan). And children all over the world make up about a half of war refugees, whilst millions die and are often the main targets in war (being seen as the next generation of 'enemies').

More than 70 countries have laws which criminalise homosexual acts, and a number of these – Iran, Afghanistan, Saudi Arabia and Chechnya amongst them, have the death penalty for gay sex. Torture is common to extract confessions of 'deviance', gays are raped to 'cure them of it', and they are sometimes killed by death squads. The rights of women, children and homosexuals are violated everywhere. We have conflicts in Iraq, Palestine, Sri Lanka, Afghanistan, Uganda, Rwanda, Colombia, Sudan, Darfur and elsewhere. Thousands are being killed daily. Transnational organised crime flourishes – with a possible annual income of over $2 trillion. And so far I have not mentioned the environment.

And yet the good news is that there has been some progress on a number of fronts. Infant mortality has fallen significantly throughout the world. World poverty is actually dramatically down (but this is very uneven): there has been more success in the war against poverty in past 50 years than the preceding 500 years. The numbers of starving and chronically undernourished in low-income societies has declined from around 40 per cent in 1960 to less than 20 percent in 2002. There is more access to drinking water and reasonable sanitary conditions than ever before in the history of humankind. In low-income societies there has been clear improvement: from 165 deaths per 1000 live births in 1960 to about 75 in 2007. Life expectancy is up: again people in low-income countries lived for just about 41 years in 1960; they now live on average to 64 years. Literacy has increased from around 16 per cent in 1960 to about 75 per cent in 2000, and education at all levels is recognised and significantly on the increase. Most of all, over the past 500 years, the struggle and gaining of freedoms and justice for the ordinary person has been placed so firmly on the agenda in ways that simply wasn't imaginable in the longer past. And more and more countries seem to be relatively more 'free' (perhaps 46 per cent of the world) – though there are real problem about what this means. Looking at the many technical developments over the past century or so also cannot fail to impress. It is probably fair to say that the last 200 years have brought both more knowledge and artistic creativity than all the previous centuries, and that the past 50 years has made all this more accessible to more people than ever before in history. The world history of art, culture, music, sport, and human creativity

*Table 3:2*  Emergent human social worlds – a classic basic typology ('ideal types') of Western societies

*We all dwell simultaneously in traditional, modern and postmodern worlds – though to very different degrees.*
Sociologists use versions of these ideas in many of their arguments, but there are many dangers of oversimplification and over-generalisation and they should never be seen as a simple evolutionary development. They are useful though as starting points for understanding deep contrasts and changes in society. Beware of the dangers of historicism – of seeing necessary, predictable change: societies develop contingently and unpredictably and are never homogenous. These models are also derived largely from the standpoint of Western cultures and will not be so applicable elsewhere.

|  | Traditional (agrarian) | Modernising (industrial capitalist) | 21st century (global postmodern) |
|---|---|---|---|
| Economy and work | Agricultural; herding; fishing; maritime | Mercantile capitalism; factory | Global capitalism; IT and service |
| Technology | Human and animal energy | Industrial energy sources | Post industrial; information; digital; energy crisis |
| Population | High birth and death rates; low population | Falling death rates; high birth rates; rapid growth | Low death rates; low birth rates; slowing populations |
| Governance | Slavery; feudal war lords; kings | Nation states and new social movements (NSMs) | World organisations |
| Environment | 'Natural disasters' | Industrial pollution | Eco-catastrophe and environmental movements |
| Religions | Superstition; polytheism to monotheism | From monotheism to secularism | Fundamentalism; diversity; secularism |
| Communications | Signs; speech and early writing | Print to electronics | Mass media and digital culture |

| | | | |
|---|---|---|---|
| Community and networks 'the plural community' | Tribal; village; face-to-face; local | Cities; associations; secondary | Networks; cyber relations; global |
| Knowledge and ideas | Religion; folk superstition | Rise of science | Relativism; reflexivity; relationalism |
| Control and law | Punitive; repressive; 'natural' | Increase of laws and formal institutions; restitutive | Massive legal system; heavily organised and financed |
| Health | High death rate | Environmental health and 'sick model' | Managed care; hi-tech medicine |
| Values | Traditional | 'Make it new' | Postmodern pluralism |
| Groups | Primary | Secondary | Cyber networked |
| Roles and self | Ascribed | Achieved | Open |
| Culture | Folk | Mass culture | Cosmopolitanism |
| Society | Simple | Industrial | Complex |
| Time and change | Very slow | Speeding up; invented traditions | Rapid – even within a generation |
| Military | Centrality of warfare but limited and focused | Mass national armies; all the people: 'Liberté, égalité, fraternité' and internal revolution | 'New wars' |

is ceaseless and we can only stand in amazement – despite all the problems – at just what societies foster.

So a balance sheet on the state of the world brings very mixed stories indeed. Sociologists are embedded in all these changes, study them and try along the way to make the world a little more of a better place.

## SUMMARY

This chapter has provided a very general guide to teeming life in the human social world – its themes have been big and wide-ranging. Everyone of them is a sub-sphere of sociological analysis: the changing nature of capitalism, the growth of population and cities, the development of science and rationality, the environmental crises, the 'secularising' and fundamentalising of religions, the emergence of nation states, social movements and the democratic turn. Ultimately, the character of the emerging postmodern world is discussed and its high spots and low spots debated.

## EXPLORING FURTHER

### MORE THINKING

Now is also the time to look a little at your own society and consider how it differs from other societies you may have encountered – through friends, through travel, through the media. Think about some of the people you know and consider what kinds of social groups they belong to. How do they differ? And what do they have in common?

### FURTHER READING

A brief history of the modern Western world is well provided in Mary Evans's *A Short History of Society* (2007); Patrick Nolan and Gerhard Lenski's textbook *Human Societies: An Introduction to Macrosociology* (2008) provides a good general account of types of society; and Robin Cohen and Paul Kennedy's *Global Sociology* (2007) is an excellent introductory text. The chapter covers a wide range of fields. Here are some good introductions to particular areas. James Fulcher's *Capitalism: A Very Short Introduction* (2004); Saskia Sassen's *Cities in a Global Economy* (2006); Robert Fine's *Cosmopolitanism* (2007); Anthony Smith's *The Cultural Foundations of Nations* (2009); Anthony Giddens's *Politics of Climate Change* (2009); Phil Zuckerman's *Invitation to the Sociology of Religion* (2003)

Overviews of the broadest changes are mentioned in the text on page 61. Of these, the shortest and easiest is Anthony Gidden's *Runaway World*; the most comprehensive is Manuel Castells's *The Information Age* (originally published in three volumes; revised edition 2009). Zygmunt Bauman's *Globalization* (1998) and Jan Nederveen Pieterse's *Globalization and Culture* (2004) are good introductions to globalisation.

4

# STANDING ON THE SHOULDERS
# OF GIANTS

For all practical purposes it is not misleading, therefore, to regard
the enterprise of nineteenth century sociology as the anatomy of a
distinctive type of modern industrial society

Krishan Kumar, *Prophecy and Progress*, 1978

To be ignorant of what has occurred before you were born is to
remain always a child. For what is the worth of human life, unless
it is woven into the life of our ancestors by the records of history

Marcus Tullius Cicero, 106–43 BCE, Oration xxxiv

Throughout the world's history, many people have puzzled about
the nature of the social world they have lived in: how did their world
come into being, what was their place in it and what might be the
great thread that holds it together? In all societies there are people
who think about the nature of their society. In the past, this social
thinking has often taken on a religious or spiritual turn – the social
is examined and explained as the creations of various gods (there are
an awful lot of them, and often significant enough to kill for) and the
place of humans in it is located within this religious canopy or arc.
Sometimes this social thinking takes a political turn – people explain
societies as the creations of powerful people or groups (key tyrants

or emperors, or groups like the exploiters and the exploited). Often too people explain social things in biological terms – as evolution, or as the result of individual wills. There are then many ways of thinking about the social world we live in.

We can trace the more formal thinking about the nature of society through many great thinkers and artists throughout history: in the Arab countries, the ideas of the fourteenth-century Muslim, Ibn Khaldun; in the East, the significance of the Chinese philosopher Confucius (551–479 BCE); and in Africa, the long history of poets and folk story tellers. Ideas about the social have developed throughout the world and its history. 'Sociology', in a sense, is just the most recent – and most Western. We stand on the shoulders of giants who have thought long and hard about the world we live in; our past is full of creative and artistic endeavours struggling to make sense of the social. There are significant histories not to be forgotten.

## A VERY SHORT HISTORY OF WESTERN SOCIOLOGY

As societies have grown in scale and as scientific thinking has developed, so it is not surprising that 'sociology' should have emerged slowly as a new intellectual discipline. Since the 'great transformations' of the early nineteenth century, it has progressively entered the Western world as a university-based research discipline, and now in the twenty-first century it is to be found in most countries of the world. The complexities of the modern global life almost demand that we cultivate serious (even 'academic') thinking about society; and that in the grand divisions of labours of life that the modern world brings, many people should now devote their time, talents and intellectual energy to providing this. At the same time, always remember that modern sociology is Western: which means that the whole of sociology is drenched with Western assumptions and values. This, as we shall see, is about to change.

### 1750: THE ANTECEDENTS OF MODERN WESTERN SOCIOLOGY: THE ENLIGHTENMENT PUZZLES

The modern Western world takes much of its intellectual shape between the fifteenth and eighteenth centuries, during the long

## THINK ON: PUZZLES OF ENLIGHTENMENT THINKING

The foundation of sociology is usually claimed to be the **Enlightenment**. This was a time for rational reflection, scientific development and the breaking free from religious and traditional 'myths'. It puzzled over a series of critical questions and amongst these were:

1 What is human nature and how should we live our lives? (The moral questions posed by Voltaire, Roussseau, Kant and others.)

2 What kinds of society exist and how are they changing and developing? Is human progress possible? Is there a move from 'savage' and 'barbaric' to 'civilised'? Bit by bit, a massive classification of types of society was starting to evolve.

3 How are societies to be ruled? Should power lie in the hands of the Leviathan – is democratic rule possible or desirable? (Often called The Hobbesian Question, after Thomas Hobbes)

4 Can diverse religions be tolerated and accepted – a freedom of religion? How much terrorism should religion be allowed to maintain its supremacy? Can religious diversity be accepted without society falling apart? (The Religious Question – discussed fully in Charles Turner's *The Secular Age*, 2007)

5 Who and what is a person? What is the emerging self like and who is the modern individual? And closely linked, are people selfish? Is the basis of society a collective concern for others or a rather more basic self interest? (What might be called the Adam Smith question)

6 What is knowledge, truth, morality? (The Cartesian, Kantian and Humean Questions)

search for emancipation from religious and absolutist dogmatism and terrorism through the pursuit of science and the struggle for human 'freedoms and rights'. Here we see the breaking away from the rule of superstition, magic, religion, the church and the various monarchies and aristocracies. Here too we find the horrors of the long history of the Spanish Inquisition, the witchcraft hunts, the Thirty Years War and the English Civil War, and the ultimate revolutions in France and America – side by side with the growth of slavery and then ultimate emancipation. This period also saw the gradual rise of mercantile capitalism and the massive colonisation (and oppression) of much of the world by Europe. Simultaneously it also saw the gradual emergence of emancipation movements fighting for their freedoms – of women, of slaves, and of minorities of all kinds.

The Enlightenment – associated with many, including Diderot, Hobbes, Hogarth, Hume, Kant, Locke, Mozart, Newton, Pope, Rousseau, Voltaire, and others – made claims for the world to be rational, scientific and progressive. We were heading to a potentially better world. Progress was on the agenda through rational thinking. Often looking back to the ancient Greeks, they posed some very major questions about society, questions that still haunt sociology today. The box 'Puzzles of Enlightenment thinking' outlines some of these big questions.

Again, in a small book like this, I cannot follow up these ideas. Many (like Adorno, Horkheimer and Foucault) have been very critical of this rational, optimistic and Western-centred view of the world. They suggest that it has led to a world that is far too instrumental, technical, controlling – the harbingers of the modern surveillance society, rationality, disenchantment and even the Holocaust. Despite this, many more have seen it as a critical advance in the development of science and rationality as tools for trying to understand the world – and changing it for the better. Sociology was born of this moment.

## 1800–1920: EARLY MODERN SOCIOLOGY

Sociology as a grand and general 'scientific discipline' is generally told as a story that emerged out of Enlightenment thinking and the great revolutions of the eighteenth and nineteenth centuries. It is seen as a discipline born out of 'the shock of the new'. Social life had seemingly never been in such turmoil. It was now confronted with the French Revolution, the Industrial Revolution, the newly emerging nation-states, the independence of the USA and the growth of ideas of democracy, as well as the escalation of populations across the word and the rise of new cities and the slums that accompanied them. We often think today that we are in periods of extraordinary social change: a little history shows that this change has been unfolding for several centuries. There was undoubtedly something in the air at this time in the Western world that saw a new world in the making, a time of rapid and even revolutionary change. The old order seemed to be (indeed was) in serious decline: a traditional life was being swept asunder.

It was in this climate that sociology was born to appraise just what was happening: to analyse the sheer complexity and scale of the new modern society arriving before its eyes. What were the key features of this new world? Why was this change taking place? How might social order be maintained in the midst of such change? And just how could this new social order be studied: was a science of society actually possible, and if so what should it look like? Many of the founders of sociology thought of sociology as a mission to make the world a better place.

Two of the earliest pioneers of this Western sociology were the eccentric Auguste Comte (1798–1857), and the odd and solitary Herbert Spencer (1820–1903). Comte, growing up in the wake of the French Revolution, is usually claimed to be the founder of sociology, coining the term sociology in 1838. For him, societies moved from being religious to philosophical to scientific societies. The earliest era, right through the medieval period in Europe, was the *theological stage* – a world guided by religion, a society as God's will. With the Renaissance, the theological approach to society gradually gave way to the *metaphysical stage* – a world understood as a natural, rather than a supernatural one. The modern world however brought a *scientific stage* and the development of technology, propelled by scientists such as Copernicus (1473–1543), Galileo (1564–1642) and Isaac Newton (1642–1727). Comte claimed that society followed invariable laws. Much as the physical world operated according to gravity and other laws of nature, so the task of sociology was to uncover the laws of society. This new approach of science was what he called **positivism**. Today the word is still widely used to refer to the scientific method.

Herbert Spencer, writing a little later, and with Darwin's discoveries firmly in sight, also saw societies as inevitably evolving – this time from the less complex or simple towards the massively, multiply complex. Militant society, structured around relationships of hierarchy and obedience, was simple and undifferentiated; industrial society, based on voluntary, contractually assumed social obligations, was complex and differentiated. As we have seen in

*Table 4.1* Rapid social change: the evolutionary typological tradition of Western thinkers

| 'Sociologist' | Earlier societies | Newer societies arriving | Explanatory dynamic? |
| --- | --- | --- | --- |
| Adam Smith (1723-1790) | Hunting, herding, agricultural | Commercial | Rise of free markets |
| Auguste Comte (1798-1857) | Theological, metaphysical | Scientific, positivist | Science? |
| Henry Maine (1822-1888) | Status | Contract | Changes in law |
| Herbert Spencer (1820-1903) | Homogeneous – simple, militant | Heterogeneous – complex, industrial | Changes in population |
| Ferdinand Tönnies (1855-1936) | **Gemeinschaft** – community based | **Gesellschaft** – association based | Community shifts |
| Karl Marx (1818-1883) | Primitive communism, slavery, feudalism | Capitalism (but leading to socialism) | Economic exploitation |
| Émile Durkheim (1858-1917) | Mechanical solidarity | Organic solidarity | Population density and division of labour |
| Max Weber (1864-1920) | Traditional | Rational-bureaucratic, secular | Changes in religion (protestant) and economy(capitalism). |
| Georg Simmel (1858-1918) | Primitive production | Money and modernity | Circulation of money, group size grows |

Chapter 2 (pp. 32–3), Spencer conceptualised society as functioning like a 'social organism', (parallel to a human body) which evolved from the simpler state to the more complex according to the universal law of evolution. He saw progress as 'the survival of the fittest' (this was his phrase, not Darwin's). He was one of a growing number of thinkers who were trying to classify and understand the emergence of different types of society. A summary of some of these positions is given in Table 4.1.

## THE MAKING OF CLASSICAL SOCIOLOGY IN THE NINETEENTH CENTURY

The nineteenth and early twentieth century saw an enormous flurry of intellectual activity around the nature of society – much of it now long forgotten (John Scott's *Social Theory* (2006) is an interesting guide through much of this now lost work which also looks for the continuities between then and now). Reading the historical documents now leaves the feeling of a large group of gentlemen struggling to look across the world to make sense of rapid change whilst dealing with the shock of evolutionary theory. They compare world societies and try to make some sense of where we have come from and are now heading. Remember evolutionary theory was influential but also shocking. It was challenging many orthodox views of the world – especially religious ones. Although they were all Western, they all had their eye on a wider global world.

There are hundreds of thinkers during this period, but the now orthodox account of the history of sociology came to be written in the 1950s and saw three key figures as symbolic of classical sociology. We have met them all already: Karl Marx, Émile Durkheim and Max Weber. They are the holy trinity of sociology, and usually taught religiously in all sociology degrees as they open up some major debates of their time which are still alive today. Marx analyses the growth of capitalism, the significance of the economy and the material world, the importance of class, exploitation and inequality – and the possibility of a socialist society. Weber finds the growth of mass rationality, the bureaucratic state and a disenchanted world. Durkheim shows the significance of the social bond examining changes in religion and the division of labour.

We have encountered the key work of Karl Marx already several times – as he examines the impoverished lives of the masses under the exploitations of industrial capitalism and analyses the class struggles of societies. His earliest writings were philosophical and often called humanist whilst his later works developed the material conception of history and the scientific analysis of the **mode of production** (see Chapter 6). In the 1850s he produced historical studies of the working class movement, and analysed the relationship between the economic base and the ideological superstructure. He saw the role of historical actors and social class living in the squalor produced by the industrial revolution saw history as central to human understanding: and marked out the role of the economic and social class as key factors in social change. Alone amongst the early sociologists (and indeed the later ones), his work played a crucial role in the development and shaping of the twentieth-century communist societies (at one point probably over a third of the globe had been inspired by his work, including Russia, China and much of Africa and Latin America). He wrote the texts that subsequently led to the major Marxist revolutions (and failures) of the twentieth century (in Russia – in 1918, and in China – in 1949).

Émile Durkheim was professor of education at the Sorbonne between 1887 and 1902, and wrote four studies of lasting significance. *The Division of Labour* (1893) traced the development of society from 'mechanical to 'organic'. *The Rules of Sociological Method* (1895) analysed the very nature of 'social facts' and how they should be studied. *Suicide* (1987) took a highly individualistic phenomenon – killing yourself – to demonstrate through the analysis of suicide rates just how socially patterned it was. *The Elementary Form of Religious Life* (1912) demonstrated through a case study of the aborigines how 'religion is something eminently social'. Durkheim leads us into key debates about the massive growth of human populations and the shifting moral order of societies. For him, the growth of dense population shifted the nature of the human bond. As society moved from mechanical to organic solidarity – from traditional similarity and bonding community to the new industrial societies based on huge scale, difference and changing patterns of divisions of labour – they became much more prone to a breakdown of norms (anomie) and a weakening of social bonds. As old forms of bonding weakened, new ways of building solidarity and community were needed.

Max Weber was more concerned with human action and their meanings. He told us that 'ideas have consequences'. The new rationality helped shape capitalism and the emergent bureaucratic world. For Weber, transformations taking place were more connected to shifts in ideas and religious belief: the modern capitalist world had a close affinity to the rise of Protestant Christianity (or as he put it 'The Protestant Ethic'). He can be seen as the sociological counterpart of Franz Kafka: for him, the modern world led to the growth of the cold, impersonal bureaucracy and ultimately to a massive disenchantment with the world.

### A CAUTIONARY WORD: CONCEALED AND SUBTERRANEAN TRADITIONS

I have so far described a rather orthodox and straightforward history that is the tale commonly told. But no histories are ever quite like they are told. Although there are key figures, sociology was a young discipline and being developed on all sides with many disparate struggles as to its nature. Often now this is hard to see. Here were fermenting yet concealed traditions trying to grasp the social through a wide range of tools: many of the earliest writers were novelists, political tract writers, reformers, politicians, photographers, journalists, historians, priests and researchers. A motley crew indeed. So do remember as I rehearse this 'short history' that there was no unity in the origins of the discipline. As we shall see, there still is not – but that is to jump ahead of my tale ...

## EARLY TWENTIETH CENTURY SOCIOLOGY: PROFESSIONALISATION

Whatever the undercurrents, by the twentieth century sociology was fast becoming 'fixed' and 'professionalised' into an academic discipline. Albion Small (1854–1926) founded the Department of Sociology at the University of Chicago in 1892 and it remained the key institution until the mid-1930s when challenged by Pitrim Sorokin (1889–1968) who established the Sociology Department at

Harvard in 1931. Durkheim founded the first European Department of Sociology at the University of Bordeaux in 1895, publishing *The Rules of Sociological Method* as a kind of manifesto stating what sociology is and what it should do. In the UK, sociology as an academic subject began life at the London School of Economics in 1907 when L.T. Hobhouse (1864–1929) became its first Professor of Sociology. London remained the centre – indeed was the only place (apart from Liverpool University) until the middle of the twentieth century. In Germany, the first chair of sociology was created in 1918, and in 1923, the influential Institute of Social Research was established. In 1919, the first Indian Department of Sociology was established at Bombay (Mumbai). But in many countries round the world, sociology hardly developed at all throughout much of the twentieth century and in some countries sociology was more or less banned.

Although much of the foundational work of Western sociology came from Europe, at the start of the twentieth century a new 'American' sociology' started to develop where the United States (believing in its own exceptional position in the world – of democratic government and economic opportunity) would assume a prime role. Indeed, it would not be too wrong to say that the first half of the twentieth century belonged to American sociology – marking a (sad) move from a global awareness of societies across the world to one that increasingly focused on the workings of one: the United States. Bit by bit, the model of social analysis becomes North American – based on North-American thinking with the United States of America taken as the normative core of social life in the world. Life in America was social life. Capitalism and individualism became core assumptions.

The foundations of this sociology are usually seen to be **Chicago sociology** – though the story is much more complex than this. Chicago has to have the credit for popularising the discipline – with its key focus on urban research and the problems generated by the city, its textbook (*The Green Bible* of Park and Burgess), and its new, well-published graduate school. For the Chicago sociologists, the city became the key feature of the newly arriving world – more and more people found themselves in the city as 'urbanism' became 'a way of life'. A key influence here had been the German Georg Simmel (1858–1918), who we have met before, and who saw the city characterised by secondary rather than primary contacts. The contacts of the city may indeed be face-to-face, but they have now become impersonal, superficial, transitory, and segmental. The reserve, the indifference, and the blasé outlook of people in the city helps immune themselves from the expectations of others. It also leads to the sophistication and the rationality generally ascribed to city-dwellers. The city gave rise to new forms of social life.

This period also marked the first great African American sociologist W.E.B. Du Bois (1868–1963). From the 1920s onwards, he demonstrated the impact of modern capitalism on the structuring of race and social differences. In his *The Souls of Black Folk* (1903) he outlined his theory of double consciousness: 'One ever feels his twoness – an American, a Negro: two souls, two thoughts, two unreconciled strivings; two warring ideals in one dark body, whose dogged strength alone keeps it from being torn asunder'. Here is 'the negro's' sense of always looking at one's self through the eyes of others. Du Bois believed in the possibilities of racial progress and conducted major empirical research in Philadelphia on the lives of city-dwelling blacks. Subsequently there has been a major strand of US work that takes the 'race divide' very seriously.

## SOCIOLOGY IN THE WAR TIMES

This 'short' twentieth century was confronting new problems: the horrors of two major world wars, two major world revolutions (China and Russia – along with many others), a coming to terms with the ravages of the colonial past, and the damage and immiseration caused by much of the ruthless earlier industrialisation. A different set of social conditions thus started to bring different analyses. In Germany, there was a creeping rise of fascism, watched as it developed by a group of thinkers who developed **critical theory** and came to be known as the Frankfurt School (where they were based). Theodor Adorno (1903–1969), Herbert Marcuse (1989–1979), Marie Jahoda (1907–2001), Eric Fromm (1900–1980), Walter Benjamin (1892–1940) and Max Horkheimer (1895–1973) have left major legacies as social and cultural critics.

Their core concerns were the application of broadly Marxist (and often Freudian) ideas to the workings of culture as they examined the arrival of mass society, the proliferating of technology and bureaucracy, and the growth of what Adorno called 'the Culture Industry' – often regulating and trivialising our lives. Karl Mannheim (1993–1947) who developed the sociology of knowledge, and Norbert Elias (1897–1990) with his theory of 'civilising process' were also at some time based at Frankfurt. But all in the end fled the rise of Nazism, most finding a home in the USA either in California (Adorno and Marcuse) or New York (at the New School), or England (Elias and Mannheim). Their writings – often hard to understand – have been crucial in shaping contemporary analyses of culture. (Today probably the most significant development of this position can be found in the work of Jürgen Habermas). During this period, sociology more or less disappeared under both Stalinism and Maoism – two vast continents for whom sociology was an unacceptable discipline.

## SOCIOLOGY AFTER THE SECOND WORLD WAR: FROM CONSENSUS TO A MULTI-PARADIGM DISCIPLINE

In the period after the Second World War, a new age of 'professional sociology' appeared to bring a maturity and for a short while a kind of consensus appeared – 'the end of ideology'(claiming the exhaustion of political ideas). It was especially associated with the work of **functionalist** theorists like Kingsley Davis, Robert King Merton and Talcott Parsons. Indeed, in the mid-twentieth century, no sociologist was more well-known than Talcott Parsons(1902–1979). Like all sociologists, his ideas changed over time, but in 1951 he published *The Social System*. This heralded the search for developing a grand, overarching explanation of how social orders worked, and here he outlined the pre-requisites for the functioning of societies in a series of elaborate typologies and boxes. For Parsons all societies must perform certain key functions: they have to *A*dapt, achieve their *G*oals, become *I*ntegrated and ultimately maintain themselves (which he called *L*atency) – a framework often abbreviated to *AGIL*. This highly abstract systematic depiction of certain social necessities, which every society must meet to be able to maintain stable social life, led to a typology and table of approaching one hundred boxes – a map of the social system and its interconnected functions, from biological systems to world systems. His work can be applied to many areas of social life – how do schools work, hospitals run, prisons function as systems? They can all be seen as systems striving to achieve certain goals, socialising their members to their cultures, and adapting along the way. Grand systems of society – an almost utopian order – were a key theme.

But not for long. Whilst Parsons was developing this abstract model of society, others became critical. As sociology became more and more formally organised in universities and professions, by the end of the 1950s, sociology had become obviously divided and suffered a number of major internal critiques about the directions it was heading. The publication in 1959 by the North American Marxist C. Wright Mills (1916–1962) of *The Sociological Imagination* has come to be identified as a kind of landmark publication (even though Mills himself was author of only a few books and died young, he gained a maverick reputation). The book opens with an amusing – if unfair – attack on Parsons and his jargon, and is famed for its critique of the state of sociology at this time, which he saw as being dominated by three main misleading trends: grand abstraction, empirical triviality and methodological fussiness. For Mills, sociology had lost its critical way. Likewise, the Russsian émigré to the USA Pitrim Sorokin – fleeing imprisonment in the Czarist regime of the Russian Empire – suggested that sociological work had now become a 'jungle of diverse and often discordant theories', spoiled by the tendency towards 'fads and foibles' (the title of one of his many books). It seems Sorokin was right – for the discipline has continued so ever since. Although professional sociologists often try to create a semblance of underlying theoretical cohesion and order in understanding society, in practice, sociology was and continues to grow into a fractured, fragmented and **multi-paradigmatic** discipline that is often guilty of following trends and fashions of the time.

*Table 4.2*    From Comte to Bourdieu: twenty landmark male Western texts 1824–1984

A landmark provides a marker by indicating the arrival of something that breaks with the past and generates new work for the future. There are thousands of studies which could be placed on a list like this but here is a small 'sampler' selection. To get on this list, you have to be dead! I have not included texts that developed from feminist work here as I do this in Table 4.3. It would be odd for a professional sociologist to not at least know about most of the following:

| | |
|---|---|
| 1. | 1824 August Comte, *System of Positive Politics* – introduced the term sociology |
| 2. | 1846 Marx and Engels, *The German Ideology* – the theory of materialist history outlined |
| 3. | 1886 Charles Booth, *Poverty: Life and Labour of the People in London* – measuring poverty in the city with a very large survey |
| 4. | 1987 Émile Durkheim, *Suicide* – suicide statistics show just how suicide varies socially |
| 5. | 1889 W.E.B. Du Bois, *The Philadelphia Negro* – first major study of the American Negro |
| 6. | 1904 Max Weber, *The Protestant Ethic and the Spirit of Capitalism* – ideas shape history, and here religion shapes capitalism |
| 7. | 1900 Georg Simmel, *The Philosophy of Money* – changes in organisation of money shift human relations |
| 8. | 1921 Robert Park and Ernest Burgess, *Introduction to the Science of Sociology* – first major textbook from a major new sociology department at Chicago University with a stress on city conflict |
| 9. | 1918–20 W.I. Thomas and Florian Znaniecki, *The Polish Peasant in Europe and America* – highly regarded five volumes of innovative method, theory and data on migrants and city life |
| 10. | 1929 Robert and Helen Lynd, *Middletown* – small town community life (Muncie) in the USA observed closely and especially through its class system |
| 11 | 1932 George Herbert Mead, *Mind, Self and Society* – philosophical foundations for bridging individual and society |
| 12. | 1944 Theodore Adorno and Max Horkheimer, *Dialectics of Enlightenment* – asks 'why mankind, instead of entering into a truly human condition, is sinking into a new kind of barbarism' |
| 13 | 1949 Robert King Merton, *Social Theory and Social Structure* – major statement of mid-twentieth-century functionalism |
| 14. | 1950 David Riesman, Nathan Glazer and Reuel Denney, *The Lonely Crowd* – society has moved from tradition directed to outer directed |

continued

*Table 4.2 continued*

15. 1951 Talcott Parsons, *The Social System* – theoretical treatise about the integrated social order.

16. 1959 C. Wright Mills, *The Sociological Imagination* – left critique of grand theory and overworked methodology in sociology

17. 1956/59 Erving Goffman, *The Presentation of Self in Everyday Life* – micro-sociological argument about social life as drama

18. 1970 Alvin Gouldner, *The Coming Crisis of Western Sociology* – another substantial and left-based critique of mainstream sociological theory

19. 1976: Michel Foucault, *Discipline and Punish* – popular discourse theory of prison and crime

20. 1984 Pierre Bourdieu, *Distinction* – key late-twentieth-century analysis of social class

## 1968 AND ALL THAT: A SYMBOLIC YEAR

Let's move on. After the war, sociology expanded in major ways, developing momentum, status and a certain kind of fashionability as it entered both the universities and the schools in a mass way. The discipline became more and more popular – almost fashionable and trendy till the mid 1970s, and the field expanded rapidly. Its expansion is often linked to the radical global student politics of 1968, a symbolic year that came to be a watershed signalling:

- The massive expansion of higher education throughout the world.
- The coming of age of the baby boomers, born just after the Holocaust and The Second World War. Like each generation, it was different – but this was the one that became the first major self designated 'youth culture'.
- A sense was 'in the air' that something new was coming premised on quite a lot of hope and optimism. The world was here to change.
- So with this: the new times (postmodern) were in the making – of individualism – the 'Impulsive self' and the 'Me decade'; of consumption – of new markets; and of informalism.
- The development of human rights since the United Nations declarations of 1948 – from the civil rights movement and the women's movement.

- Continuing war and international conflict – notably in Vietnam.
- The dawn of the spiritual 'Age of Aquarius' and the growth of countercultural moments.
- The simultaneous rebirth and slow death of the Marxist world.
- The spread of global awareness largely through the mass media. More and more, as Todd Gitlin put it, 'the whole world was watching'. Symbols had gone global.

These are very big themes. '1968' signified not a year but a whole period (roughly the late 1950s to the early 1980s) when significant social changes were settling in. And the massive development of sociology was bound up with this period. Sociology now became a popular university discipline (and the butt of many jokes!). This period really marks the rapid development of professional sociology and the arrival of sociology's widespread incorporation into university syllabuses. A key mid-twentieth-century UK sociologist, A.H. Halsey has provided a detailed (if very traditional) account of British sociology and marvels that whereas there could have been no more than 200 undergraduates in the 1940s, by the year 2000 there were 'as many as 2,000 sociologists teaching and 24,000 students in the universities of the United Kingdom'(Halsey 2004, p. 3). Sociology was introduced in to the school curriculum in the mid 1960s and become popular in the universities during this period (and especially in the then 'new' universities of Essex, Warwick, Kent, York, Sussex and Lancaster).

The sociology that started to flourish in this time became much more critical of the traditional canon or orthodoxies of sociology – indeed became much more influenced by the work of Marx than that of Durkheim and Weber. One sociologist Alvin Gouldner (1920–1980) wrote of *The Coming Crisis of Western Sociology* (1970), and it seemed a new era was being ushered in. Gouldner argued for a greater reflexivity in sociology – that sociology needed to see itself in the same ways as it saw society. Sociology was always bound up with the contexts of its times and these needed to be fully incorporated into sociological thinking. This meant the serious analysis of capitalism which structured sociology as much as everything else.

## WIDENING THE BASE OF SOCIOLOGICAL THINKING: BREAKING DISCIPLINARY BOUNDARIES

One of the striking features of post-1968 sociological thinking has been the gradual widening of its intellectual base and its questioning of its traditional assumptions. Some sociologists have buried their heads very deeply in the sand about such developments; others have been very critical and condemnatory of such trends. But like it or not, the study of the social has broadened out: no longer is it simply in the hands of sociologists, there are now many other pathways into sociology and scholars outside the mainstream of sociology have challenged the supremacy of the sociological profession in looking at the social. Amongst these new inquiries are cultural studies, feminism and gender studies, media and communication studies, post-colonial studies, multiculturalism, race and anti-racism studies, queer and LGBT (lesbian, gay, bisexual and transgender) studies, global studies, cyber-cultural studies and human rights studies. Bridges have also been made to many linked disciplines – geography has become 'space studies', history has engaged with the new cultural and social histories as well as oral history, and anthropologists have been developing 'cultural anthropology'. You can soon see these shifts in major book shops: the old sections on sociology have become somewhat smaller whilst these new sections have developed into sections all of their own – and often overtaking and even replacing those of sociology. Although professional sociologists have tried to hold its traditional claim over the field of the social, in practice it has now massively diversified and people can be found studying the social within many other fields.

### ENTER POSTMODERNISM, MULTICULTURALISM AND FOUCAULT

There are many influences on this diversification. Postmodernism became a buzz word in sociology by the mid 1980s for a deep sense of transformation and the movement into a world where the search for one grand truth is over. Likewise multiculturalism also arrived during the 1980s – most significantly in the USA, though it spread everywhere – and critiqued the idea of a monologic culture i.e. one that speaks with only one voice. From the discovery of a black history and a woman's history in the heady days of 1968, it soon became clear that there had been a tremendous bias in academic life in favour of white, middle-class men. The voices of many had been silenced. It could be seen simply by looking at the people who taught and ran the universities and schools – women and women's views of the world were rare; black voices very few. One path here was the direct recruitment of more women and more ethnic groups to the universities to teach (a point which is now highly visible when looking at many US universities). But the content of study and academic disciplines also changed, leading to much conflict on the campus over what should be taught – the so called 'culture wars'. The challenge over the syllabus and what constituted knowledge was on. And it influenced sociology. Certain new writers appeared who started to have a major impact on social thinking but who were not sociologists (Michel Foucault (1926–1984), for example, who we met in Chapter 2 has had a major impact on all of the humanities and social sciences).

## FEMINISM UNBOUND

A good and prime example of this broadening out is the arrival of feminism in the academy. In the 1970s, sociology was roundly criticised for overwhelmingly being *by men, about men and for men*. The hidden agenda of much early sociology was 'masculinist': not only had there been few women sociologists (and those there had been were 'hidden from herstory'), the subject matters (and many assumptions) had been tacitly largely about men: men and industry, men and class, men and education, men and power were its themes. It was time to bring women in. And we can see this shift over the past fifty years or so. Many old topics have been given new slants – religion (why are gods and priests overwhelmingly male) or criminology (why are so many criminals men?). Methodologies and theories have been scrutinised for their male slant on objectivity. And there has been a major revisiting of past theories to see why women have been ignored. Indeed it has led to a discovery of many women sociologists who have been written out of history. Harriet Martineau (1802–1876), Jane Addams (1860–1935), Charlotte Perkins Gilman (1860–1935), Marianne Weber (1870–1954), Anna Julia Copper (1858–1964) and Beatrice Potter Webb (1858–1943) are examples. But above all, feminism has brought many new concerns to the sociological agenda: care, emotions, domestic violence, childbirth and reproduction, housework/domestic labour – as Table 4.3 illustrates.

*Table 4.3*  Expanding the concerns of sociology: the impact of feminism

| *Feminism expands sociology to look at* | *Illustrative author and book* |
| --- | --- |
| Housework – domestic labour | Anne Oakley, *Sociology of Housework* (1984) |
| Emotional work | Arlie Hochschild, *The Managed Heart: The Commercialization of Human Feeling* (1983) |
| Caring | Virginia Held, *The Ethics of Care* (2007) |
| Sexual violence | Liz Kelly, *Surviving Sexual Violence* (1988) |
| Mothering | Nancy Chodorow, *The Reproduction of Mothering* (1979) |
| Young women and girls | Angela McRobbie, *Feminism and Youth Culture* (2000) |
| Women and crime | Carol Smart, *Women, Crime and Criminology* (1976) |
| Rethinking men and masculinity | Raewyn Connell, *Masculinity* (2nd edition, 2005) |
| The state and women | Sylvia Walby, *Theorizing Patriarchy* (1990) |
| Lesbian life | Arlene Stein, *Sex and Sensibility: Stories of a Lesbian Generation* (1997) |
| Rethinking race | Patricia Hill Collins, *Black Feminist Thought* (1990) |
| New families | Carol Smart, *Personal Lives* (2008) |
| Feminist methods | Liz Stanley and Sue Wise, *Breaking Out* (2nd edition, 1993) |
| Colonialism | Chandra Mohanty, *Feminism Without Borders* (2003) |
| Feminist epistemology | Sandra Harding, *The Feminist Standpoint Reader* (2003) |

*THE RISE OF CULTURAL STUDIES*

The last decades of the twentieth century saw an unmistakable 'cultural turn' in the social sciences. In Europe, its inspiration came from Gramsci, Foucault, Bourdieu, Habermas and others – all of whom we will briefly meet in this book. In the UK, an interest grew out of a literary socialism associated with Richard Hogart and Raymond Williams, and leading to the work of Stuart Hall and the so called Birmingham Centre of Cultural Studies (BCCS) prominent in the 1970s for its research on cultures, identities, class, race and gender. In the US, a more mainstream focus on culture – its symbols, language and civil society – started to develop in the work of Jeffrey Alexander, Steven Seidman, Ann Swidler and others. Different as they all were, understanding the conflicts and changes found in the workings of culture became more and more a core concern.

*ASCENDANT POST-COLONIAL VISIONS*

Post-colonial theory is another example. Post-colonialism looks at countries that were once colonised by others – notably the invasion or influence of Britain, France and Spain over many countries in the eighteenth and nineteenth centuries. In this process, indigenous peoples lost their own sense of who they were along with their own histories in the wake of the dominance of these colonising thinkers. Shaped heavily by Edward Said's book *Orientalism* (published in 1978), **post-colonialism** shows how the knowledge of colonised (subordinated, subjugated) peoples is often shaped by the coloniser. Very often in the past the sociologist's own approach had legitimated the coloniser's position, indeed even masking the assumptions of the ruler. Now, coming from many traditions, post-colonialism highlighted the voice of the neglected ('**subaltern**') others. Much sociology it has argued has been complicit in this earlier science – indeed Enlightenment thinking itself may well have been a central tool of the colonisers, holding as they did to Western view of science, rationality and progress as the key to future thought. Sociology itself then may here become a tool not of scientific advance but of complicit, colonial oppression. Taking this seriously in effect means a much more careful listening to other voices from other cultures.

*COMING OUT OF THE CLOSET IN SOCIOLOGY: THE ARRIVAL OF*
*LESBIANS, GAYS, TRANSSEXUALS, QUEERS AND OTHERS IN THE*
*UNIVERSITY*

During most of sociology's two hundred year history, sociology paid
no attention to the complexities of sexuality and took for granted
the punitive polarity between homosexuality and heterosexuality,
in which homosexuals were presumed sad, sick, sinning criminals.
Homosexuals – a term invented in the 1870s – had been a classic
case of the stigmatised outsider we met in Chapter 1, even within
sociology itself. But with the new wave of sociology since 1968,
the arrival of the Gay Liberation Front and the Queer Movement
eventually started to change this. As with women, blacks and post-
colonial groups, gays and lesbians have started to find a voice in
many countries around the world. This also challenged the blatant
**homophobia** and **hetero-normativity** of much sociological
writing.

## SOCIOLOGICAL IMAGINATIONS AND THE FUTURE OF SOCIOLOGY

This chapter can be seen as providing a synoptic, straightforward
and inevitably superficial account of mainstream sociology for
beginners. It is a fairly classic telling – most introductory textbooks
would tell the story a bit like this. Mainstream sociology has been
shaped by the Enlightenment and the modern industrial-capitalist
world – a world in which white, Christian (sometimes Jewish) men
held all the prominent positions. Whenever it has had a global eye,
it has usually managed to keep the Western world as its baseline: it
has focused overwhelmingly on only a limited number of societies
associated with the rich – often colonising – West, leaving all
other countries either to anthropology or to a specialist area called
'development studies'. To put it bluntly, *over three-quarters of the world
– China, the Islamic countries, Africa, much of Asia and Latin America – go
missing from much of the mainstream Western sociological account of the world.*
This was less so in the very early days and is starting to be corrected
again now; but for much of the twentieth century, the arrogance of
much Western sociology is really rather surprising. Today sociology
is at least looking outwards from the West to a more international

world. There are other changes too shaping the new sociology – not least the developing cyberworlds – as we shall see.

Sociology is (and always has been) a fragmented discipline. It can hardly be otherwise. At a simple counting, I can see over fifty different theoretical positions, hundreds of different methodologies, and a vast arena of areas of interest (see Table 4.4). Textbooks try to simplify this into various schools of thought, but the point really is that *sociology is a very messy discipline*. At the very least we can say it is **multi-paradigmatic**. Does the future of sociology lie in more and more specialisms, fragmentations and new 'disciplines'? Almost certainly. But a word of caution is now needed.

For all its multiple varieties, sociology is held together by a common awareness of the significance of the social. Sociology is an imagination, a way of thinking, a critical consciousness. And as such it will always be needed. What the rest of this book tries to show is that despite all the variations and disagreements – all the various theories and methods – doing sociology always means the development of this common critical consciousness. The next three chapters aim to tell you what to look for in developing this sociological imagination. Areas of interest, theoretical tendencies, methodological skills may come and go – there will always be trends and fashions. But the essential wisdoms of sociology will always be needed.

## SUMMARY

Sociology was born of the Enlightenment and industrialisation and has been around for some 200 years in its 'professional form'. This chapter provides a conventional brief history of it. Currently, it is being reshaped by new 'postmodern trends' like multiculturalism, feminism and queer theory. A caution is sounded: recent world developments challenge much of 'Western' sociology (dominated by Europe and the USA). We can expect in the near future that this history will be reworked when a proper focus is given to all countries and regions of the world.

*Table 4.4*   Subject sections in the American Sociological Association in 2009

This list gives some idea of the major areas of specialism and contemporary interest in sociology today – at least in the U.S.A. These sections attract a lot of interest and hold their own meetings and newsletters. They are listed in alphabetical order. Nevertheless, they far from exhaust the range of interests in sociology.

1. Aging and the Life Course
2. Alcohol, Drugs, and Tobacco
3. Animals and Society
4. Asia and Asian America
5. Children and Youth
6. Collective Behavior and Social Movements
7. Communication and Information Technologies
8. Community and Urban Sociology
9. Comparative and Historical Sociology
10. Crime, Law, and Deviance
11. Culture
12. Economic Sociology
13. Education
14. Emotions
15. Environment and Technology
16. Ethnomethodology and Conversation Analysis
17. Evolution, Biology and Society
18. Family
19. History of Sociology
20. Human Rights
21. International Migration
22. Labor and Labor Movements
23. Latino/a Sociology
24. Law
25. Marxist Sociology
26. Mathematical Sociology
27. Medical Sociology
28. Mental Health
29. Methodology
30. Organizations, Occupations, and Work
31. Peace, War, and Social Conflict
32. Political Economy of the World-System
33. Political Sociology
34. Population
35. Race, Gender, and Class
36. Racial and Ethnic Minorities
37. Rationality and Society
38. Religion
39. Science, Knowledge, and Technology
40. Sex and Gender
41. Sexualities
42. Social Psychology
43. Sociological Practice and Public Sociology
44. Teaching and Learning
45. Theory

## EXPLORING FURTHER

MORE THINKING

Start to build up your own time line charts of the history of sociology. Think of key theorists, countries, ideas, and historical phasings. A quick look at the appendices in Donald. N. Levine, *Visions of the Sociological Tradition* (1995) may be useful.

READING

On the Enlightenment tradition, see Paul Hyland, Olga Gomez and Francesca Greensides, *The Enlightenment: A Sourcebook and Reader* (2003), a wide-ranging collection of original statements and commentaries. Alan Swingewood's *A Short History of Sociological Thought* (2000, 3rd edition) was first published in 1984 and has been updated regularly. It is one of many, but provides a short and orthodox account of what the history of sociological theory is usually agreed to look like by most sociologists. John Hughes, Wes Sharrock and Peter Martin's *Understanding Classical Sociology* (2003) gives a good introduction to the Big Three. A.H. Halsey's *A History of Sociology in Britain* (2004) is a very valuable account of the whole of British sociology – though it also shows the problems of writing such an account. There are many collections of readings but Charles Lemert's *Social Theory: The Multicultural and Classic Readings* (2004) is well organised, with useful short commentaries. It provides extracts of all the major thinkers which are very short and provides an excellent starting source book.

Critical commentaries on the development of Western sociology to look at include Raewyn Connell, *Southern Theory: The Global Dynamics of Knowledge in Social Science* (2007); Patricia Hill Collins, *Black Feminist Thought* (1990) and Gurminder K.Bhambra, *Rethinking Modernity: Postcolonialism and the Sociological Imagination* (2007) On feminist sociology, see the valuable account by Patricia Madoo Lengermann and Jill Niebrugge-Brantley in *The Women Founders* (1998). Sara Delamont's *Feminist Sociology* (2003) is a clear and helpful contribution. Rosemarie Tong's *Feminist Thought* (third edition 2008) clarifies different positions. On sexuality, see Jeffrey Weeks's *Sexuality* (third edition, 20009). On race and racism, see the admirable collection *Theories of Race and Racism: A Reader* (2007) edited by Les Back and John Solomos.

# CULTIVATING SOCIOLOGICAL IMAGINATIONS

> The sociological imagination enables us to grasp history and biography and the relations between the two within society. That is its task and its promise.
>
> C. Wright Mills, *The Sociological Imagination*, 1959

> Only connect! ... Only connect the prose and the passion.
>
> E.M. Forster, *Howard's End*, 1910

So now we reach the Holy Grail. Just how are we to make sense of this enormously complex, ever changing, politically laden flow of human social life that I have been locating in this book so far? How are we to sociologically understand this world we live in? Or at least some small parts of it? And, maybe even, ultimately, how can we use this knowledge to help create a better world for *all*? Here indeed are the challenges of sociology. *How can sociology be done so that it gives us better accounts of the social world than everyday life provides us with?*

This question leads sociologists to academic courses and debates on what is called **methodology** or **theory**. Sociology can now be studied in schools and colleges where to think theoretically and develop methodological skills is what sociology is all about. Indeed, sociologists can often be split into empiricists, methodologists and theorists. Empiricists are often passionately obsessed with the minutiae of social life and seek to describe as much as they can in great detail. 'The truth of the story lies in the detail'. Methodologists give their intellectual energies to rendering the tools and statistics of social research ever more sophisticated: 'good measurement and sophisticated research design' – that's what needed, they say. And theorists are often beautifully obsessed with the intricacies of human thought and thinking and how to make as precise and logical as possible the general and abstract principles of social thought. It is in fact an old, old story – between those more comfortable with facts and those happier with abstractions. Studying sociology will almost inevitably mean doing a course or two in 'methodology' (often run by the empiricists) and a course or three in 'sociological theory' (usually run by the male theorists). Methodologists will tell you how to do research in an ideal world, and theorists will tell you how to search for more general laws and understanding the rules of the game.

## SIGNS AND ROAD MAPS FOR DOING SOCIOLOGY

In the next two chapters, I aim to look at some of the basics of these approaches. But here I also want to argue *against* the fetishes of methodology and abstract theorising. Of course 'methods' and 'theory' will always be significant issues for any serious research and thinking in *any* field or discipline from physics to music. But they are often overstated: *theory and methods are simply tools, means to an end.* Sadly, for many social scientists they become ends in themselves and often create little worlds of academic infighting and obscurantism to be avoided by most. The challenge for sociology is to develop a deep understanding of the empirical social world we live in through whatever routes this can be achieved best. In this chapter I suggest some guidelines for cultivating a way of thinking about the social; in the next I hope to foster some skills in both doing research and thinking about the adequacy of research you read. As always, these are just starting points – the basics. The box overleaf summarises these.

THINK ON: GUIDELINES FOR CREATING A
SOCIOLOGICAL IMAGINATION

Put simply, here are the eleven key tips discussed in the chapter:

1   Search for underlying structures and social patterns
2   Understand social actions and meaning
3   Bridge actions and structures
4   Empathise with lived cultures
5   Interrogate the material world
6   Develop an awareness of time and history
7   Keep moving on: look at contingency, change and flow
8   Locate social life in place and space
9   Be biographical
10  Ponder power
11  Live with complexity and contradiction.*
*12 *analyse the matrix of inequalities. (This 12th issue is
    not discussed in this chapter, but Chapter 7 is devoted
    exclusively to it.)*

## 1  SEARCH FOR STRUCTURES: WHAT ARE THE UNDERLYING PATTERNS OF SOCIAL LIFE?

The first ingrained habit of the sociological mind is to keep looking for social patterns. Social life has many random and chance factors as we shall see: but if we look hard enough we can usually find a sense of order beneath much of it. Terms capturing this include **structures**, **institutions**, **forms**, **habits**, and **habitus**. For the moment, let's simply see them as the patterns of social life.

### THE DAY AND ITS HABITS

The simplest start is to think about a typical day in your own life – or anyone else's for that matter. It is not usually a completely chaotic mess, even if it sometimes seems like that. Indeed, some people can be very tight and rigid about their day. In the film *Stranger than Fiction* (2006) the hero, Harold Crick – a dull auditor for the tax office, is shown as a man ruled by his clock (and who hears the narrative of his life). He counts the number of times he brushes his teeth in the morning (38!), knows the precise time he should leave for the bus each day, which he catches every day for the office and has never missed. At work, every event is timed and structured by time. He is a man dominated by ritual, time and narrative. Likewise the film *Groundhog Day* (1993) shows a man who gets up every day to do exactly the same things. He is – as the tag goes – 'having the worst day of his life – over and over'. The hero, the meteorologist Phil Connors, awakens each day to find it is again February 2: it starts each morning at 6:00 a.m. with his waking up to the same song, Sonny and Cher's 'I Got You Babe' on his alarm clock radio. His memories of the 'previous' day intact, he seems to be trapped in a seemingly endless 'time loop' to repeat the same day in the same way in the same small town.

Now look at your own day, your own environment and chart its own patterns or structures. Even if you party every night, get up very late and spend most days just lazing and grazing around you are probably caught in a pattern. Most Western people most days follow the same daily routines – getting out of beds, stumbling to bathrooms, having some kind of breakfast, setting out on some kind of work or day 'schedule of events' – seeing friends, going to work, dropping the children off, cooking the meals. The influential late nineteenth-century pragmatic social philosopher William James called this the flywheel of habit. He suggests that most of our lives are lived in habits and routines and that this is indeed what makes social life work.

## THE STREET AND ITS SOCIAL ORDER

Now go a little beyond your own life – but not far. Look around your neighbourhood. Sociologists have long strolled around cities and streets looking at the patterns of life that appear before their eyes. And what becomes clear is that the spaces we move in develop definite ways of life.

Elijah Anderson is an African American Professor of Sociology and author of *Code of the Street* (1999). His study looks at the rituals, values and social etiquette to be found in the multicultural neighbourhoods along Philadelphia's Germantown Avenue, a major artery of the city which reflects the vast social and economic difficulties confronting many urban centres throughout the world. In the opening chapter, Anderson invites the reader to take a stroll with him along this road. It is a long road, and as he moves along, it changes its shape and culture from the richest of the posh folk to the poorest of the poor. As he moves the social patterns of the street – which groups go where, their shifting values, their street codes – change. He looks at the differences between the 'decent' families and the rougher 'street' families – the smart parts and the parts shaped by urban decay. Anderson's study is part of a tradition of urban sociology which has long been mapping out the shapes and structures of city life for the past century and a half. In a way you will already know this intuitively: some parts of the city are no-go areas; others are stinking rich! Streets tell you what is expected of you. Strolling around Mayfair in London you will meet very different people to when you are strolling around Brixton. Sociologists have long mapped the features of many cities. Thus, the pioneering Charles Booth (1840–1916) mapped out poverty in London, and the Chicago sociologists became famous for their analysis of 'zones' during the 1920s and the 1930s. And these days there is also a whole industry devoted to mapping out life styles attached to postal areas and zip codes.

## THE WORLD AS A PRISON

Having gone so far, we can now we can take our mapping of social orders much further. We can look at all of society as a flow of social orders and patterns constantly being generated and regenerated around certain 'problems' – in families, schools, workplaces, churches, governments, stock exchanges and prisons. What is the pattern here?

Consider for example families. All societies have structures which help organise the raising of children, the regulation of sexuality, and the organisation of identities and generations etc; but, as is well documented, the variety of family organisation across different times and places is considerable. People enter marriages for example by contract, coercion, force, choice. They marry opposite sex and same sex partners. They have many partners (polygamy) or one (monogamy); they marry within the same category (endogamy) or outside of it; they have large families and small families, raise them on their own or with the aid of all kinds of others. And they may be close to the wider family (extended family) or not. Nevertheless within all this variety, there will always be patterns and structures.

And it goes yet further than this: all societies across the world develop definite identifiable patterns. French society is not Thai society is not Australian society. **Social structures** are the patterns of predictable human actions that cluster around key problems in living and they vary in all societies.

## 2 EXAMINE SOCIAL ACTIONS AND MEANINGS: HOW DO PEOPLE ACT TOWARDS OTHERS?

Sociology's first task is to lay out these broad patterns of social structure, and ultimately attempt to understand how they work. But if we just stayed with this question all the time, it would not get us very far. For people would soon object to the way society is seen as a prison in which they are trapped and patterned. People are much more *active* than this. Human beings engage continually in social action and interaction with others – changing their own lives and others, challenging what they find around them. Human lives are never passive but always in perpetual motion. And, indeed, they are often enabled to act because of this structure.

In this sense, a basic unit of sociology to think about is human social action and interactions. People act in the world towards others, they create social worlds with others; they are not the mere passive recipients of presenting social orders, structures, prisons or patterns. Indeed their actions keep changing the world and keep social life in perpetual motion as they engage with others. We are historical actors always making our worlds: never ever static but always moving, and never blindly determined, but always in perpetual creative action. We are never solitary individuals, and always depend on others for a sense of who we are. Sociologists work hard on examining human **actions, habitus**, and **selves**.

## SOCIAL ACTIONS

The most celebrated account of social **action** was provided over a century ago by Max Weber. Put simply, he claimed that social actions refer to human life when it takes into account the meanings people have of other people. It is linked to what is sometimes called '**inter-subjectivity**', whereby people make sense of social life through entering the minds of others they interact with. Charles Cooley saw this too when he claimed that 'We dwell in the minds of others'.

So, one task of the sociologist is to investigate the different kinds of social actions, each with their own reality and properties. A quick listing of such social actions might include (the list is not exhaustive):

- Rational actions, where our actions are shaped by ends and means (e.g. science; some – especially economists – also say that following paths to maximise our own self interests is rational).
- Value actions, where our actions are shaped by (often personal) values (e.g. when we take moral or ethical positions).
- Practical actions, where our actions are guided by solving daily problems.
- Instrumental actions, where our actions are shaped by pursuing one's own ends (e.g. we use a teacher as a means for getting access to knowledge or learning).
- Emotional actions, where our actions are shaped by feelings (e.g. when we cry at funerals).
- Traditional actions, where our actions are shaped by habits (e.g. cleaning our teeth, driving a car).
- Embodied actions, where our actions are closely linked to the functioning, movement and projects of our bodies (e.g. washing activities, sex play, the clothes we adorn ourselves with: see Chapter 2, p. 26–7).
- Innovative actions, where our actions are guided by creativity (e.g. art, music, much writing).

Of course, such a list is just a start and these areas often overlap. You may like to note the sheer range of these actions – they include feelings, bodies, creativities, values, practicalities. Much social science has a tendency to focus on rational actions; but very often much of social life is not shaped by this at all. Nevertheless sociologists do like to study these actions – in science, in the gym, in schools, in street behaviour, in love and conflicts. Note this is not psychology – the psychologist would study the individual's motives: here we are looking at the creation of social actions and how people orientate life to others. You may like to review some of the 'social actions' you encounter during an afternoon or evening. How do people orientate themselves to others and how does meaning arise? Remember: you are never alone in a social action.

PRACTICES AND HABITUS

Indeed, taking these actions further we might also see them as clustering into patterns themselves. Here some sociologists speak of the logics of practice (Pierre Bourdieu is a key figure here: see page 167), and, again, these emphasise the importance of the body and practices within the social world. This view stands against the absurdly naïve view that people simply act in rational and coherent ways. Just ask yourself if you do? Instead social actions are usually practical – they operate according to an implicit practical logic for them. This is a practical sense with certain bodily dispositions which functions differently in different environments with different people. Sociologists often speak here of **habitus** to indicate a system of habits acquired through social life which we carry around with us. We develop rituals, a sense, a 'feel for the game' of whatever we are doing. This idea gets us beyond the simple notion of *individual* habits – and on to a wider sense that we dwell all the time within our *social* habits. One major task of sociology is to understand the workings of these everyday logics, these common sense forms of social action – because this indeed is what we live with all the time. They are, in a sense, what makes the world go around.

## 3 BRIDGE ACTIONS AND STRUCTURES: HOW DO WE CONNECT INDIVIDUALS WITH SOCIETY?

We have seen that sociologists look at 'social structures' and the big patterns which organise social life deeply, whilst at the same time examining 'social actions', their orientations to others which keeps changing and challenging the structures. Sociologists see people as prisoners and puppets but also as people. The interest of sociologists in social things soon leads them to the *collective, the broad, the wide* concern with how societies work – with the nature of inequalities, the economic organisation of different kinds of society or the post-colonial world. But we also soon find that such issues leads us straight back to the *concrete lived lives of individuals.*

### INDIVIDUALISM AND THE SOCIAL

So here you find one of the major recurrent problems of all sociological thinking: *how to cope simultaneously with constraining structures and creative actions?* How can we link together action and structure? This is often called the **'action–structure'** debate. Throughout sociology you will find this tension between the broad mapping of *general social structures* and the *concrete and social actions of individuals.* It is sociology's abiding tension.

Here you will have to struggle with the *humanly creative* and the *socially determined,* with *individuals* and *societies.* In sociology this puzzle is never far away. How can individuals function as individuals within a society that must take away their individuality if it is to run for other individuals too in a well and orderly fashion? How can a society develop a cohesion and a collectivity whilst fostering an individuality and cultivating a unique humanity? How can there be individuals within society and a society with individuals? How can we have freedom yet constraint ? How can the individual dwell in the social and the social dwell in the individual? How can we have communities and bonding which do not overreach themselves into totalitarianisms and despotism? How can we have creative and caring individuals who do not overreach themselves into selfish, narcissistic egoists? How, in short, can we develop and maintain *a balance of individuality and sociality in life and society?* Too much focus on individuals leads to accusations of *individualism and reductionism;* too much focus on structures will lead to accusations of *determinism, holism and abstraction.*

It would be hard to find any sociologist (or indeed any thinker about the social from any discipline) who does not in the end have to deal with this question. Although discussions take many forms and may be partially resolved in many ways, it is the big social question. If 'individuals' triumph, we can so often sense a crumbling anarchy of egoism and selfishness taking over; if the 'social' triumphs, we can so often sense a painful loss of individuality as we are stalked by collective terrors. The roll call of thinkers on this issue is enormous: Plato, Aristotle, Hobbes, Rousseau, Montesquieu, Adam Smith, Kant, Goethe, De Tocqueville, Marx, Durkheim, Weber, Simmel, Dewey, Mead and on to major contemporary sociological works such as David Riesman's *The Lonely Crowd* (1950), Robert Bellah *et al.'s The Habits of the Heart* (1985), and Robert Putnam's *Bowling Alone* (2000).Welcome to the club!

## THINK ON: SIX OPENING WAYS INTO THE ACTION–STRUCTURE PUZZLE

The action–structure debate is a complex one and has produced many major and often dense theoretical studies dealing with it. Here are a few of the ways sociologists try to resolve this puzzle. Look out for them.

1   *Biographical life history*: start studying human biography and work out the ways in which social structure constrains you (see Mitch Dunier in *Slim's Table*)

2   *Structural analysis*: start with external social facts of structure but then work down to real people and how their lives are shaped (see Raewyn Connell especially in her book *Masculinities*)

3   *Cultural configurations*: look simultaneously at cultural meaning and individual meaning and move between them (see Norbert Elias in his *The Civilizing Society*)

4   **Structuration** *theory*: see the *duality of structure* in motion: social structures make social action possible, and at the same time that social action creates those very structures (see Anthony Giddens, *The Constitution of Society*)

5   *Positions and relations*: study relationships and practices in their habitus (as in the work of Bourdieu, see Beverley Skeggs, *Formations of Class and Gender*)

6   *Ethnographies*: get close to what you want to study and see both action and structure at work in the real situation (see Paul Willis, *Learning to Labour*).

## 4 EMPATHISE WITH LIVED CULTURES: HOW CAN WE GRASP MEANINGFUL SYMBOLIC WORLDS?

We have often seen though this book that social life for humans is invariably bound up with meaning. Whether we are looking at the societies of the Atzecs, the Romans or the Enlightenment; in the largest cities of the world or the smallest tribes on a Peruvian hilltop; humans – from birth to death – are engaged in a constant search to make sense of the world around them. Crucial to grasping this meaningful world is the idea of culture (revisit Chapter 2). Culture is uniquely human. Every other form of life – from ants to zebras – behaves in more uniform, species-specific ways. It is culture that makes us truly distinctive from most other animals. *We are the meaning-making animal*. And meanings have consequences. How people give meaning to their lives becomes a key reality for them.

Cultures might be seen as 'ways of life' and 'designs for living', as 'tool kits' for assembling 'webs of significant meanings', as 'the scraps, patches and rags of daily life'. They can be seen as a set of creative tools and responses, lived daily in a flow and a flux to try and help us resolve our daily problems of living. At the heart of cultures are such things as the languages, symbols, narratives, stories, rituals, values, roles, identities, myths, beliefs, practices and material objects which make up any people's way of life – the recipes for us to make sense of it all. Never tight, fixed or agreed upon, it is dangerous to think of cultures as unities, wholes or fixed in any way. They never are. Instead they are always alive and changing – contested, debated, modified, supported and rejected by their members in a vast stream of practical actions. They are always messy, multilayered and multiple mosaics; and are bridges to the past as well as guides to the future.

Cultures suggest innumerable social worlds that are constantly contradictory and full of tension. When we are looking *across* cultures, we should never be at all surprised to find their enormous differences. But this is so also when we look *inside* specific cultures. Cultures do not speak to consensus and uniformity: by their natures they cannot. Thus to speak of cultures as harmonious well-ordered consensual wholes is sheer nonsense. Shorthand talk of 'Muslim culture', 'working-class culture', 'women's culture', 'British culture' or even 'gay or queer culture' is in truth to construct a lie. Immediately sociologists can recognise that human social worlds are stuffed full of massive ambiguities, contradictions, tensions – never worlds of agreed upon consensus. Social life as lived by all peoples at all times grows out of these tensions. It is extremely important to grasp this – because views of cultures which flatten them, homogenise them and turn them into monologic, monolithic and mono-moral overly stable forms are very dangerous to sociological thinking – they foster the stereotypes of much everyday thought.

One of the most striking features of human cultures is the sheer range of things that people come to believe in at different places and times. The religions we encountered in Chapter 2 are a good example. Sociologists are not in the business of making value judgements about what people come to believe and how they make sense of social life. Rather their concerns are with showing how such beliefs come to arise (historical questions), with the ways in which they have come to be learnt and organised into people's lives (socialisation questions), and the overall roles and tasks that they play (functional questions).

These cultures are everywhere. As well as attempting to capture mainstream and dominant cultures, sociologists have paid much attention to studying a mass of different cultures. Basically, they enter these worlds and try to understand the language, the stories, the rituals, the identities within them. This task is often called **ethnography** – literally describing ways of life. Think of the way of life with which you are familiar. Here are some that sociologists have studied:

> astrology cultures; cyber cultures; drug cultures of all kinds (dope cultures, heroin cultures, LSD cultures, etc.); ethnic cultures (black, Asian, Muslim, etc.); environmental groups; feminist groups; flying saucer cults; gay, lesbian and queer cultures; gun rights cultures; leisure cultures; music cultures (rock groups, jazz bands, orchestras, opera, etc.), political cultures (right, left and middle); racial supremacists (Nazis, Ku Klux Klan, skinheads, Black Panthers, British National Front, etc.); religious and spiritual cultures of all sorts; school cultures; sports cultures (boxing, football, running, swimming, etc.); and youth cultures (teddy boys, mods and rockers, punks, goths, heavy metal, raves, etc.).

And on and on: the list could be extended massively. This is what many sociologists do – they study little social worlds and their ways of life. They get close to them, live in them and see what is going on. They conduct ethnography and interviews. Such attempts to analyse the cultural then requires thinking about language, symbols, stories, role-taking, feelings, bodies, identities and values. A core task for all sociology is to understand the meanings that people construct. Everything a sociologist looks at always has to take into account these contested meanings that drench all of life: in signs, gestures, languages, narratives, and the stories that people give to their lives. They employ the method of **Verstehen**. See Table 5.1.

*Table 5.1*  Doing a cultural analysis

| *Think about* | *Question* | *Discipline linkage* |
|---|---|---|
| Language | What are the words, the slang, the special meanings of terms in this culture? | Linguistics |
| Signs and symbols | Examine key symbols, look at the chain of signs and the process of signification? | **Semiotics** |
| Stories and narrative | Listen to the stories (narratives, myths, accounts, etc) that people tell | **Narrative** theory |
| Verstehen and role taking | Understand the ways people come to see others: see the world through others' eyes | Max Weber used the term '**Verstehen**'; G.H. Mead developed the idea of role taking |
| Emotions and empathy | Appreciate what others are feeling | Sociology of emotions – Cooley, Hochschild |
| Identities and roles | How do people come to see themselves (who are they?) and what roles do they perform? | **Dramaturgy** – see Goffman; and role/performance theory; modern identity theory |
| Bodies | What are the key projects in which people use their bodies? | Mind/body dualism debates; the new 'body theory' |
| Values | Know the values that guide lives | Studies of attitudes and values |

## 5 INTERROGATE THE MATERIAL WORLD: JUST HOW ARE WE CONSTRAINED BY OUR BODIES, THE ECONOMY AND THE ENVIRONMENT?

Human social worlds then are certainly symbolic, cultural and **perspectival**; and sociology is directed to their study all the time. But this is *never* enough. For we also live in worlds that are undeniably material and have a brutish, physical reality about them – 'red in tooth and claw', as the poet Tennyson put it. Think of your own life and social world. You know that you are a physically biological bounded animal with definite needs to be met (like food, water, shelter, safety and health). You live on the land in a universe shaped by vast physical forces – evolution, environments and economies (including your 'land', the intense population, your 'property' and 'technologies' surrounded by the ultimate power of law and governments). Here too are your human capabilities waiting to be cultivated or not (to flourish, be extinguished or be regulated?). Here are things you most certainly cannot lightly wish or think away. They will exist independently of us giving them meaning. They are what we might call the material social world. It is a ' kickable world', a really real world, one which exists beyond our own wishes, beyond the realm of ideas and culture. This is a physical world not of our making, and not simply made of ideas and symbols. We confront these material conditions of our existence every day. Two modern thinkers (of many) who have played a major role in sensing this world have been Darwin and Marx.

At its most general level, **materialism** (and its often linked pal, **realism**) is a philosophical stance that explains the nature of reality – in all its aspects – in terms of matter. The world is first and foremost material, physical, tangible: a world of bodies and resources. The earliest material philosophers (like Democritus, around 460–370 BCE) were atomists who thought that universe and matter are only made up of atoms assembled in a purely mechanical way. The formation of world and life are explained by the associations of these atoms that are the only reality. Here the social world is an external world with an absolute existence independent of ideas and consciousness. At its extreme it stands in opposition to any kind of idealism – or any theory that gives primacy to meaning. At this point sociology enters one of the oldest debates in philosophy – the controversy between **idealists** (who give attention to the world of ideas and ideals) and materialists (who give attention to matter and materialism). By contrast, the earliest idealist philosophers from Plato through to Kant argued that social reality is based on mind or ideas. As we shall see, this helps also to generate one of sociology's core and continuing tensions: the realist–idealist debate.

Never mind all this. At the most direct and concrete level, the material world directs you to study the evolutionary, the economic and the environmental (the three 'E's as I like to call them). Evolutionary thinking directs us to see our bodily tensions and limitations; economic thinking directs us to the resources we work for and live through (the minerals, the oil, the land), and the technologies of production that are generated; and environmental analysis make us aware of the wider universe and the severe limits it places upon our actions, as well as the competition for land and scarce resources on the earth now. All these forces work largely over and beyond our own control. We cannot (usually) control our own brain functioning and hormones – our animal-like nature. We do not control the wealth and work situations we initially find ourselves in – whether our technologies are ploughs or computers, and the ways in which everyday things get turned into sellable commodities (commodification, as it is often called). And as we know these days, the environment and its four key elements of air, fire, earth and water, may rage into human disaster and environmental degradation. Everyday we hear of another catastrophe – a tsunami, a fire, an earthquake (There is, of course, a sociology of disasters).

## 6 DEVELOP AN AWARENESS OF HISTORY AND TIME: HOW CAN WE CONNECT THE PASTS, PRESENTS AND FUTURES OF HUMAN SOCIAL LIFE IN THE FLOW OF TIME?

The social always has a past, a present and a future and it is always on the move. Whether you study migration, music or mass movements, sociologists will want to understand their histories, the way they are lived dynamically in the here and now, and ultimately sense their movements – even where they might be heading (though they are not futurologists – the future can never be known). They are always on the go.

Sociology is a bit like contemporary history. It focuses on the detail of the world – but as it is lived now, at this moment. This is never enough though. All social things have a past and sociology needs hence to look at the archaeology of all social things. More than this: the past is plural and ever present in the moment – there is the perpetual haunting of all social things in their multiplicities. And this history is both big and bold, and small and trickling. Major studies have been done on the histories of nation-states (in the work for example of Michael Mann on genocide; by Charles Tilley on social movements). But it also looks at the smaller histories of every damned thing – the social histories of toilets, telephones and tomatoes! – along with, we might now add, sleeping, sex and salsa! Look at the social things of the present and ponder how they are haunted by the past. But central as history is for sociology, sociologists also know that we live in the present. We are concerned with the ways in which the pluralising pasts – other countries – live in the present. The past itself is always constructed in the present moment, which then itself turns back into a lost past.

And this raises the issue of time. There is, as we would expect, a sociology of time which looks at the whole shaping of 'the temporal order'. Time itself cannot be fixed and given but a very problematical humanly produced thing too. We have not always had clocks, they are not all the same across the world, yet once they were invented arguably they significantly changed the way we lived. (Yes, there is a sociology of the clock too.) A sociology of time looks at the ways in which we construct our sense of time – *objectively* through clocks and various measures, but also *subjectively* – how we experience the daily flow of time (the phenomenology of time, as we say) and indeed construct our memories (social memories) of the past. Memory in sociology cannot be seen as simply an individual psychological trait but rather as something that is partially structured by the groups we are moving in. Memory is collective.

## 7 KEEP MOVING ON: HOW TO EXAMINE THE CONTINGENCIES, MOBILITIES AND THE FLOWS OF SOCIAL LIFE?

Closely linked to the above is the need to always view human social life (and sociology) as a process: everything changes, life flows and nothing stays. Whether we are analysing harassment, homicides or health systems – all change by the moment. Sociology's subject matter – even its very categories – are *never* fixed or stable. A comment made one moment can be changed the next. A group formed one hour changes the next. A situation moves on. A biographical life is transformed from second to second. Societies are bubbling cauldrons of never-ending change. Nothing stays the same. Every sociological finding is out of date the minute it is done. All 'findings' are short-lived – they last for the moment they are found. In this sense, sociology is permanently out of date as the world moves on. Hence a major challenge often arises: what in the midst of the vast flow and flux might just be of stable and recurrent value? Where is the permanence in all this perpetual change? We live now in continual permutations of social actions.

Like most of what I am saying, this is not a simple idea. Life is a flow, and it flows through all manner of chance and unforeseen events that then have enormous social consequences. Life is simultaneously hugely determined by major biological, personal and social forces; yet it is also much less determined than some science suggests. Small chance factors can have huge causal power. And equally many contingencies can pile up into regular sequences and patterns to become almost unnoticed. Oddly this idea of contingency – deserving surely of a full blown sociological theory and philosophical account – lacks one. Life is fragile and precarious. *We all suffer all the time from contingencies*. Chance happenstances are the stuff of our everyday lives.

The central role of contingency is a popular theme in history, literature and art. Consider Peter Howitt's film *Sliding Doors* (1998), which stars Gwyneth Paltrow and John Hannah. Here the central character Helen is sacked from her job and returning home at an unusual hour, she rushes to catch the tube train. And in one moment the film depicts one reality in which she just manages to squeeze through the sliding doors and get on the train; and in another depiction – a second moment or reality shows her missing the train. But it is a decisive moment. With the first moment she meets James on the tube but gets home to find her boyfriend, Gerry, cheating on her with his ex-girlfriend. Following the other moment, Helen misses the tube train, gets mugged, goes to hospital and eventually arrives home to find her partner all alone! At that one moment – that one contingency – her life is full of different possibilities. And in the film, the two moments – shaping two realities – move forward in parallel with radically different outcomes. The first moment means that Helen leaves Gerry and forms a positive delightful loving relationship with James; the other shows Helen's life taking bad turns, as her boyfriend continues to cheat on her. A moment in life makes a huge difference. Classically, it is that moment when we cheerfully leave the front door of our house, and are then run down by a passing lorry. You can never tell; anything could happen. Moments really do matter. Possibilities are everywhere for things to be different from what they are.

There are many films and stories which tell similar tales. The fragility of the moments of life is a persistent and popular theme. One recent writer, Nassim Nicholas Taleb in *The Black Swan*, has turned the idea into a bestselling one. And yet most of the time – most days of our life – we stave off the wider possibilities of our existence and their shaping through chance occurrences because of our persistent tendency to make social habits. The huge potential and risk of human existence is persistently narrowed by the fly wheel of habit. The buzzing booming confusion of the world is persistently narrowed down so that most of our lives – most of our days – we follow well patterned habits. We cannot stand too much life and we have to narrow and restrict our daily potentials into well formed, routines – in behaviour, in thoughts, in feelings. Crudely we become zombie like. But this does not stop the many precarious moments harbouring full scale chance possibilities of change.

## 8 LOCATE SOCIAL LIFE IN PLACE AND SPACE: HOW IS HUMAN SOCIAL LIFE SHAPED BY THE SITUATIONAL, THE GLOBAL AND THE PUBLIC?

All of social life flows and moves with places and spaces. There is a geography – and a geometry – of social things. Nothing happens outside of the flow of situations or context; and sociology is always asking questions about the construction, organisation and impact of these spaces. We have already seen something of this when we were looking at the habits of the street and in the mappings of cities earlier. Well over a century ago, Charles Booth mapped out the streets and life of the London poor; whilst in the USA, a strong classical tradition of sociology – known as the Chicago ecological school – documented the importance of city zones in our lives, making major contrasts with the spaces and lives conducted in rural areas. It matters whether you live in cities or the countryside – and as we know, more and more people have now come to dwell in the space of 'the global city'. Today we live in the postcode society where regions, city, province, street become clues to life styles. We have also seen how the roles people play differ across various settings. And we have sensed the ways in which the world is moving from being a local place to a global one (see Chapter 3).

To start thinking about space and the social, it might help for a moment for you to do an exercise. Consider yourself, your body and your mind as a kind of vehicle driving gently through – and at the same time, constructing – different social spaces, situations, settings. You might encounter five spaces moving out from your body. First there is the phenomenology of space – this is the mental map you make of the world you live in. If you think about the area you live and move around in, you will find you have your own sense of space which is not one that anyone else has. Second, as you move into any social situation – a school classroom, a street corner, a workplace, a church, a public toilet – you will find that awaiting you there are some expectations of how you should behave: that you may not behave that way is another matter. What is certain is that some general ways of behaving are tied up with almost all spaces. There is a sociology of situations and co-presence. Broaden this out and we can find that people often connect with each other through various groups – social worlds and their perspectives. In this sense a society can be mapped out as different kinds of worlds, a bit like the different cultures I have outline above. Society is not a homogenous whole but a series of intermeshed social worlds. It is also a network – a chain of relations through which we live. With the arrival of the internet, more and more people live their lives through virtual spaces that can only be called the network society. Finally we can sense that social life moves from being located within specific social worlds to a much wider sense of the global world (see Chapter 3). Now much of your life can be seen as part of a chain which connects to others round the world. Spaces have become more and more globalised – and sociology has to search out these connections.

## THINK ON: THE PUBLIC, THE PRIVATE AND THE SURVEILLANCE SOCIETY

Here is one example of space at work. A key way to understand space is to view it through the complex dichotomy of public and private. The public usually refers to the world of work and politics that takes place outside of the home which is the private world. It can also indicate the divide between the state and government in a divide with the civic sphere – the world of friends and encounters. But simply put, public worlds are *out there* and private worlds are the ones *in here* – the more intimate ones we create for ourselves. In many past societies, this divide is clear and abrupt. In some – like feudal society – the world of the home was the core; in others, like ancient Greece, the world of the public was prime. What matters for sociologists these days is the shifting nature of this divide. Where for example is cyberspace in this – it seems to be a very public system which is also very private? Likewise, what happens when public spaces are connected to CCTV systems – when public spaces become privately observed? This is one basis of what is called the surveillance society.

## 9 CONNECT WITH EMBODIED, EMOTIONAL BIOGRAPHICAL NARRATIVES: HOW TO LISTEN AND EMPATHISE WITH REAL HISTORICAL LIVES AND THEIR LIFE STAGES

The billions of people on Planet Earth cannot all be studied by sociologists (perish the thought!). But if we lose sight of real, lived, biographically fleshy, feeling lives then we easily can get lost in abstractions divorced from social life. Sociologists can never afford to forget that it is a dense moving biographically grounded web of human life that is the baseline of their study. Hence whatever else they do, they need to return regularly to real bodily lives, observe their experiences and listen to what they have to say. This is the corrective needed to prevent sociology becoming far removed from social life, as it can so easily. Sociology always connects life histories with the wider workings of actions, structures and histories. A wonderful display of this can be found in Pierre Bourdieu's *The Weight of the World* (*La misère du monde*) (1990) – a study made up entirely of interviews with downcast Parisians telling of the contradictions of their lives.

Every human life is touched deeply by the social as it moves from birth to death, and this is hence always a proper focus for sociologists. They can examine a life closely to see how within one life many features of the social world are put to play. Unemployment in a life here becomes not simply a matter of personal failure but of the workings of the wider economy; homosexuality is not a personal pathology but something deeply shaped by laws and the social meanings of gender; our bodies are not simple biology but connect to the body projects and emotional structures of our time (see Chapter 2 again). A central tool for sociology is hence always the **life narrative** – listening with empathy to the stories that people tell of their lives. However broad ranging your study may be and however many people may be studied (often in their thousands), sociology always needs the in depth study of one concrete life to remind itself of the actual impossibility of grasping the whole situation.

## 10 PONDER POWER: WHO IS CONTROLLING WHAT'S GOING ON HERE?

How does power touch your social life? Sociology sees power as a prominent – if contested – feature of the social. Loosely defined as the process by which people are able to influence and exert control over their own lives and resist the control of others, **power** comes in many forms and spawns many debates raising matters of domination and subordination.

### BIG POWER, LITTLE POWER; VISIBLE POWER, INVISIBLE POWER

Power is identifiable in a big sense – most societies have governments who exert different kinds of power (and come in different forms as authoritarian, monarchic, theocratic, totalitarian and democratic states). It is also present in a myriad little ways – in the choices, rules and regulations that face us in everyday life (at school and work, between men and women, in the family, amongst friends, or in field of discrimination like race and sexuality). The former is generally the topic of 'the sociology of power' whilst the latter is often seen as a 'micro-politics' of everyday life. Either way, power is omnipresent and ubiquitous in the study of social life. It asks the question: *who is controlling what's going on here, and how?*

Some forms of power are highly visible and we can see them at work straight away. Think of the despotic ruler and tyrant, of slavery, or even the prisoner and his guard. It is upheld through coercion, physical control and ultimately brutal violence over others' bodies. Some forms of power are given over to others – we concede the power we give to a democratic government who is chosen initially by us and who is supposed to act on our behalf; or to our parents as children – who are supposed to act in the best interests of the child. And some forms of power come to work in hidden ways – we consent to others regulating our lives without really realising we are doing this. Very frequently, the workings of power is the key feature to grasp behind the workings of stratification.

The most apparent account of power is that which highlights a dominant group over another and it probably gets the most attention in sociology – maybe too much attention. With a long history of theorisation, stretching back (via Plato and Machiavelli through Pareto, Mosca, Weber and Marx), this 'elite theory of power' holds that in every society there must be a minority who rules over others (a political class or governing elite) though just what nature of this minority is in question – it could be an economic group (Marx's ruling class), or a religious leader (as in Iran, a theocracy), or intellectuals (in China under the rule of the *literati*), or a combination of groups (C. Wright Mills' famous study of the US power system in 1956 – *The Power Elite* – distinguished three major elites: the corporation heads, the political leaders and the military chiefs). These are the people who occupy the 'command posts'. And Marxist sociologists of various persuasions ultimately connect these ruling groups back to a class – the ruling class is the dominant economic class (in writings such as Ralph Milliband's *The State in Society*). Others have argued for a long time that power is more dispersed than this and is connected to a much wider range of groups. (This was for a long time called the pluralist theory of power and was identified with Ronald Dahl's *Who Governs?* (1961))

A key problem in thinking about power is the ways in which people dwell in systems of domination and subordinations *without really thinking about them*. It has been called 'non decision making' (how people do *not* make decisions about their lives). How are some issues organised into politics whilst others organised out? A key concept developed here has been that of hegemony – an idea developed (from the Greeks) by the Italian Marxist Antonio Gramsci (1891–1937), in his *Prison Notebooks* (1929–1935) to suggest the way in which people come to accept the coercive roles of the state unthinkingly and uncritically. How do people come to consent to governments that act against their interests? For many political theorists there comes a crucial wider turn to culture and the workings of what the French Marxist Louis Althusser (1918–1990) called ' the ideological state apparatuses' – those crucial mechanisms such as the media, organised religion, the schools (educational curricula), and the commercialised popular arts (cinema, music, etc.) which work to influence the citizens to be subordinate to the state and accept its dominant values – hence maintaining the **hegemonic** *status quo*. This kind of approach means that sociology needs to focus a great deal upon these media as a way of understanding the workings of power and ponder when consent might cease.

And we ask what stops people rebelling? A long list of reasons can be provided: inertia and habit hold it all in place; ideological manipulations by the media prevent people from seeing their true interests; people get sufficient satisfaction from the government to go along with it much of the time; rebellions of an extreme kind are just too damn costly for people's lives (think of the tragic consequences of most revolutions where thousands, sometimes millions, die). And, perhaps most intriguingly, many people do indeed resist their governments and others' power every day – there is a permanent grumble and resistance in society. In all societies there are subterranean traditions of resistance and fighting back in a myriad little ways. Once we start analysing this, we can see that power permeates through the everyday life of a society. It is everywhere (and nowhere)! It was Foucault who puts power right at the centre of his theory and power is for some sociologists the central feature of social life.

So back to your own social life. It might help to think of how power is ubiquitous in your own social relations – pervasive and circulating through all situations. Even more, it may actually enter your body and mind: how is your everyday life organised through power relations (in families, with friends, in schools, at work)? This is not a matter of brute force or simple repression, but a matter of the way in which society saturates our being with a host of minor regulatory forms and practices. From childhood onwards we are, so to speak, made out of this power: all our ideas, our bodies, our behaviours are inside a system of power that regulates us. We find it operating in families and schools, in prisons and hospitals, in streets and media, in our knowledge and daily encounters. Power is diffused everywhere. And of course we resist it: 'where there is power, there is resistance' says Foucault. But even as we resist, we enter new fields of power and control: our social movements have their own regulations. It seems we are trapped. And it is another sociological challenge to grasp it.

## 11 LIVE WITH COMPLEXITY AND CONTRADICTIONS: HOW ARE THE CONTESTATIONS AND CONUNDRUMS OF SOCIAL LIFE TO BE LIVED WITH?

One of the most irritating myths about sociology is that it is an easy subject! If you take seriously the ten little points I have suggested as guidelines for studying sociology seriously, then I think you will by now being feeling very intellectually challenged – even threatened. Sociology raises endless conundrums and intellectual puzzles – in a sense it struggles with the meaning of life! And there are problems with everything I have said above. You will not travel far in sociology – or society – without sensing that life is a series of conundrums. Everything seems to harbour its opposite. Life is a paradox. Amongst the most common tensions we face are:

- Are societies free or determined? They are both.
- Are societies material or ideational? They are both.
- Do societies progress or regress? They do both.
- Are societies wholes or individualist.? They are both.
- Is the social unique or general? They are both.

We can continue. Human social life – including sociological thinking – is incorrigibly contradictory and contested. All social things seem to be contested. We have *Contested Cities, Contested Nature, Contested Communities, Contested Identities, The Contested Self, Contested Environment, Contested Meanings, Contested Histories, Contested Citizenship, Contested Knowledge, Contested Space, Contested Futures, Contested Justice* and *Contested Values* (all these are recent book titles!). Such tensions are ubiquitous in sociology and indeed you will find whole books built around them – classically in Robert Nisbet's *The Sociological Tradition* (1966) where it sets out major tensions such as secular and sacred and authority and power; more recently Chris Jenks's edited collection *Core Sociological Dichotomies* (1998) discusses over twenty of these major tensions. We will find contestation at the heart of Marx's theory of materialism and class conflict; it is there when Durkheim claims that the normal seems to be inextricably bound up with the abnormal or pathological – you can't have one without the other. Opposites and tension seem to thrive on each other.

Again, there is nothing new here. A long history in world philosophies recognises these contradictions and tensions. For Heraclitus, a perceived object is a harmony between two fundamental units of change, a waxing and a waning. For Plato (c. 424–348 BCE), it was the spectre of idealism and materialism. In Chinese thought, the notions of yin and yang (or earth and heaven) describe two opposing aspects of reality which then complement each other, or create a unity. And in the work of the German philosopher G.W.F. Hegel (1770–1831), ideas and societies can be seen as inevitably moving through contradictions or opposing tendencies. He speaks of these as dialectics – when two opposites clash (thesis and counter thesis) and a new form emerges (synthesis). He analyses, for example, how an event like the French Revolution brought both great ideas of equality and a major upsurge of violence (the Reign of Terror), but these clashes could ultimately lead to the possibility of a new constitutional government (which then itself becomes the next part of an endless dialectical process).

So here comes the big difference between these theoretical and philosophical debates and the sociological project: *sociologists always have to return to the empirical world in order to see what is happening in lived human social life. They look at contradictions as lived.* Sociology is an empirical discipline, and sociologists always have to come back to ground from the theoretical heavens. And in that sense they find they have to show how people in societies live with these contradictions – philosophers may, in their heads, sort them out but daily practical social life is not so easy. We live in a pluralistic universe and human social life is incorrigibly stuffed full of contradiction, difference, tension, and ambiguity. Sociologists have to recognise this sooner or later. They have to observe these tensions, think them through, negotiate and struggle between opposing paths, and learn ultimately the hard trick of dealing with them in their thinking. They are ever-present – it is a fine balancing act – we have to live with them. It is some of the ways of doing this that will be our concern in the next chapter.

Living with these tensions is not easy, but doing sociology necessarily means the recognition that social life is a paradoxical affair. There are no easy answers, and although we may take sides, in the end life is always and everywhere flushed full of tension, contradiction, and paradox. Sociology is charged with thinking through – and living with – the continuous, contradictory and contingent social world we live in. Like life, sociology is a conundrum.

## SUMMARY

Sociology is a form of imagination and this chapter maps some of its complexities and contradictions. Sociologists need to look at action, structures and the tensions and bridges between them. They simultaneously examine material and cultural worlds. They see social life as located in time (history) and space (geography) and the flows and movements between them. They search for the power relations behind the social – asking who is shaping what? And they try to connect all this to the grounded connections of lived lives, biographies and the stories that people tell of them. It is hard for any sociology study to do all this but the more you can examine in any study, the better. In this chapter are a number of the key entrance points to thinking about the social. Figure 5.1 suggests some of the key elements for any sociological analysis.

## EXPLORING FURTHER

### MORE THINKING

I have suggested here a road map with eleven signposts to help develop a sociological imagination. You should think a little about each, but you will find some more interesting and suited to you than others. Try and apply them all initially to your sociological work and thinking and then develop those which interest you most. Nobody can do it all!

### FURTHER READING

'To be a literate person today is like living in the library of Jorge Luis Borges, where near-infinite corridors of books contain the universe but we lack a key to their contents.' So says Randall Collins as he traces the world's history of intellectual life in his magisterial and wonderful *The Sociology of Philosophies* (1998). The field that this chapter covers is so truly vast that I have decided here to just list a

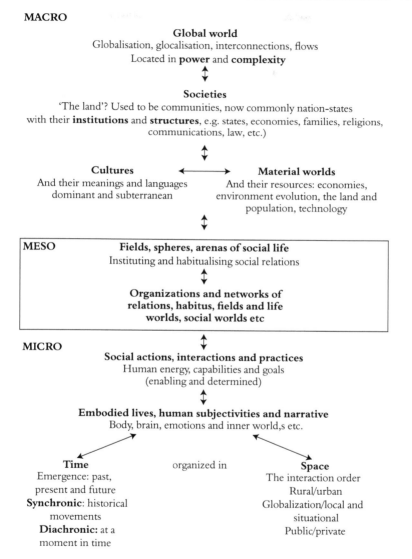

**MACRO**

**Global world**
Globalisation, glocalisation, interconnections, flows
Located in **power** and **complexity**

**Societies**
'The land'? Used to be communities, now commonly nation-states
with their **institutions** and **structures**, e.g. states, economies, families, religions,
communications, law, etc.)

**Cultures** ←——→ **Material worlds**
And their meanings and languages           And their resources: economies,
dominant and subterranean           environment evolution, the land and
population, technology

**MESO**   **Fields, spheres, arenas of social life**
Instituting and habitualising social relations

**Organizations and networks of
relations, habitus, fields and life
worlds, social worlds etc**

**MICRO**

**Social actions, interactions and practices**
Human energy, capabilities and goals
(enabling and determined)

**Embodied lives, human subjectivities and narrative**
Body, brain, emotions and inner world,s etc.

**Time**           organized in           **Space**
Emergence: past,           The interaction order
present and future           Rural/urban
**Synchronic**: historical           Globalization/local and
movements           situational
**Diachronic**: at a           Public/private
moment in time

*Figure 5.1*   Putting it together: mapping out the flows of 'the social'

few books that do some of the above but which have fascinated me. I hope you might like some of them too:

Elijah Anderson (1999) *Code of the Street: Decency, Violence and the Moral life of the Inner City* looks at race and inner city trouble.

Stanley Cohen (2001) *States of Denial: Knowing About Atrocities and Suffering* looks at the ways we ignore the atrocities of the world.

Clifford Shaw (rev edn 1966)*The Jack Roller: A Delinquent Boy's Own Story* the life story of one boy, a classic Chicago study.

Arlie Hochschild (1983) *The Managed Heart* introduces the significance of emotion through a study of flight attendants.

Pierre Bourdieu (1990) *The Weight of the World* his important theoretical work is 'fleshed ' out with interviews.

Arthur W. Frank (1995) *The Wounded Story Teller* who draws on his own illness to develop an account of the stories we tell of our illnesses.

On a more abstract level, see:

Jürgen Habermas (1989) *The Structural Transformation of the Public Sphere* – a highly influential theoretical work on space and politics

Jeffrey C. Alexander *The Civil Sphere* (2006): a major recent account of the way societies work

# ENGAGING THE EMPIRICAL

Imagination is more important than knowledge
Albert Einstein, *The New Quotable Einstein*, 2005

A blank page, so full of possibility.
Stephen Sondheim, *Sunday in the Park with George* , 1984

Sociologists are often seen as people who do interviews, conduct social surveys, design questionnaires or study little groups. This is not so: many other groups use research tools. What make sociologists distinctive is that they bring a critical attitude to the wide range of data that they use. The practical task of the sociologist is to become aware of the world we live in – to look carefully at it, engage with people and their plights, and think deeply about it. In the midst of this, the struggle is on to tell the truth with an adequate objectivity – or fair enough neutrality. We observe the world in many different ways, come to appreciate its multiplicities, complexities and inner meanings, and engage with it through all our senses. And in doing this lies the excitement and challenge of sociology. But this is simple to say and so much harder to do: there is much controversy between sociologists as to just exactly how this can or should be done. This is the focus of this chapter, dealing again with introductory, but difficult, matters.

## THE PRACTICE OF SOCIOLOGY: THE TRICKS OF THE TRADE

To understand the world sociologically is like any skill: it requires practice, and it means learning some of the 'tricks of the trade' – Howard Becker's term – from others who have been there before. Sociologists – like all scientists and artists – need to cultivate certain crafts, imaginations and ways of thinking: to be critical, dialogic and reflexive. We need to attend to complex human biographies and actions in emerging times and spaces; to grasp human subjectivities embedded in power relations and material worlds; and we need a calm distance – struggling for adequate objectivity – whilst maintaining a personal passion. Some parts of doing sociology are a bit like learning to play the piano, a new language, or acquiring the tools (and subsequent knowledge) of a biologist or chemist. There are layers of skill involved in all of these from the novice to the expert: at the start, there is much to be learnt and many skills to acquire. Bit by bit, levels of competences are acquired.

One difference with sociology from other skills lies in the fact that we are all already 'novice sociologists' by virtue of us living in society: to navigate our ways around the social world everyday requires some modicum of knowledge about how the society works. We can, though, mistake this early and basic knowledge as being enough to say we are sociologists. In fact, becoming a sociologist is a slow process of acquiring a sociological imagination. It is the difference between a pianist who can vamp out a simple tune on two or three notes and distinguish a crotchet from a quaver, and someone who can read music, appreciate scale and chord complexities, and play concerts.

There are hundreds of books and courses on all aspects of sociological research methodology and this book cannot serve as an introduction to much of this (but see the reading suggestions at the end of the chapter). What I propose instead is to provide a very basic schema to guide you through some of the big issues. Broadly, doing sociology means cultivating some of the following kinds of skills:

1  epistemological work: learning how to think socially, grasp the kinds of truths that social science can produce, and develop the road map I outlined in Chapter 5;
2  empirical work: learning how to get close to what is going on in the world – developing an intimate familiarity with your topic in all its 'sources' and 'forms';
3  analytic work: learning how to dissect social life (a bit like a zoologist might an animal!) and make good sense of it all.

## 1  EPISTEMOLOGICAL WORK: THE FRAMING OF SOCIOLOGICAL KNOWLEDGE

As with all intellectual work, sociology requires serious thinking. Earlier chapters have suggested the many pathways into sociological thinking. The previous chapter alone suggested eleven key areas to scrutinise. At every stage of study, sociology asks you questions about the very nature of the kind of knowledge being assembled (**epistemological** questions), puzzles your sense of what is really real in the social world (**ontological** questions) and examines your own personal location in the research process (known in the trade as '**reflexivity**').

### SOCIOLOGY AS A HISTORICAL, SCIENTIFIC ART

For two hundred years of its history, sociology has struggled to define itself as the science of society. Yet since its inception, there have always been long and heated debates as to just what is meant by this very idea. This 'debate on methodology' (sometimes called – in German – the *Methodenstreit*) between the human and natural sciences (*Geistwissenschaften* and *Naturwissenschaften*) arose significantly in Germany between the philosopher and cultural historian Wilhelm Dilthey (1833–1911) and the neo-Kantians Heinrich Rickert (1863–1936) and Wilhelm Windelband(1848–1915) in the late nineteenth century. What an intellectual buzz there must have been in those days as they debated the true nature of social science, history and human knowledge. These were modern rehearsals of old philosophical debates. But they influenced all who followed them (including Max

## THINK ON: WHAT IS KNOWLEDGE?

Epistemology is that branch of philosophy which studies the nature of knowledge – and its various versions of truth. There are major debates on epistemology within sociology, and four can be listed here:

- **Positivism:** The classical and traditional view of science: measurements of observables, as in classifying animals or doing laboratory experiments. Common tools are surveys, statistical data.
- **Interpretivism:** Human life differs because of meaning and hence a key task is to understand these meanings through '*Verstehen*', empathy, intimate familiarity. Common tools are life stories, in depth interviews and field work, participant observation/ethnographic work (these three words are often interchangeable).
- **Standpoints** and perspectives: Recognises that all science and serious analysis is conducted from a socially grounded point of view and we need to be clear what this standpoint is. It has led to a wider array of standpoints: feminist, queer, post-colonial and others.
- **Realist:** Stronger and more theoretical view of science. Claims that science does not depend simply on observation and measurement, but seeks deep underlying causal processes. A physicist may observe planets, but a theory is then needed to explain them; a biologist may observe plant and animal life, but then needs to explain them e.g. with Darwin's evolutionary theory or Marx's theory of materialism, both are grounded in observations but also develop much grander and wider explanatory tools.
- For a wonderful collection of readings on this – and more – see Gerard DeLanty and Piet Strydom (2003) *Philosophies of Social Science: The Classic and Contemporary Readings.*

Weber). And such debates have not gone away in the twenty-first century.

Dilthey wanted to produce what might be called a cultural science and he aimed to show that the knowledge of the world of humans could only be gained through close inspection of lived experiences (*Erlebnis*) and gaining understanding (*Verstehen*) of them, rather than through mere observations of the external observable world. As we have seen before, a central data for sociology is human meaning; and Dilthey claimed that we need to develop good ways to grasp the meanings and spirit of the times and place we are studying. Sociology must definitely *not* be the same as the natural sciences since cultural sciences always needed to understand these experiences through re-experiencing (*Nacherleben*) the meanings carried by historical actors or cultural objects. And these world views (*Weltanschauungen*) are relative to cultures. Windelband and Rickert agreed with much of Dilthey but they argued that real distinctions did need to be drawn between those who wanted to establish universal laws and uniformities (the so-called nomothetic sciences) and those who thought that history could only give specific probably unique constellations of action (the idiographic sciences). Following Kant, they argued that the human sciences should indeed look for universal laws (leaving history to look at the unique cases).

Now this is a complicated debate of the kind in which many sociologists revel. Be warned, if you want to study sociology to any advanced level, these are the kinds of questions that are constantly addressed. But let me be simple: sociologists are always busy pondering questions like:

- Are the social sciences really like the physical sciences (which in turn raises the issues of what the physical sciences are)?
- Does the subject matter of social science differ so much from that of the physical sciences that it requires a very different method? Do human meanings make a big difference?
- Should the social sciences really be a branch of history – and hence idiographic, focusing upon unique and specific instances?

- Should social sciences seek out universals and be capable of making generalisations? Is abstract theory a good way of doing this?

I can tell you now: there are no simple answers to these questions, much ink has been spilt on them, and academics take very different stands on them today. But to start out in your own thinking, it might help if you go back to your own experience (probably in school) of three things: science, art and history. Science – be it biology, physics or chemistry always involved some kinds of *observations* of what is going on in the world. Personally, I always think of David Attenborough's many television series of nature watching – of the scientist watching carefully his animals and their behaviour. But usually they go beyond simple observations and classify, conceptualise, and attempt a few generalisations. Nowhere is this clearer than in the astonishing theories of the origins of the universe. Physics may have created the Hubble Space Telescope to observe the heavens, but it has not observed the famous 'Big Bang' theory. Drawing from evidence, there is a lot of imaginative speculation in science too. Sometimes sociologists invent a rather simple-minded view of science as observation and testing when it is always so much more than this.

So now consider history. Again, at school, you always learn a lot of very specific facts about the past. But – if you were taught well – you will soon also know that a lot of these facts pose very real problems of interpretation. These days – with a lot of history programmes on TV, the problems here really do become much clearer: how do historians get their facts? Often historians are manifestly opinionated people telling a good yarn, trying to persuade us how the world is – alongside the truth of what they have found. Think how the history is bound up with the presenter (at the present time in the UK: think of the two most famous tele-historians, Simon Sharma and David Starkey, and how different their styles and approaches are). There is so much more to history than a straightforward presentation of the facts.

Finally think of art – a piece of music, a painting, a play or poem. What do you learn from this? At the very least, I hope, something about human imagination and creativity; and more – just maybe something about humanity and its lot? So much literary writing (Shakespeare, Tolstoy), visual art (Hogarth, Warhol) and music (Mozart, Mahler) address the great social themes of their times and our times. And this can shift imaginations, perhaps more than science. As Keats waxed lyrically: 'Do not all charms fly at the mere touch of cold philosophy?' ('Lamia', 1820).

So there is art, history and science. If we want to understand what is going on in the world, is one better than the other? Should we junk art in favour of science? Favour history over science? See art as the supreme entrance to the condition of humanity? Science as the gateway to the stars? Well that is your choice: but for me, we need all three equally. They are not incompatible and each is there to check the worst excesses of each other.

All of which is why I think it is best to see sociology as engaging with multiple methodologies and as a historical, scientific art which aims to understand what is going on in the human social world. *We struggle with understanding our unique pasts (history); we seek to make connections and generalisations from observations of the world in order to understand what is taking place in the empirical world (science); and we need our imaginations to make sense of it all (art)*. Of course, individuals might specialise in one or other styles of doing sociology: but ultimately to grasp a depth of understanding of society, we will always need the three bubbling around: a science for objectivity, a history for unique understanding, and an art for critical imagination.

Sadly, contemporary knowledge is often divided into what the scientist and novelist C.P. Snow – back in the 1950s – called 'the two cultures': the arts (humanities, arts, history) versus the sciences. You can see this in the ways in which contemporary universities award degrees (Bachelors of *Arts*, Bachelors of *Sciences*) and organise their faculties (The Faculty of *Science*, The Faculty of *Arts*). Even in schools, students are often asked to choose a scientific or artistic path at ridiculously early ages. Indeed, in modern times, it has become almost a divide – societies get organised on this split. You can see it in an omnipresent tension between 'philistine scientists' and overly 'romantic artists'! But it has not always been so. If you look for example at the work of Leonardo da Vinci (1452–1519), you will find his work was variously that of a painter, a sculptor, a musician, an architect, a scientist, a mathematician, an engineer, an anatomist, a botanist – the list goes on and on. He was not concerned with the petty divides that modernity has made for their convenience. There were no mutually exclusive polarities between the sciences and the arts. His studies of science and engineering fused with art and philosophy – and filled some 13,000 pages of notes and drawing. He is of course the classic Renaissance Man. But he shows, so vividly, that the worlds of science and art need not be kept as apart as the modern world tries to do. Table 6.1 suggests some of the false splits that need bridging.

*Table 6.1*    Only connect: bringing together science and art

|  | *The artistic pole* | *'History' and sociology as mediating forces* | *The science pole* |
|---|---|---|---|
| Task | Interpret and understand | ⟷ | Measure and find causes |
| Focus | Worlds of meaning, feeling and experiences | ⟷ | Outer structures, objective causes |
| Tools | Empathy, imagination, familiarity | ⟷ | Trained research skills |
| Values and politics | Everywhere | ⟷ | Neutral, value free |
| Presentation | Film, novels, drama, art, music | ⟷ | Technical papers, reports, tables |

## 2 EMPIRICAL WORK: GETTING INTIMATE WITH DATA

All good sociology is **empirical** in the sense that it engages closely with what is going on in the social world (if it does not, then it becomes something else). But there are multiple ways of pursuing these common goals. Another chart may help here in clarifying two major and very different logics of research. In practice of course there are hundreds of variations on these and the task again is to bring these varieties together. Still, it is useful at the outset to sense a divide (see Figure 6.1).

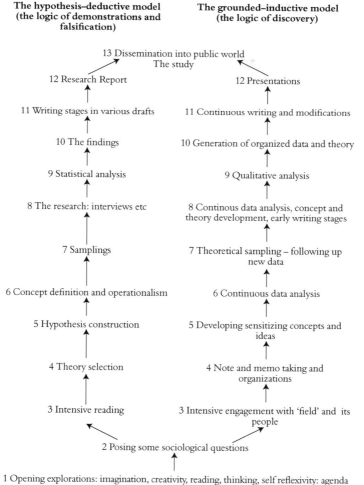

**The hypothesis–deductive model** **The grounded–inductive model**
**(the logic of demonstrations and** **(the logic of discovery)**
**falsification)**

13 Dissemination into public world
The study

12 Research Report 12 Presentations

11 Writing stages in various drafts 11 Continuous writing and modifications

10 The findings 10 Generation of organized data and theory

9 Statistical analysis 9 Qualitative analysis

8 The research: interviews etc 8 Continous data analysis, concept and
theory development, early writing stages

7 Samplings 7 Theoretical sampling – following up
new data

6 Concept definition and operationalism 6 Continuous data analysis

5 Hypothesis construction 5 Developing sensitizing concepts and
ideas

4 Theory selection 4 Note and memo taking and
organizations

3 Intensive reading 3 Intensive engagement with 'field' and its
people

2 Posing some sociological questions

1 Opening explorations: imagination, creativity, reading, thinking, self reflexivity: agenda
setting

Caution: I have dangerously oversimplified these positions of the research process. Life is much more complex than our simple schemas of them: both approaches are often combined, and there are many other stances. But as an opening way of thinking about the choices available in social research, this does suggest some key different pathways

*Figure 6.1* Two 'ideal type' logics of research processes: deductive and inductive

The first route starts with the big hypotheses and the search for generalisations; it makes the ideas in it measurable (often called 'operational concepts'); searches out data to 'test' or falsify their hypotheses (the key principle of falsification); and rigorously scrutinises the hypotheses to find false cases where it does not hold or work. Probabilities of their conclusions being true are then calculated mathematically through various procedures. Such studies usually read like technical reports – usually evidence will appear in a fair amount of statistical reporting with much technical analysis. It is a 'top-down' approach moving from the 'general' to the 'specific'. Most big survey and 'scientific sociology' uses this as its basis: we collect observations to accept or reject hypotheses.

The second route begins with observations and experiences and is based on a logic of discovery. Concepts emerge that are much less measurable but which seem to make sense of the observations and which aim to foster deeper understandings (often called sensitising concepts). Out of such observations and concept development, small scale theory starts to develop. Research does not establish hypotheses or even concepts in advance of various kinds of field work (observations, in libraries, looking at visual media etc). Usually the final study appears that contains much verbatim speech – from the people interviewed, from books, from other sources. It reads in an easier fashion and some emphasis is placed on the writing craft. There is always a problem here as to whether you can truly start observing anything without prior generalisations or assumptions. It moves from observations towards case studies and only ultimately – if at all – to generalisations, abstractions and theories: it is a 'bottom-up' or grounded approach. The former is often called '**deductive**', the latter '**inductive**'.

Sociological data are the various bits of information that sociologists analyse. When sociology was developing, it often had to 'invent methods' like 'the survey' and indeed 'the interview' to get this data, but these days the tools they use are in widespread use in society. We see interviews in the press and on the media all the time; we complete survey forms from any and every organisation we are likely to encounter. Most major organisations now have 'research and development' units. There is no longer anything really specifically sociologically significant about research methods for sociology –

they are everywhere to be found. In the past, the sociologist may have been characterised as a person who uses interviews, surveys and statistics: not now. Research tools are used across a wide range of fields, and sociologists work is much broader than this.

Still, to give you a quick idea of the tools available for gathering data, the focus box provides a quick listing of some of the tools that sociologists use – very few will cultivate skills in more than two or three of them. When sociologists use a range of these tools (as they should), the process is often called **triangulation**. In alphabetical order these include the tools listed in Figure 6.2.

Each one of these sources requires its own skills in analysis – and there are numerous books published that provide such advice on all of them. To repeat: whilst they are used in sociology, they are also to be found across many disciplines and many practices in everyday life. They are common features of everyday life and there is no longer anything remotely special about them as sociological tools.

Archival documents (historical, personal, all kinds); artefacts and things ('stuff': personal possessions, archeological 'finds', consumer objects); art (painting, sculptures); attitude scales; autobiographies and life stories; auto ethnographies; case studies; census; content analysis; conversation analysis; cyber material (web sites, emails, blogs, YouTube, Second Life, social networking sites); diaries; discourse analysis; documents of all kinds (eg school records, club magazines); documentary film; experiments (laboratory studies); field research (participant observation, ethnography); fiction (novels, television drama (eg soaps); films and video; focus groups; historical research; interviews of all kinds (short, long, focused, survey, in depth, analytic); letters; life stories; maps; personal experiences; photographs; post codes; questionnaires; social surveys (national, local, longitudinal, panel); texts of all kinds; visuals (photographs, film, documentaries, videos, paintings and art).

*Figure 6.2*  The research tool kit

## EXCURSUS: NEW TOOLS OF A DIGITAL INFORMATION AGE

But if the old methods have become commonplace, the digital revolution has provided new challenges for sociology. We have moved on dramatically from the methods and worlds studied by the earlier sociologists. Sociology may have been born of the Industrial Revolution and early capitalism, but it has fast moved into the twenty-first century. In contrast with past worlds, we now live in social worlds saturated with information about society and a startling array of new ways of obtaining it. Much of human social life can now be traced through a click of your mouse. Studying society has never been easier or more widely and fully accessible. At least for starters, what used to take sociologists years to dig out, and often cost millions of pounds, can now be found in a few minutes or hours and cost virtually nothing. The ways of doing sociological work are dramatically changing. These newer resources were just never available to sociologists in the previous two centuries. There is now a cyber-generation that will inevitably shift the everyday practice of sociology. Old methods and old theories are inevitably, if slowly, having to change.

Consider how we can now access large amounts of data about social life at the press of a button, something our ancestors could hardly have imagined. We can now find massive world statistical datasets gathered by diverse agencies on every nook and cranny of social life – data that earlier sociologists could only have dreamt of. We can interconnect with all kinds of people, researchers and groups through the network, blogging and twittering pages of the internet. We can access people across the world at any time or place through our emails, our faxes, our mobile phones and our network pages. We can photo, video and camcorder almost anything instantly – living in a visual and screen culture where digital images and on line podcasts make retrievable millions of slices of social life – awaiting the sociologist's critical eye. We are surrounded by television, films, documentaries, public interviews, everyday press reportage, reality television and the documentations and research of a myriad of pressure groups, social movements and NGOs. We increasingly have to live with the algorithmic formula which calculates our every need on the bar code at the supermarket checkout. There are the new tracking systems for information management – such that computers can predict what you will buy and what your interests are – based on previous sales and decisions taken. We can Google Map and satnav the spaces people dwell within; and deploy closed circuit television (CCTV) to capture life as it is lived in everyday life *in situ*. We can find out the life styles of people through our consumer studies using zip codes and postal addresses. And we can do all this globally and in an instance. In short, there is now such a staggering amount of stuff about society available in digital form that it can overwhelm. The contemporary world is a very different world from that of earlier generations of sociologists; and it brings startling and very different resources available for research and study. Everybody can now easily be their own sociologist as resources about society await us in cyberspace simply awaiting exploration.

But the sociological questions become even more pressing. Given that there is now so much social stuff out there, what is to be made of it all? It is precisely this thought, this serious *thinking*, which is now required when oh so much stuff sits at our finger tips. No data or information is just the automatic truth about society. The new technologies may change patterns of communication, create new virtual worlds and generate access to much data. *But data overload and indiscriminate media saturation now becomes more and more of a problem.* We can YouTube our lives away watching simulated entertainment and live out imaginary lives in games and 'second lives'; but as sociologists we now need to ask just *how* these newer technologies and 'cyber-knowledges' may be profoundly reshaping our relationship to information and knowledge. *Tweeting* is not in-depth knowledge (no one has ever claimed this!). We need to ask firstly how these new technologies can inform our understanding of the social, but more importantly we need to ask how sociological thinking can help us make sense of this explosion of data stuff.

## THINK ON: USING CYBERSPACE TO STUDY THE SOCIAL

Let me just give three examples, from many. All are controversial with traditional sociologists, and yet I think here to stay and be developed.

### 'GOOGLING SOCIOLOGY': SENSITISING THE FIRST APPROXIMATION OF A FIELD OF INQUIRY

Search engines such as Lycos (formed in 1994), Google (formed in 1998, and the world leader) or Bing (formed in 2009) have helped provide ways of accessing data on all manner of worldwide issues. Typing key words helps access world maps, library catalogues, archived newspapers and journals, official government documents, social movement archives and all manner of cultural phenomena. In many ways this is a good starting point for almost any social research, and sometimes it may prove to be all you need for basic research: data on the Web is like secondary data that is open to analysis (e.g. crime statistics). But there is much more to be found: the complete works of many early key sociologists are available free of charge in their full original glory (look up The Marx/Engels Library for example). Virtually every social activity now has its web site (from sports and pets to crime and politics). Reaching data overload comes quickly, and the challenge is to make sense of it.

### WIKIPEDIA SOCIOLOGY AND THE DEMOCRATISATION OF KNOWLEDGE

Wikipedia is the web's ever-expanding encyclopedia and many students rush to it – it seems to have all the answers, and can easily be cribbed for essays! But this whole site also raises the question: *Just what is an Encyclopedia and what is it for?* Conventionally, an encyclopedia provided stable answers to problems provided by 'experts' carved in stone. With Wikopedia, anyone can provide information and it will be as up to date as anyone wants to make it – the fragile nature of a traditional encyclopedia is profoundly revealed. But it is also wide open to abuse: anyone could put anything on it. A lot of errors could be posted. And this raises the issue about what knowledge is? Is it to be fixed by experts – as in the past; or is it to be more open, fluid and even democratic? But if this is to be the case, do you really want to be filling up your minds with false and misleading information? What this raises in an acute form is the idea of *a sociology of knowledge* which asks questions about how ideas, data and knowledge are always the products of particular times and places. We have to know about the social organisation of knowledge: it is knowledge from where and whom? Wikipedia puts these issues squarely on the agenda.

VISUAL SOCIOLOGY: YOUTUBE, WEBCAM IMAGES AND VISUAL CULTURE

Sociology was born at roughly the same time as photography, but over the past two hundred years their histories have not touched a great deal. A few sociologists have included photos in their books and some have become connected to documentary film making. But sociology has not taken much interest in the image. Yet now the new technologies have made the visual a focus – we have digital cameras and webcams and click away happily snapping the features of everyday social life. We can study the visual at the click of a button – and store it, analyse it, and debate its meanings and its roles in social life. New forms of visual communication are everyday experiences and sociologists will in the future ignore them at their peril. The visual image is becoming central to understanding the social – and sociologists have only just started to take it seriously.

## 3 ANALYTIC WORK: DATA IN SEARCH OF SENSE

Welcome to the interview, survey and questionnaire society. There are multiple ways of securing data for sociology: nowadays we can find such data in many places. It is there in the newspapers, on the internet, on television and in the myriad documents found in daily life. We are quite familiar now with observing the lives of others – we do it all the time when we watch 'reality programmes' like *Big Brother*, or in the many documentary films. Indeed some of these are quite extraordinary in giving us 'fly on the wall' accounts of life. Many of these media programmes and everyday interviews – and the reflections that go on around them – can often take you closer to what is going on in contemporary social life than a great deal of sociology published in the sociological journals! So the skills of sociology do not basically lie in their research tools. The world is now stuffed full of data for everyone to examine, and the case could now be made that we no longer need sociologists – they served a purpose in the transition from the industrial to the late modern world, but now we are all data collectors and analysts and sociologists have become dinosaurs.

This is obviously not my view; for there is a method in sociology's madness. *Sociology provides ways of making sense of this mess of data*. We know that much data in the material is garbage, dross, that 'reality' programmes put on a show for us and are not the one 'reality', and that many surveys are biased by the commercial interests behind them (they are, after all, *market* research). The challenge for sociology is to provide *analytic tools* (as opposed to data tools) for thinking about such 'data'. In the everyday world, we might just take the 'reality' of the interview, the 'truth' of a questionnaire, the 'facts' of a survey for granted – as given. But good sociology cannot do this. It always needs to inspect the data to make critical sense of it. Sociology's cardinal methodological rule is that *truth is never easy*. In understanding social life, truth rarely simply announces itself. Social truth is a struggle arising from many perspectives and disagreements in social life. Never expect to find the truth of any social situation to simply await you from research.

## THINK ON: NUMBERS AND THE SOCIOLOGIST

Sociologists are sometimes mistaken for statisticians. This is not so. True, many will have to learn the use of statistics for various research projects and run programmes that do this – like the Social Science Statistical Package (SSSP); but this is not sociology. Yet sociologists do need to be sophisticated about numbers and acquire a critical numeracy which enable them to ask serious questions about how we use numbers in society. This is a big topic, but here are just three starting questions to ponder.

1  Is everything measurable – indeed should we try and measure everything? Can we really make sense of many things – like love, happiness, anger or God – through counting. What are the limits of numbers?

2  What do numbers really mean? Is a billion big and one small? Not necessarily so. Numbers are often banded around for political points and can be used for very misleading ends. Develop your benchmarks for making sense of numbers.

3  How are statistics – of crime, of suicide, of health, of finance – produced? What are the agencies behind them? Some sociologists actually study the work of statistic producing agencies and show the everyday assumptions (even biases) they work from in making statistics. Consider the idea that statistics only really measure the work of statistic agencies. Who created it, when, where and why? (For more, see Joel Best's *Damned Lies and Statistics*).

### THE DATA OF CRIME

Here is a quick example: crime and sexual violence. We are all used to hearing the saga of rising (and nowadays falling) crime rates. Here we have accounts presented by official government agents of crime statistics: huge agencies and much money is devoted to keeping these records. Indeed, how can a modern society think about crime without some large-scale statistics like these? We need them. But sociologists can *never* simply take them for granted. Instead they have to ask just how did some people come to assemble these statistics (and not others) in these ways (and not others)? Who reports, defines and logs a crime? How do people come to make sense of what is – and is not – a crime? Once you start posing these questions, it becomes clear that statistic construction depends on a long interpretive chain of many people at different stages of vulnerability and officialdom making crucial decisions over time, often shaped by organisational needs, over time. More than this, once a report is made, and crime statistics are reported to the public, we then find a whole bunch of other interpretations are made of it – the media interprets it selectively, the public has to make sense of it, and the official government responds and re-interprets it. In other words, there is *a moving process of interpretation and reinterpretation of these crime statistics and there is absolutely nothing simple about them. Criminal statistics are the work of human agencies and bureaucracies that lead to sedimented human meanings.*

There are other lessons to learn from this simple example. First, whatever crime is going on in a society, crime statistics are only one perspective or angle for getting at it: crime statistics bear a moving and difficult relationship to real or actual crime. Some crimes like rape are notoriously under-reported and suffer from severe problems of interpretation; others – a street homicide seems much clearer to define. Processes of interpretation are done from a point of view. We can never tell or grasp the full picture. Every bit of data is told from a point of view, a perspective, a **standpoint** – and sociology has to locate this. This is the Rashomon effect – named after the famous Japanese film where one story of murder and rape is told from many perspectives and the very nature of what is true is held under a microscope. *There are always multiple perspectives on social life.* To stay with the example of rape, we can immediately see a wide range of perspectives that are available to us here. Figure 6.3 shows just a few of the angles, perspectives or standpoints that rape could be described from.

This is very simple: but surely, the more perspectives and angles we can get on this, then maybe the better our sociological account will be? Few sociologists can ever do all of this and instead we often get descriptions of the fragments that fail to connect up. The task of sociologists is to unpack as many of these different perspectives as possible.

| | | | |
|---|---|---|---|
| • The Rape Victim | • The Rapist | • The Rapist's Family | • The Victim's Family |
| • Police responses | • Neighbours | • Rape counsellors | • Community responses |
| • Media reactions | • Support groups | • Politicians | • Court officials |
| • Men's responses (but which men?) | | • Women's responses (but which women?) … and so on. | |
| *In looking at any social thing, always consider the range of different perspectives that could be brought into its study* | | | |

*Figure 6.3*  Whose perspective? The Rashomon Effect

NARRATIVE QUESTIONS?

Two linked questions follow from this. How does the perspective get organised and shaped, and what is the wider context of the perspective? Here we enter another important feature for sociological analysis – that of **narrative** and story. Human beings are always creating meaning and they do this through stories and narratives. We are the narrating animal and sociology becomes the study of social narratives – of the ways in which people code and organise their experiences though discourses. In one sense then sociology is the study of social life through the representations we produce of it. Sociologists study the narratives that people write and make around their lives, and then in turn reproduce new narratives of theses narratives. There is a constant flow of narratives within society and sociology.

But this raises the next issue. Are all **perspectives** and narratives equally valid or dependable? If we line up all these different perspectives – as in the rape example, or analyse an array of different narratives as above, surely sociology falls into extreme relativism. It just shows different views and has no base line for adjudicating truths. Well this is not so. *Sociology looks at the relations between things, recognises the different standpoints and perspectives, senses the narrative organisation of life, and then tries to balance, match and keep an eye on truth.*

We know this kind of issue from blogging or watching a reality TV programme. We see the narratives; we hear the different perspectives; but ultimately we want to find a way of bringing them together. People are different. How can we make sense of the ways in which such things interconnect and relate? How can we provide a wider, higher, broader, deeper narrative that brings these things together? This is just what sociology wants to do and it does its job when it reveals and tells these contrasting perspectives and standpoints. It is working well when it jostles contrasting standpoints together. And sociology does its job best of all when it brings together all perspectives and works to transcend them (a happy day that will never ultimately come along!) We must do the best we can and sociology's ideas of perspective and narrative help a lot.

### MAKING SENSE OF DATA: GAINING ADEQUATE OBJECTIVITY IN A SUBJECTIVE WORLD

The classic way of handling method problems is derived from the adoption of the *scientific method* itself. For example, a very basic feature of science is that it tests or *falsifies data*. It does *not* accumulate more and more data that just supports a view; rather it tries to knock down any statement, to falsify and show where conjectures are not true. It looks for negative evidence. A key tip for being scientific is usually to ask three simple questions: does this data 'measure' or truly capture what it purports (*validity*); do researchers use the same kind of tools so that like is being studied with like (*reliability*); and finally are the subjects typical of their wider group – or not? (*representativeness*). Many research manuals flag the importance of these three key evaluative tools, and it is worth knowing about them. If, for example, you are studying, say, rape – then are you 'measuring' rape, is it actually tapping into what rape is? This raises serious questions about the meaning of rape. Further is the rape a typical one – and how can we know this? Would another sociologist be able to repeat this study and come to the same kinds of conclusions?

### SOCIOLOGY AS A CRITICAL IMAGINATION

But science, vital as it is, it is not without problems. Thus, sociologists cannot take for granted that the 'scientific questionnaire' will get at the facts, the interview will dig out the true story, the documentary will 'tell it as it is', or that the survey will provide accurate statistics of our world. These methods often imply that there is indeed an objective, well ordered universe out there – one we can trap and tell the truth about. But things may not be so straightforward. Even physicists do not see the world in this simple way. Good science and good art always knows this. Human social worlds do not lend themselves to' easy' truths or findings.

What we need therefore is always *critique*. Think about the social life as we have been discussing it in this book (or the case of rape we have just raised above). It is dense with contradictory and ambiguous meaning; it is always embedded in historical worlds and emerging in different spaces; there are structures and actions; there are multiple social worlds never unitary ones; power is everywhere and hence lives, meanings and sense have to be negotiated in conflictual situations. It is lodged in worlds of intense human suffering and social inequalities. All this we have seen in this book: so how then can we study it all at such an objective and neutral distance? What we are measuring is on the move all the time and we cannot trap the ambiguity and contradiction of social life simply through research tools. What people say at one second is often contradicted seconds later, what people say may not be what they mean – or do, and as people change, so may their 'truths'. Now I am *not* suggesting that sociology goes down some relativist impasse where we cannot get at the truth and anything goes. Not at all. Read on. Here are more challenges.

First all data needs to be placed in wider *contexts* – locate the wider contexts of both history and what is going on now. Knowledge never stands on its own: it needs to be related. For example, the trouble with much internet data is that it comes to us as mere 'bits'. In order to make sense of it, *we need frameworks to provide a wider sense of it.* Thus it helps to know where this bit of data can be located within debates about it (controversies usually exist and need to be used as a frame). More it needs also to be given some sense of historical sense – no data arrives out of the blue. There are precedents and histories – what are they? Ultimately, a range of different perspectives and narratives around it will become transparent; and these then need connecting to the wider patterns and social actions found in the wider culture as it shifts in time and space. Here I am harking back to some of the themes we saw earlier in creating a sociological imagination. Without *puzzling* these things you are lost in the moment, floating with nowhere to go. This 'puzzling' is just what good education can now help to provide.

Important here too is what is known as the **comparative method**. If we have an interview finding, we can compare it with what others have said in the past as well as comparing it with a more abstract ideal type. A very general idea to help in all this draws upon a nineteenth-century idea (prominent in the work of Max Weber) of the **ideal type**. Ideal types are *not* meant to be seen as ideals (or perfect types), nor are they meant to be seen as simple statistical averages. Rather they signal the key characteristics of any phenomena – which may not actually exist in reality. It is an abstract type against which real phenomena can be matched. As Weber (1978: 20) says:

> An ideal type is formed by the one-sided accentuation of one or more points of view and by the synthesis of a great many diffuse, discrete, more or less present and occasionally absent concrete individual phenomena, which are arranged according to those one-sidedly emphasised viewpoints into a unified analytical construct ...

Another part of this wider critical approach is to investigate *the spirals of meanings*: how can we make sense of the meanings here and how do they connect up with the wider culture and even the research process? *Data is always about human meanings – and as such it needs interpretations.* As we have seen, over and over, one of the key features of the social world is that it is dependent on communication, is dialogical and inter-subjective. We depend on others and their meanings. Sociological data is always congealed human meaning and somehow we need to see how these meanings were made and then how we make sense of them; that social life is encircled in meanings. Everything you touch in social life comes loaded with meaning – and hence this is always a key starting part of making sense. For Weber the challenge was *Verstehen* (understanding); for Scheler it was empathy; for Thomas and Zaniencki it was the cultural coefficient; for Bourdieu, it was habitus. Never mind the terms: I hope you will see the importance of grasping the layers and complexities of meanings that flood social life and social research. Sociologists often refer to this as a **hermeneutic** analysis and by this they refer to the complex ways in which humans come to make sense of their world.

## THINK ON: EVALUATING DATA.

Whenever you are confronted with social data – in sociology books, in the press, on websites, in reports – ask the following questions.

1 *Science*: What is the evidence against this – try and falsify it. (Do not simply accumulate more and more evidence in its favour, but try to falsify it). How typical is this (ask about the representativeness of the sample)? And the validity and reliability?

2 *Context and comparison*: Locate the evidence in wider frameworks: historically (put it on a time line of similar 'facts'), geographically (how might this appear to other nations and cultures?) and theoretically (how might this appear with different thinkers and theorists approaching this same fact).

3 *Standpoint and perspective*: What is the 'angle' here – what other perspectives might there be? All accounts are written from 'angles'. Think in particular of the background and assumptions of the researcher and authors as far as you can. Even the most neutral of writers (a rare and not very interesting breed) work with assumptions.

4 *Language, rhetoric and narrative*: Think about how the data is being presented – usually it is trying to persuade you of its truth by using various devices. Since Aristotle's *Rhetoric* (and his debate with Plato on this) we have known about the significance of languages, and the power of the poetic and storytelling to persuade audiences. Social data is a special form of rhetoric and narrative that needs understanding and examining.

5 *Hermeneutics*: Enter the circle of meaning. Data never speaks for itself – is has been given meaning by its researcher and its presenter, and is now is open to further interpretation. More, the data text itself can only make sense by connecting its parts – the philosopher Paul

Ricoeur (1913–2005) talks about a hermeneutic circle of knowledge. As we have seen, truth and knowledge are not the straightforward things we might like to think!

6  *Reflexivity*: Consider the social impact and role of this data. Social findings feed back into social life and change it. There is no neutral presentation of findings – social facts are part of the social. This feedback needs to be considered. Crime statistics for instance are never simple reflections of crime, but become social ideas that then change the way we think about crime (for example, they might generate 'fear of crime').

## BEING PRACTICAL

I might have scared you a little in this chapter by raising some rather difficult questions about truth, meaning, knowledge and how social research is never a straightforward matter of interviewing or gathering statistics. My main aim indeed has been to make you aware of what you might do, and to be critical whenever you find data. But it can be carried too far and I have known students give up when they found that this process was so complicated and difficult. So a balance is needed and as usual people muddle through. Seeing sociology as an imagination, a science and a craft you need to work on developing the tools of its trade; and learning requires patience: the voyage is from information to knowledge to wisdom. It takes time. Let me end with a series of rather more down-to-earth tips to help you on your way:

1  Get close to whatever you want to study. Stick to the concrete and ask: What is going on – by who? where? when? and why? Wherever possible stay engaged with people in their worlds and avoid becoming cut off or aloof from them. Keep yourself grounded.

2  Keep asking questions about the quality of the kind of material you are working with – your data. Think about what it is you are 'measuring', 'observing', 'describing' – are you getting at this as best you can?

3  Think about the kind of knowledge you are aiming for – and where you might stand in relationship to this. What is your own perspective, your standpoint? Maybe you are completely neutral, but this is unlikely. Learn to describe social realities from as many angles as you can. Draw some social maps of different perspectives around your topic and sense what your perspectives are leaving out.

4  Make sure your choice of research tools – websites, YouTube, media content, interviews, etc – are the most appropriate tools for your study. There are a wide range of possibilities out there. You do not have to stay with the survey or the interview.

5  Cultivate both good language and good concepts. Avoid jargon and shun pretentiousness and pomposity. Stay intelligible as far as you can in your thinking and your writing. New words can be helpful – but go for the simpler word wherever you can. Do not be too easily impressed by complicated expressions – many academics are very poor at expressing themselves! Read George Orwell's classic little book *Why I Write* (1940), and his line: 'Break any rule rather than saying anything outright barbarous'.

6  Cultivate basic skills of numeracy, writing, thinking and 'seeing' the world. The best way to do this is to practice the skills a little every day. Develop good work habits.

7  Be sensitive to the political and ethical relations inside your research and outside of it. Recall the old adage that 'knowledge is power' (Pope), but also the significance of ethics and remain empathetic to the ways you engage with people. Respect people and their worlds.

8  Stay open. Things will change and your proposals will change. This is normal. Keep a flexible eye on what you are finding and change with it. Never stick to fixed protocols if your study takes you elsewhere.

9  Know yourself and be comfortable with who you are in relation to your study. Unlike many areas of study, sociology is social. And it means you need to know a bit about what you want to study, how it links to your own life, what your reasons are for studying this, how it might be shaped and indeed impact your own life.

10 Nobody can tell you how to do research – and reading guides on how to interview, design questionnaires and do content analyses etc are pointless until you have a project in mind. Research tips devoid of a project mean little. But once you know your project, read and study voraciously on how others have used these methods and practice them in dummy runs. Never unleash yourself on others or make data without detailed preparations.

Finally, the cardinal rule: let methods be your servant. Read widely, think a lot, keep critical, stay grounded and be passionate about what you do. Aim for adequate objectivity. And to thy own methodology be true – but make sure you have one!

## SUMMARY

We look at methods and see that sociology straddles art, science and history. Methods requires you think hard (about what kind of knowledge you want to produce), do empirical investigation (the need for a logics of gathering data – inductive and deductive – and a wide range of research tools to draw from), and skilfully analyse and make sense of data (a check list for evaluating research is provided). The importance of the new information technologies for doing this research is emphasised.

## EXPLORING FURTHER

### MORE THINKING

Start to evaluate some of the research findings you find everyday reported in the media and elsewhere about the social world. Look back over the book and its key arguments and develop your own checklist of issues that need to be considered in such an evaluation. Match it with the one in this chapter (see the box: Think on: Evaluating Data). Perhaps start with some items you find on the internet, maybe on Wikipedia, and try to evaluate them? More ambitiously, try and conduct a small scale study of your own using ideas from this chapter and the previous one.

READING

The starting point may be to look at some of the very large textbooks that guide you though many of the issues I have only lightly touched upon in this chapter. There are many, but two standard books are: Alan Bryman, *Social Research Methods* (2008) and Earl Babbie, *The Practice of Social Research* (2009). On field work, see: John Lofland, David Snow, Leon Anderson and Lyn H Lofland, *Analyzing Social Settings* (2004). To get a grasping of some of the philosophical issues, two classics on the philosophical problems of the social sciences are great starting places. They are Karl Popper, *The Poverty of Historicism* (1957) and Peter Winch, *The Idea of a Social Science and its Relation to Philosophy* (1958). A good text guide to these issues is Gerard Delanty, *Social Science: Philosophical and Methodological Foundations* (2005) and the accompanying collection of readings in *Philosophies of Social Science: The Classic and Contemporary Readings* edited by Gerard Delanty and Piet Strydom (2003). I have found the work of Howard S. Becker very illuminating on all these issues: see especially *The Tricks of the Trade* (1998) and *Telling About Society* (2007). Finally, a lively new challenge to the orthodoxies can be found in Les Back, *The Art of Listening* (2007)

7

# SUFFERING INEQUALITIES

We are threatened with suffering from three directions: from our own body, which is doomed to decay and dissolution and which cannot even do without pain and anxiety as warning signals; from the external world, which may rage against us with overwhelming and merciless forces of destruction; and finally from our relationships to other men. The suffering which comes from this last source is perhaps more painful than any other.

Sigmund Freud, *Civilization and its Discontents,* 1930

It's the same the whole world over, it's the poor wot gets the blame;
It's the rich wot gets the pleasure, ain't it all a blooming shame.

1914–18 war song/music hall ballad

We have seen that sociologists look at both the joys and the sufferings of human social life. Yet very often students come to sociology with a dream to make the world a better place and their concern is less with what might be positive and enjoyable in the world than with what is troubling. They are disturbed, worried or aggrieved about something – either in the wider world or their personal life. They see injustice or social problems that they want to help remedy. There is a media report on children dying in the third world; a trade union father worried about the conditions of work; a feminist mother appalled at the abuse and powerlessness of many women across the world; a film which shows injustice and brutality in life; despair at perpetual war; anger at homophobia and racism; a worry about the environment. What, they ask, is to be done? They want to understand what is going on and turn to sociology for help.

There is indeed undeniably an awareness of the social sufferings of the world in much sociological work and in this chapter, I want to focus a little on just one as a kind of case study. There is a lot of suffering in the world, a lot to choose from, but I have selected probably the most central of all areas studied by sociologists: that of the sufferings connected to inequalities.

## THE ARCHAEOLOGY OF SUFFERINGS: MAPPING DIFFERENCES AND DIVISIONS

One starting point for sociology must always be an awareness of vast human **differences**. We dwell in an incorrigibly plural universe. As the Irish poet Louis MacNeice beautifully put it: the world is 'crazier and more of it than we think, the drunkenness of things various'. Human worlds are lush with multiplicities and possibilities. We have seen throughout this short book how differences abound and proliferate in nations, cultures, peoples, ethnicities, religions, ages, histories, languages, meanings. Everybody's world is most certainly never just like yours, your friends or your neighbours: even though most days we might act as if it is. It is the persistent recognition of these differences and the pursuit of their understanding that is one driving hallmark of a sociological awareness.

But everywhere we look we can see these human differences growing into disagreements and conflicts; and soon differences congeal into structures of division and hierarchies. All societies – human and otherwise – are distinguished by patterns of inequality. Ants have their workers, apes have their grooming rituals; and chickens have their pecking orders. In most known human societies, there are always a few high in the pecking order whilst the masses are cast asunder to the lowest regions. Some have privileged and flourishing lives; some are rebellious, resisting or resilient; many lead wasted or damaged lives. Indeed, the history of human societies can well be read as a history of billions of people going quietly to their graves with lives of almost unspeakable suffering delivered upon them from the raging inequalities of the differences given to them by the society where they were born.

Societies then are homes to social divisions, hierarchies and structured social inequalities. There are always it seems the rich and the poor, the slave owner and the slave, the black and the white, the migrant and the host, the educated and the ignorant, the

## THINK ON: THE INEQUALITIES OF THE WORLD

The leading Swedish sociologist Göran Therborn in his book *Inequalities of the World* (2006) has expressed his own personal concern about inequality so well that I will quote him: he reflects my view and that of many others too (p. 5):

> Why shouldn't a new born child in Congo have the same chance to survive into a healthy adulthood as a child in Sweden? Why shouldn't a young Bihari woman have the same autonomy to choose her life pursuits as a young white American male, or an Egyptian college graduate the same as a Canadian? Why shouldn't all Pakistani and Brazilian families have the same access as British or French to good sanitation, air conditioning and/or heating, washing machines, and holiday tickets? Why should many children have to work? Why shouldn't a black HIV-positive person in Southern Africa have the same chance to survive as a white European? Why should a handful of individual 'oligarchs' be able to expropriate most of the natural resources of Russia, while a large part of the population have been pushed into pauperism? Why should big business executives be able to pay themselves hundred of times more than the workers they are constantly pushing to 'work harder', more flexibly and at lower cost? In brief, there is inequality in this world because many are denied the chance to live their lives at all; to live a life of dignity, to try out their interests in life, and to make use of their existing potential. The inequalities of the world prevent hundreds of millions of people from developing their differences.

diseased and the healthy, the man and the woman, the gay and the straight, the able and the disabled, the terrorist and the terrorised, the pathological and the normal, us and them – indeed the good, the bad and the ugly. And sociology cannot fail to see this. In human societies, differences are used as moral markers to establish how some are better than others. Moral worth is often attached to this labelling as boundaries are established of the normal and the pathological. The elite are superior; the mass are downcast. Borders become hierarchically arranged and a ranking or pecking order is established: outsiders, underclasses, dangerous people, marginals, outcasts – the scapegoats – are invented. And sociologists ask: just how are these 'outsiders' and ranking orders created, maintained and changed? This is the problem of social exclusion, the social 'other; and social stratification. In this chapter, I will review a few key themes found in the vast literature on the sociology of inequality.

## THE STRATIFICATIONS OF THE WORLD

A very good question for any sociologist to ask early on is: what is the basic map or organisation of this society's pecking order? Who are its excluded and devalued 'outsiders' and 'others'? Here we look at the most basic layers – the shapes of hierarchy – that a society has. All societies will have such a map. The most common ones you will see are the strata or layers of the slavery system, the caste system, the class system, and the world poverty system. In all cases, there is a small elite at the top and various other groupings in the middle and the bottom. Here the idea of stratification draws on the imagery of layers: just as there are layers of the earth, so we can depict societies as falling into layers. Crudely there are always a few at the top and many at the bottom – with quite a lot in between. Sociologists study these in great detail but they can be briefly summarised. They are:

### CASTE

Perhaps nowhere is this more clearly seen than in the formal caste system. There is a long history of the **caste** system – notably in India. Here, people were ranked in a rigid hierarchy at birth, and this alone determined social position. Although the system has been officially abolished in India, there is significant evidence that it is still alive in many traditional Hindu villages (and in the big cities too). At it simplest, the system denotes four major categories: Brahmans (priests and writers) who claim the highest status, Kshatriyas (warriors and rulers), Vaishyas (the merchants and landowners) and Shurdas (artisans and servants). People outside the system become 'untouchables' (nowadays called the Dahlit), and they have the most unpleasant work – handling sewage, burning corpses, scavenging. It is estimated that there are some 150 million untouchables in India (about 20 per cent of the population), whereas the Brahmans at the top make up just 3 per cent. This makes them one of the most subordinated and neglected groups in the world.

### SLAVERY

This has been throughout history a major pattern of social organisation – not just a blip of Western life. Its origins can be found deep in prehistoric hunting societies; it is dominant in ancient society – the Greeks, the Romans, the Persians, the Etruscans – all had major systems of slavery. In modern times, slave trading reaches a peak in the United States with a pre-Civil War slave population of 4,000,000; and then it is found again through the forced labour of the Nazi regime and in the Soviet gulags. And it has not vanished today. Today it has been estimated there are still some 27 million slaves found in forced labour, forced marriages, debt bondage, and sex trafficking – along with an organisation dedicated to its eradication.

### SOCIAL CLASS

This is the major system of stratification identified with capitalism. Classically, sociologists draw upon the contrasting ideas of two key early thinkers: Marx and Weber. Broadly, Marx highlighted **class** as an economic issue and identified two major social classes (there were others) who corresponded to the two basic relationships to the means of production: individuals either owned productive property or worked for others. Capitalists (or the *bourgeoisie*) own and operate factories, and use (exploited) the labour of others (the proletariat). This led to huge inequalities in the system, and in Marx's view would lead ultimately to class conflict. Oppression and misery would drive the working majority to organise and, ultimately, to overthrow capitalism. A process would take place in which the poorer classes would become more pauperised, polarised and aware of their class position. This would lead to a class consciousness of their true economic exploitation. Max Weber saw things a little more widely; and identified class as lying at the intersection of three distinct dimensions: class (economic), status (prestige) and power.

### GLOBAL POVERTY

These days it is often common for sociologists to identify another (probably linked) system at work which divides the world. Here we find that the world's countries are massively unequal. Strikingly, a divide is often seen between the bottom billion who live on less than US$2 a day, and the top 'super rich': the richest fifth of the world's population who enjoy an income thirty times greater than the poorest fifth. Whilst a few luxuriate in private yachts and planes, billions of others have fallen into the 'black hole' of slums and poverty. They have become what the Caribbean French philosopher-revolutionary Frantz Fanon (1925–1961) called ' the wretched of the earth'. Here are those who experience either the poverty of landless labourers and traditional peasants or who have become the 'urban poor' – who seek out an existence in the slums and *favelas* of the earth: migrants, garbage pickers, beggars, handcart pullers, sex workers, the disabled of all kinds.

## THE STUDY OF UNEQUAL LIVES: OBJECTIVE AND SUBJECTIVE INEQUALITIES

A great deal of sociology has been concerned with investigating the ways in which this inequality can be measured. Some has aimed at a more scientific account of measuring aspects of social class, racial discrimination or gender inequalities to reveal its *objective existence*. Others have been more concerned with observing and listening to the *subjective experiences*.

## THE 'FACTS' OF WORLD INEQUALITIES

There are major inequalities, documented from many sources, on income and wealth, life expectancy and health, education and literacy, work and housing. The inequalities can be traced between countries around the world and within countries. The statistics are always problematic. Studies usually acknowledge large margins of error: it is hard to measure many of these issues in rich countries yet alone poor ones. Still, trends are unmistakable and quite extreme. We live in a world of staggering inequalities – though it is uneven across countries. Here are just a few examples:

The world poverty line is now defined as living on the equivalent of $1.25 a day. With that measure based on latest data available (2005), well over a billion of people live on or below that line. Furthermore, almost half the world – over three billion people – live on less than $2.50 a day and at least 8per cent o of humanity lives on less than $10 a day. And linked to this are many other inequalities: more than a billion people lack access to safe water, and over two and half billion lack adequate sanitation. While hunger and under-nutrition is the fate of one third of all Africans and one quarter of all South Asians, in the West, we have food disorders around eating and obesity. Recent economic events have exacerbated all this

At the other end of the scale, the income of the richest 1 per cent of the world's population is equal to the income of the poorest 57 per cent. This happens within countries as much as between countries. In the USA in 2008, there were 469 billionaires while over 51 million people were living in poverty. The top fifth of earners receive over half of the national income whilst the bottom fifth receive only 5 per cent. Indeed, the top 10 per cent of American households take in 42 per cent of all income and hold 71 per cent of all wealth. Famously, two men in the US (Bill Gates and Warren Buffett) have as much money between them as 30% of the entire US population. In rich countries, life expectancy is about eleven years longer than for the world generally; in poorer countries (a third of humanity) it is nine years shorter. A baby in a high-income society (like Japan or most of Europe) lives some 20 years longer than a child born into a low income society.

Never mind the precision of these figures: the figures are so strikingly extreme that we know that vast billions of people live in absolute or abject poverty, whilst a few million live in almost unimaginable wealth. This is a very unequal world.

See Göran Therborn, *Inequalities of the World* (2006).

## THE OBJECTIVE REALITY OF INEQUALITIES

Objective inequalities have been measured by a large array of devices. To come to their conclusions, sociologists spend a great deal of time discussing the most appropriate ways to measure inequalities and to provide objective measures for tapping into them. They have developed many classifications of the class system in different countries – using occupations as a key factor. They have elaborated on ways of measuring wealth and income. Much has been written on the measurement of poverty – both as an absolute and as a relative measure. They have developed all kinds of scales for showing different levels of literacy and education, the degree of sickness and the varying rates of death, the extent of the 'gender gap' and for levels of political engagement. And key statistical measures like the **Gini coefficient** have been evolved to help track the changing levels of inequality. This has been done at both national and international levels. As you study sociology, you will encounter and critically assess all these (for an introduction to all this Geoff Payne's *Social Divisions* (2006); and a clear example of the use of such scales to develop arguments around inequality is to be found in Kate Pickett and Richard Wilkinson's *The Spirit Level*.)

Broadly, on all these objective measures, there seems to be massive world wide evidence of huge inequalities across countries, and an inequality that in many countries (like the UK and the US) is growing (see Table 7.1).

*Table 7.1* The facts of world inequalities

| Rank | Country | HDI | Rank | Country | HDI | Rank | Country | HDI |
|---|---|---|---|---|---|---|---|---|
| HIGH | | | MEDIUM | | | LOW | | |
| 1 | Norway | 0.971 | 87 | Thailand | 0.783 | 160 | Malawi | 0.493 |
| 2 | Australia | 0.970 | 88 | Iran | 0.782 | 164 | Zambia | 0.481 |
| 3 | Iceland | 0.969 | 92 | China | 0.772 | 167 | Rwanda | 0.460 |
| 4 | Canada | 0.966 | 100 | Jamaica | 0.766 | 171 | Ethiopia | 0.414 |
| 5 | Ireland | 0.965 | 104 | Algeria | 0.754 | 175 | Chad | 0.394 |
| 10 | Japan | 0.960 | 106 | El Salvador | 0.747 | 180 | Sierra Leone | 0.365 |
| 13 | United States | 0.956 | 123 | Egypt | 0.703 | 181 | Afghanistan | 0.352 |
| 21 | United Kingdom | 0.947 | 129 | South Africa | 0.683 | 182 | Niger | 0.340 |
| 24 | Hong Kong | 0.944 | 134 | India | 0.612 | | | |
| 41 | Poland | 0.880 | 150 | Sudan | 0.531 | | | |
| 83 | Lebanon | 0.803 | 158 | Nigeria | 0.511 | | | |

HDI refers to the United Nations Human Development Index, which has been measured annually since 1990. It is a composite measure of three concerns: *longevity* – life expectancy at birth; *knowledge* – adult literacy and enrolment in schooling; decent *standards of living* – income per head. The least unequal parts of the world are Nordic, and the most unequal are in Latin America and Sub-Saharan Africa. The former measure around 25 on the Gini Coefficent, whilst the latter measure in at around 60. Source: United Nations, 2009.

## THINK ON: THE VOICES OF THE POOR

Here are some *Voices of the Poor* (Narayan, 2000):

> Poverty is pain; it feels like a disease. It attacks a person not only materially but also morally. It eats away one's dignity and drives one into total despair.
>
> (a poor woman in Moldova)

> Children are hungry, so they start to cry. They ask for food from their mother and their mother doesn't have it. Then the father is irritated, because the children are crying, and he takes it out on his wife. So hitting and disagreement break up the marriage.
>
> (poor people in Bosnia)

> Poor people cannot improve their status because they live day by day, and if they get sick then they are in trouble because they have to borrow money and pay interest.
>
> (a poor woman in Vietnam)

> There is no control over anything, at any hour a gun could go off, especially at night.
>
> (a poor woman in Brazil)

> It is neither leprosy nor poverty which kills the leper, but loneliness.
>
> (a woman in Ghana)

### THE SUBJECTIVE REALITY OF INEQUALITIES – THE ETHNOGRAPHY OF DAMAGED LIVES

Sociology's task is not only to measure the *objective* situations of inequality, but also to ask just what are the consequences of these differences *subjectively* for those who experience them? What does it mean to people to be poor, to be excluded, to be outcasts? Just how is stratification actually experienced by people who live devalued, even dehumanised, lives? How is their sense of self and self esteem shaped and how indeed might they fight back, resist and negotiate the insults, abuses and neglects they experience in their everyday lives? Studies show a string of feelings and responses not just to poverty and hardships but also the mundane trials of everyday life – of being kept waiting, rendered invisible and made to live through symbolic assaults to their own sense of self worth.

Study after study (see Table 7.2) have shown the ways in which people at the lower end of the pecking order – shaped by class, gender, **ethnicity**, nation, etc. – live their lives enduring various deprivations, degradations and defilements while deploying strategies to survive them. Several striking features stand out:

1  The worlds they experience and the lives they lead are likely to be insecure and unstable. Work and wealth is never guaranteed; each day can be a struggle for survival. At the heart of their lives is a basic lack of any necessities for a life. There is little money, little work, a scarcity of food, housing is minimal – and every day requires living with this. The main task becomes a struggle for survival in a world of great instability. They become *insecure lives*.

2  These worlds are often closely linked to danger: there is the presence of violence and violent threats. Brutalisation is built into the fabric of the daily life. War is often a backdrop; domestic violence is prevalent; women may experience special forms of violence such as genital mutilation; children may become soldiers. Homosexuals will be shot. Here we have *brutalised lives*.

3  Their lives of quiet desperation can become trapped in a sense of devaluation and dishonour – they experience 'class contempt', racism, sexism, homophobia and the rest. All of which potentially tells them how awful they are. 'They' are accorded little respect from outside worlds and made to feel uncomfortable in the presence of the privileged. All this can bring a low sense of worth, poor self esteem, a sense of shame, a dishonouring. These are the *shamed lives*.

4  Closely linked, they experience a basic lack of recognition – of who they are. Their lives are surrounded by people who simply

*Table 7.2*    The subjective side of inequality

There is a long history of studying the subjective experiences of those at the bottom of the pecking order. See:

1.  Oscar Lewis's *Five Families: Mexican Case Studies in the Culture of Poverty* (1959, new edition 1975)

2.  Richard Sennett and Jonathan Cobbs' *The Hidden Injuries of Class* (1977)

3.  Lillian Rubin's *Worlds of Pain* (1977)

4.  Pierre Bourdieu's *The Weight of the World* (1993/1999)

5.  Abdelmalek Sayad's *The Suffering of the Immigrant* (2004)

6.  Barbara Ehrenreich's *Nickel and Dimed: Undercover in Low wage America* (2002)

7.  Simon J.Charlesworth's *A Phenomenology of Working Class Experience* (1999)

8.  Elijah Anderson's *Code of the Street* (1999)

9.  Mitch Dunier's *Sidewalk* (1999)

10. Nancy Scheper-Hughes' *Death Without Weeping*(1992)

refuse to see them, who ignore them. There are the millions of people who clean offices at night, who we walk by as they beg in the street, who live in the no-go areas of slums unvisited by most, and the sick and poor whose sufferings are almost nightly displayed as 'victims' in other lands on television. These curiously are the *'invisible people'*: the great unseen.

5   But even if they are seen, it will often be through the lenses of charity and patronage, and often locked in a language of degradation. They become the 'disreputable poor', the 'deserving poor', the 'dirty immigrants', the 'underclass', the 'pathological'. Visible, or invisible, lives are put down: they are *demeaned and dehumanised lives*.

6   People have little control over what will happen to them and choices are restricted. But do not get me wrong. People are never passive automatons: they respond and deal with their situations. Over and over again, people respond in a number of ways. While some acquiesce and retreat in their plights, many fight back and rebel. They search for ways of dealing with their plight actively. They live *lives of resistance and fighting back*.

## INTERSECTIONS: STANDING AT THE CROSSROADS OF LIFE'S OPPORTUNITIES

So there is much evidence of massive inequality in the world. But how does it happen? Think for a moment of the seven billion people on earth at the moment (in 2010): each has a window (or structure) of opportunities open to their life. For some it is wide and expanding; for others it is narrow and restricting. Life's little opportunities in the end cluster into seven major 'forces' that help organise the wider social orders we live in, and which interconnect and intersect. Table 7.3 outlines these forces.

Whatever social thing you are looking at – schools, social work or senility – always try and ask questions about how it interconnects with these 'social orders' which shape our lives. Sociologists are interested in the ways they work individually (or autonomously) and the ways in which they dynamically feed into each other. Sometimes one will dominate over the others (for example, in slavery the racial formation has often played a significant role; in the exclusion of homosexuals, the sexual order works as a priority: but in both cases, they are also shaped by the other six forces to some extent). In many societies a gender order (some call it a patriarchy) works in which women are usually denied the same access as men to public social life – most religions are organised around ideas that women should *not* play significant roles except as mothers in the home. Ancient Greek and Roman societies were organised so that women were not only usually slaves, but were also excluded fully from recognition in public life. Neither the Catholic Church nor the Muslim faith will allow women to function in any key role. Likewise, most societies organise themselves around an age hierarchy: children and youth, young people, middle and old aged: in some societies, the old are highly valued; in others they are subordinated. Any specific order will be historically specific and unique and need careful study for all the elements outlined.

*Table 7.3* The intersecting orders of inequalities

| | | Social orders (channels of opportunities) | Supporting ideas and identities (discourses / positionalities) |
|---|---|---|---|
| Intersecting orders of social inequality: a structure of life opportunities | 1 | Class order | Classism and class consciousness |
| | 2 | Gender order (and patriarchy) | Sexism and gender identity |
| | 3 | Racial formation (ethnicity and race) | Racialisation, racism and ethnic identity |
| | 4 | Age stratification and generational orders | Ageism and generational self |
| | 5 | Nations | Nationalism and national identity |
| | 6 | The sexual order | Heterosexism, homophobia and heteronormativity: sexual identity |
| | 7 | The disability and health order | Sickness and 'disablement' ideologies: health/ability identity |

## THE CLASS ORDER

> The history of all hitherto existing society is the history of class struggles.
>
> (Karl Marx, 2000)

As we have seen (p. 156), class is based on economic factors. Most societies seem to be characterised by extremes of wealth and owning property at one end and masses of people in abject poverty and lacking in almost everything at the other. With many fine gradations, people fall into advantaged (upper, rich), intermediate (middle), subordinate (lower, working-class) groups – as well as those who seem to fall outside the whole system (the underclass). Sociologists have spent much time evolving ways of measuring social class, mainly focusing on different opportunities in work and income. Some also stress the importance of cultural differences. There is a vast literature on all this which cannot be covered here. But sadly overall, it is a picture that suggests class constantly reproduces itself – though to varying and shifting degrees – between most groups over the life cycle in most times and places. It is both global – with huge discrepancies across nations – and also local. There are *banlieus* in France, *favelas* in Brazil, *villa miseria* in Argentina, *degradati* in Italy: the stigmatised neighbourhoods of the lower classes are everywhere to be found.

## THE GENDER ORDER

> He is the Subject, he is the Absolute – she is the Other
>
> (Simone de Beauvoir, *The Second Sex*, 1949)

All societies divide their populations into men, women and others (who do not quite fit – like hermaphrodites and others). Sex itself has a biological foundation (chromosomes, brain structures, hormones, etc.); but the social expectations and the roles associated with being a man or being a woman are deeply social (and it is this which sociologists refer to as **gender**). They have an ambivalent relation. The precise content of what is expected of a man and a woman varies across history and across societies; but common to most is the ways in which women are placed in subordinate roles in

## THINK ON: BOURDIEU AND THE PERPETUAL REPRODUCTION OF PRIVILEGE – AND UNDERPRIVILEGE

Inequalities of all kinds are everywhere and they go on reproducing themselves from one generation to another. Of course there is some leakage – mobility – between the unequal groups, so that some people in each generation rise and some fall. Sociologists are keen to study this, and they usually conclude that there is much less mobility than people might think. The core problem then becomes the mechanism by which the differences keep getting reproduced – over, and over, and over again.

In general, it seems to be reproduced unthinkingly in the routines of everyday life – in families, schools, universities, work places, media. Pierre Bourdieu has been a key theorist to show that it is in the daily practices of choice, in liking the things that we like rather than others (heavy metal rather than opera, *Coronation Street* over the National Theatre), our fate is partially sealed. The habits – or **habitus** – of class for instance becomes settled. We may not see them as class, but they tacitly work their way through to reproduce this order.

You can find the classic discussion by Bourdieu in his book *Distinction* and he features prominently on YouTube. A recent application to the UK can be found in the work of Tony Bennett, Mike Savage and colleagues in their book *Culture, Class, Distinction* (2009)

relation to men. For instance, in general, women get lower pay, have less opportunities to achieve and earn (the glass ceiling), do different kinds of work (domestic work and care), and are much less likely to get on 'the rich list'. There are very few women in official positions of power – though in some countries this has increased. The rights to vote for women came much later than men's in most countries (and in many they remain disenfranchised).

Men and women do indeed have different opportunities. Women simply do not fare as well as men. To try to capture this, social scientists often speak of the Gender Gap: a measure of the levels of inequality between men and women. This is measured by four key indicators: (a) degree of economic participation; (b) level of educational attainment; (c) physical health, longevity and survival; and (d) political activity, participation and empowerment. There are many controversies about such a measure – but usually the Scandinavian countries (such as Norway, Finland, Iceland and Sweden) hold top places, whilst Muslim countries (notably the Yemen, Saudi Arabia, Pakistan, and Turkey) come out worst.

## THE ETHNIC AND RACE ORDER

> The problem of the twentieth century is the problem of the color-line
>
> (W.E.B. Du Bois, *The Souls of Black Folk,* 1903)

Members of an ethnic category share a cultural history – with common ancestors, a language or a religion that, together, confer a distinctive social identity. Most societies round the world are composed of a range of different ethnic cultures: histories of conquest, migration and war have seen to that. In this sense all societies are *hybridic* (combining different things). In England, for example, the forebears of Pakistani, Indonesian, Irish, Caribbean, Hong Kong or Chinese Europeans – to name just a few! – may well retain cultural patterns rooted in particular areas of the world. But in each of these ethnic orders a hierarchy of 'others' seems to emerge. There always seems to be a fear of outsiders – of the others – which runs deep. Each country and time seems to have its ethnic group which is cast out and around which all kinds of stereotypes, symbolic systems and mythical stories are invented.

The idea of a **racial formation** is helpful here to suggest complexes of how race organises social relations at both a micro level (a person's individual identities and interactions with other people), and macro level (the structures and ideologies generated by businesses, media and the government). Omi and Winant (1994) also believe that 'race [is] an unstable and "de-centred" complex of social meanings constantly being transformed by political struggle'. Alongside this is a process of **racialisation** – a process in which people come to be placed in ethnic /racial categories.

## THE ORDER OF NATIONS AND THEIR OTHERS

Any selected society is *never* a unified whole. True, there is often a sense of unity that is presumed to be a national identity – but this is what social scientists call an 'imagined community'. In reality societies are usually made of historically different groupings who over time have settled and developed – there are movements and migrations of settled peoples and the newly arrived everywhere, and they criss-cross over traditions, ethnicities, religions, and politics. This is the **diaspora**. People outside their nation often develop subaltern identities.

You will be hard pressed to find any society in the world where there are not such schisms between minority-outsider groups, usually with long histories and troubled identities. From Sarajevo to Sri Lanka, Jerusalem to Djakarta, it seems that much of the world is engaged in a war pitting one ethnic group against its rivals. In Australia sociologists study the tensions between aborigines and the new Asian immigrants; in America, the focus is often on American Indians, the blacks 'up from slavery', and a host of new immigrant groups (Mexicans, etc). Most societies and communities are disparate and bring their own conflicts and practices from discrimination to outright genocide.

## THE DISABILITY ORDER

Disabilities – from deafness, blindness and wheelchair mobility through chronic long-term illnesses like AIDS to mental health breakdowns of all kinds – often have some kind of biological foundation and can be seen as impairments and individual differences. But how these differences are treated socially is the sociologist's core concern. The disabled have been treated differently throughout history and given an array of names: cripples, subnormality, wierdos, mad and sad people, monsters and freaks. Deformed children have been killed at birth. Freaks have been used for entertainment in circuses and films. Many have been 'put away' in asylums and made to vanish from society. And even at their best they have been patronised by charity and welfare systems.

Sociological studies such as Erving Goffman's *Stigma* (1961) suggest how the disabled get categorised, stereotyped, socially excluded and discriminated against in myriad ways. Worse, social exclusion means disabled people often experience profound levels of poverty and deprivation. It is not just the disability that causes problems but the presence of a negative, hostile or patronising attitude from the wider society that makes life hard for them.

### THE SEXUALITY ORDER: HETERONORMATIVITY AND HOMOPHOBIA

Sexuality is much more than simply a biological drive. Sociologists looking at sexuality suggest that it is far from being a simple animal-like drive, but is something that only functions for humans when it is weaved into social relationships and meanings. We can never just do sex – it is always enmeshed in wider rules and understandings of just *who* we can have sex with (the opposite sex?), *where* and *when* it should be done (at night in the bedroom?), just *what* can be done (vaginal–penis intercourse?) and indeed even *why* we can have sex (to have children?). The long history of religions is partially about the regulation of sex – of making acceptable contexts in which sex can be done; and histories of sexuality show enormous variations both in the kinds of sex that people have, and the kinds of rules they make around it.

So sociologists are interested in such questions as how rules are made and developed about sexuality, about the range of sexual differences and how some come to be acceptable whilst others are not. They ask about the way human sexuality is given meaning – and how it often leads to the making of particular kinds of sexual identities (gay, straight, bisexual, sadomasochist, paedophile, queer). They ask about the ways in which sexuality connects to other institutions like the economy, religion, family and above all in the ways in which it intersects with other inequalities such as class, race and gender.

With this in mind, it soon becomes clear that some sexualities can be incorporated easily into a society whilst others are excluded. Homosexuality has been a key focus in recent decades and it can be shown that there have been massively contrasting social attitudes towards it across different cultures and times. In much of the Western world, gay life has become more and more acceptable over the past twenty-five years or so – recall that in many countries it was against the law in the 1960s. Yet by the start of the twenty-first century these same countries were legislating for gay marriages and civil partnerships, signalling 'new families of choices' and major changes in the public representations of same sex lives. At the same time, in many other countries, hostilities to homosexuality was great: in 2010, homosexuality is still against the law in many countries, and in a good few, is liable to the death penalty.

## THE GENERATIONAL AND AGE ORDER

A final key organising difference of all societies is age. Again, at the simplest level this is biological and the differences between infancy, youth, maturity and old age are obvious. But age is never simply a biological process though, and every culture also generates social expectations and roles which are geared to specific ages. Child rearing and infancy patterns vary enormously; not all cultures lead to the youth cultures we now find in the West (and which many sociologists have claimed grew in extent and variety with the development of consumer capitalism after the Second World War); and in some cultures the elderly are highly valued for their wisdom, in others they are more or less discarded.

Sociology suggests that all of human social life is generational. That is the social meanings of any life are profoundly shaped by a specific set of historical and personal experiences which are unique to their lives and which anchor their lives as they move through it. All lives might be seen as organised through a specific age standpoint: those born in the depression years, or who lived through the Second World War, or who grew up during the Chinese Revolution, or who lived under Stalin, or who were survivors of the Holocaust – all share a common experience which bonds them together as an age cohort. Nobody else can move though life with these experiences and they can be deeply formative of key differences. We speak nowadays of various generations – Baby Boomers, the

X generation, the Millennials. Generational lives are the escalators of our lives: whole groups of people are in perpetual motion – moving onwards together within a particular generational cohort or set of experiences, common to them and them alone, bonding them with each other, but also creating major differences with others who are not part of this generation. As they move further and further along this escalator, they become more and more distant from those at the other end who are just alighting upon it. Major generational differences generate different structures of opportunities.

## SUBJECTIVE FACTORS AGAIN: IDENTITY FRAGMENTS IN INEQUALITIES

As we have seen, objective, measurable inequalities (low income, poor literacy and the like) are always accompanied by subjective experiences. Part of this has been the idea of our relationships, positions and identities with others. **Identities** help provide a sense of (a) where we come from ('origins stories' as they are sometimes called), (b) who we are in the current moment, and (c) who we might be in the future. Our identities help give coherence to the past, present and the future. Yet whilst they help us locate our positions in the world, they are open to change as we encounter different situations and relations (recently this has often been called 'positionality').

In an early series of observations about this, Marx identified the importance of class consciousness in understanding the working of the class system. For Marx, people had to become aware of their class situation as they moved from a class 'in themselves' to a class 'for themselves'. An awareness of where we are positioned in the class system becomes crucial. Class consciousness and awareness of class are key components of class analysis. But each one of our social orders provide opportunities and potentials for new identities. Thus for example although women and ethnic minorities are often treated unequally, history suggest that often these differences are ignored: there is little awareness of this inequality. Once a group becomes aware of itself, change becomes more possible.

## DIVISIVE SOCIAL PROCESSES: HUMANITY'S INHUMANITIES

> Man's inhumanity to man makes countless thousands mourn!
> (Robert Burns, 'Dirge: Man was made to mourn', 1784)

When we start to look at these seven forces of difference and potential inequalities, we soon find there are underlying common processes of division at work. Sociologists ask: *how do social processes shape our position in social life*? Ask yourself about what opportunities you have been given (or not given)? Of how your own life choices have been narrowed or widened? How have you been honoured and respected or shamed and treated with indifference? How have you been celebrated or stigmatised? How have you been in the mainstream of things – or banished to the margins? Some lives face perpetual danger, violence and risk and others do not. Which is yours? Think in short, how some lives are treated humanly whilst others are dehumanised and ask where you lie in all this? When we start to think about this, several key processes raise their head.

### DISEMPOWERMENT: RESOURCES AND FUNCTIONING IN THE WORLD

Max Weber (1978) defined power as 'the chance of men to realise their own will ... even against the resistance of others', and saw it as shaped centrally by social class and status. Marx by contrast equated political rule with economic control. Whichever emphasis is given (they have never seemed to be incompatible positions to me), it is important to see that power is a process which flows through society – and that some people simply gain little access to it and others gain much more. The powerless come to lack the resources, the authority, the status and the sense of self that the powerful have. They lack respect. The privileged move around in different worlds: their bodies are confident, they can wear different clothes, they speak in different ways and they can cultivate a sense of respectability that marks them as valued – to themselves and in the eyes of others. They usually have autonomy and choices over their life which the powerless simply do not have. A key feature of this power is its legitimacy and the respect that others give it.

Ultimately, *the study of inequalities is about different access to resources to live with. Some people have an abundance of access to these resources; while others have almost no access.* The most obvious 'resource' is capital or wealth or economic resources. And power is an issue too – people with power usually have greater access to resources. But it goes beyond this, and these days (following often under the influence of the French sociologist Pierre Bourdieu), sociologists locate a wide array of resources. Table 7.4 (opposite) is a list of key resources and, again, you might like to think about your own opportunities in relation to them:

Understanding your own resources can perhaps help you start to see the different positions of others. Sociologists show the critical role of each of these in shaping our position in social life. Each one of the above constitutes a major area of research and thinking in sociology. Increasingly sociologists try to put these separate dimensions together and see their linkages and interconnections.

### MARGINALISATION, EXCLUSION AND THE MAKING OF THE 'OTHER'

We have seen that much social life seems to be that groups divide themselves into insiders and outsiders, creating the system of binaries – of good and bad. Many social scientists recently have called this the problem of *'alterity'* – of otherness. How do societies cope with the others? First, there is *stereotyping and stigmatisation*: people devalue others and respond negatively to them – to race groups, to the disabled, to sexual minorities. Second, they *discriminate:* creating policies which exclude and dishonour. Apartheid in South Africa or racial segregation in the USA are noted examples. Third, there are processes which physically separate people and eject them from the mainstream – a classic example is the creation of *ghettoisation*. But sometimes a people may become completely lost and absorbed through a process of *colonisation*. Ultimately, they are *excluded*. Finally they may be *exterminated*: the striking case of genocide. Here then are key processes for a sociologist to study: stereotyping and stigmatisation, discrimination, ghettoisation, exclusion and colonisation, and extermination. All work to reproduce inequalities in many societies.

*Table 7.4*   The resources of a stratified life

---

- Economic resources: how much income, wealth, financial assets and inheritance do you have access to? How much does your work provide for your needs?

- Social resources: how much support do you have from family, friends, community and networks?

- Cultural resources: how much access do you have to the knowledge, information, skills, education of your society? (Over time, such 'skills' can become part of a person' s very sense of being, 'in their body', through their qualifications and sense of self.)

- Symbolic resources: how much access do you have to people giving you legitimacy and recognition; and privileging your life over others?

- Political resources:how much autonomy do you have in your life? Are you able to control much of your day or do others control it for you?

- Bodily and emotional resources: in what way does your body or feelings seem to limit or control your life? How far do others regulate your body?

- Personal resources: how much has your own unique life and life history helped you generate personal skills for you to move easily in the world?

---

## THE PROCESS OF EXPLOITATION

Exploitation suggests people are used as means not ends; that one group benefits from another. Its most common form is economic, whereby a person's labour is used without adequate pay or compensation. A key account here suggests that a person's labour is the ultimate source of wealth (the labour theory of value). For Adam Smith (in his famous *The Wealth of Nations* Book 1, Chapter V):

> The real price of every thing, what every thing really costs to the man who wants to acquire it, is the toil and trouble of acquiring it. What every thing is really worth to the man who has acquired it, and who wants to dispose of it or exchange it for something else, is the toil and trouble which it can save to himself, and which it can impose upon other people.

Within sociology, it was Marx however who developed this idea arguing that a small minority came to monopolise the labour of others (who cannot survive without working), who subsequently earn much less than is due to them whilst the owners – the capitalists – gain at their expense.

Slavery is a blatant example. But exploitation is to be found everywhere in the world. It is found in the sweatshops of unskilled, menial low paying labour working long hours around the world. It is found in families where women work in the home, raising children and caring for the family, without any kind of remuneration – except their husband's benevolence. It is found amongst migrating groups willing to work in dangerous jobs for low pay. And it is found in child labour. In all this, race and gender are often markers of exploitation.

## VIOLENCE AS THE DIVISION OF LAST RESORT

Finally, violence may be seen as the mechanism of last resort: when all else fails, violence maintains the order. It is the ultimate mechanism to sustain inequality and difference – from state violence and war right through to the everyday bullying in families, gangs and small groups. Examples here are legion: the mass slaughtering of indigenous groups as they were invaded and colonised throughout the world's history; the chains and deaths of slaves as they were transported to their destinations; the long history of warfare between rival tribes and nations; the deaths of ten or more millions in the concentration camps and elsewhere between 1939 and 1945 – Jews, gypsies, homosexuals, vagrants, women, children. The list of such brutalities is long.

But there are also much less apparent mechanisms – many feminists for examples have claimed that 'rape is the mechanism by which men keep all women in a constant state of fear', and that it is the ultimate way in which the gender system is maintained. Others suggest there is a continuum of violence against women – from rape through pornographic representations of women as abused and on to the daily thousand little abuses and verbal harassments which keep women in their place. The system against homosexuals and transgender people in some countries is ultimately upheld through the death penalty, and in others there is the perpetual fear of queer bashing and bullying. Abuse is also levied against children and old people. Nationhood, gender, class, ethnicity and sexuality are ultimately policed by violence.

## SUFFERING, INEQUALITY AND THE SEARCH FOR SOCIAL JUSTICE

So here, in a nutshell, we have a world in which for most of its human history and across most of its lands we find human beings who have managed to organise their differences into systems of stratification, hierarchy, or social exclusion. *Human social worlds tend to be unequal worlds*. There is nothing hugely surprising about this – most animal societies are organised this way. It seems perfectly natural to many for there to be this hierarchy, appalling as this may be in terms of human suffering! So think a little more. The human animal manages to transcend many other things that animals do: animals do not compose symphonies, create democracies, or use mobile phones. Surely, we might have thought that human beings over millennia would have transcended these crude and restricting systems of inequality in some way? We might have thought that human beings would have tried to move beyond the brutalising pecking order? But no: over and over again, we find cultures with a few people who have 'a lot' at the top and the many – the mass – who live 'without' at the bottom.

It is here that sociology touches many issues of social philosophy and the problems of justice, freedoms, rights and the search for human equality. Should we put up with this kind of inequality? The modern world is persistently haunted by these debates and sociology is very much part of this. At least since the French Revolution, equality has served as one of the leading ideals of Western societies – placed often, if falsely, in conflict with ideals of freedom. Jean-Jacques Rousseau famously suggested a social contract and wrote his *On the Origins of Inequality* (1754). Karl Marx went on to write his massively influential work on class exploitation that became a major influence on the Communist revolutions of the twentieth century. And more recently, the philosophers like John Rawls (1921–2002) and others have searched for principles of social justice. Rawls, for example, wanted to ensure that people with comparable talents could face roughly similar life chances, and that where inequalities did occur they nevertheless worked to the benefit of the least advantaged. He drew upon the idea of a 'veil of ignorance' whereby people – unaware of their talents and abilities, class, race, gender or religion – would be assigned a position at birth and on the basis of not knowing any of this, be asked to choose the moral position for all to live with. Having no choice in the world we are to live in at birth, we would all probably want some kind of equality for all?

Now this is not the place to develop what has become one of the most central, complex and controversial debates in philosophy in the twentieth century. The debates between conservativism, liberalism and Marxism on equality have been long and furious and the issue of equality has never been far away from being a central debate of our times in which sociologists have participated.

## HUMAN CAPABILITIES AND FLOURISHING AS A GOAL OF HUMAN LIFE

At the start of the twenty-first century, one of the many lively debates has focused on human rights and human capabilities (though it is far from new – its roots go back to Aristotle). It has asked questions about just what human potentials and capabilities are, and then linked these to ideas of a human rights based society? Here we go right back to basics and consider an **ontology** of the human being: what is a human being and what is a human life for? And it might help to begin this deep search with a simple answer. Human beings are bundles of needs, potentials, capabilities and differences which need appropriate social conditions in order to develop and flourish. Without the right social conditions, human life becomes flawed and damaged and prone to too much suffering: lives become 'damaged' or even 'wasted'. If the goal of a human life is to flourish and develop its potentials, we need to think about the right conditions to foster this. This seems to me to be as good as any starting point, even though there are many who disagree.

In the influential work of the Indian Nobel Prize winning economist Amartya Sen and the world leading philosopher Martha Nussbaum on famine and poverty across the world, we find a major provisional listing of what these human **capabilities** could be for all human beings. They include the capability to live a *life* (being able to live to the end of a human life of normal length); for *health*;

for *bodily integrity* (which means being able to move freely from place to place, being able to feel one's body secure against assault and violence, and having opportunities for sexual satisfaction and for choice in matters of reproduction); for *senses, imagination, and thought* (an adequate education and with guarantees of freedom of expression: political, artistic and religious); for *emotions* (to be able to have attachments to things and persons outside ourselves and to love those who love and care for us); for **practical reason** (critical reflection on the planning of one's own life – and what indeed is a good life); for *affiliation and recognition* (being able to live for and in relation to others, to recognise and show concern for other human beings); the ability to *play*; some *control over one's environment*; and finally an ability to *live with other species* – a concern for and in relation to animals, plants, and the world of nature.

Although such a list is open to change, refinement and development, it seems to me to be a very good starting point for thinking about what a human life needs to develop if it is to flourish on this earth. You might like to think about your own life and how each of these 'capabilities' appear or do not appear. Some of them – good health, etc. – seem more basic than others; but all human beings are surely in need of and capable of developing in each sphere. A life where this cannot be done is a diminished life. Still, this account does not say we are all the same. It stresses that although we do all have common human capabilities, for a good life, these all need to be developed in our own unique ways. And for many people in the world, there is currently no chance that they could develop most of them at all. It is indeed an unfair and unjust world.

One way of doing sociology is to ponder this idea of 'flourishing lives for all' and to ask what social conditions might help create this? The crucial idea here is a flourishing *for all* – not as is so often the case, for just the few or just the elite. What of most people? What must the world look like so that *all* people can live 'flourishing lives'.

## SUMMARY

Social life displays enormous differences, much of which is organised into inequalities. Four key themes can be summarised: (1) human capabilities are (2) structured through divisive processes into (3) structured inequalities which (4) have damaging effects on our lives. Sociologists study the intersections and institutions of class and economy, gender and patriarchy, ethnicity and race, age and generation, nation and culture, sexuality and heterosexism, disability and health, nations and nationalism. They investigate the beliefs (ideologies) which support them and how they might change. Key processes such as disempowerment and resources, marginalisation and exclusion, exploitation and violence shape the process of divisions. Figure 7.1 attempts to bring this altogether. Finally, philosophical ideas about human capabilities and a 'flourishing life for all' are raised.

## EXPLORING FURTHER

### MORE THINKING

Look closely at Figure 7.1 and try to make sense of it. Ponder the list of capabilities and how they work in your own life. Then connect these to the 'seven forces' and see how they shape human opportunities. Consider how we can set about understanding these inequalities best – look at some of the measuring tools, and some of the subjective studies. Finally, make a small leap into philosophy and debate with friends the idea of 'a flourishing life for all'. What do you think about the list of human capabilities listed in Figure 7.1? Are you flourishing? Who is not?

### FURTHER READING

The writing on inequalities is vast. Good general introductions include: Evelyn Kallen's *Social Inequality and Social Injustice* (2004), which is broad and sets the scene in a lively way. Geoff Payne's *Social Divisions* (2006) contains a great deal of material on all the major forms of inequalities – including disability. Wendy Bottero's *Stratification* (2005) is a dynamic rethinking of many issues. Göran Therborn's *Inequalities of the World* (2006), quoted in the chapter, has a fine introductory essay which reviews the world data of inequality. A useful and popular book is Richard Wilkinson and Kate Pickett's *The Spirit Level: Why More Equal Societies Almost Always Do Better* (2009). Severine Deneulin and Lila Shahani in *An Introduction to*

*Figure 7.1*  The matrix of inequalities

**UNEQUAL ORDERS**
**Which organise our resources and differences**
(What are the forces which push and locate unequal positions?)

1  Gender and patriarchy
2  Class and economy
3  Ethnicity and race
4  Age and generation
5  Nation and culture
6  Sexuality and heterosexism
7  Disability and health

**SOCIAL SUFFERINGS**
**The social impacts on lived lives**
(What are the subjective and objective consequences to people of inequalities?)

A: *Objectively*
Poverty, mortality, illnesses, malnutrition, violence
B: *Subjectively*: the thwarting of human capabilities and potentials
Insecure lives – Brutalised lives
Invisible lives – Shamed lives
Demeaned lives – Resisting lives

**DIVISIVE PROCESSES**
**Which structure inequalities**
(How are we hindered in our capabilities and potentials?)

1  Exclusion
2  Dominance and subordination, exploitation
3  Marginalisation, stereotyping, discrimation and stigma-tisation
4  Ghettoisation and segregation
5  Colonisation
6  Violence
7  Pauperisation
8  Dis-empowerment
9  The silencing of voices; 'othering'
10 Dehumanisation

**HUMAN CAPABILTIES**
**Human meeds and capabilities**
(What are human needs to be met and flourish? No one list is the only route)

1  Life
2  Bodily health
3  Bodily integrity
4  Senses, imagination and thought
5  Emotions: to love and to belong
6  Practical reason: form a sense of a good life and be able to plan it
7  Affiliation: living with others with recognition and respect
8  Live with other species and the world of nature
9  Play, laugh, enjoy
10 Control of own environment – politically and materially

Literally thousands of papers and books have been written on these areas since the beginning of sociology, and to some extent they constitute the largest and major areas of inquiry within sociology. This table simply directs the reader to some of the key issues which need attending to and brings together as a scheme research that is often kept separate. The simplest challenge for the reader is to understand the key terms, ponder how they interconnect and flow, and then link to their own life and the life of different others. In this chapter I simply amplify on some of these concerns.

*the Human Development and Capability Approach* (2009) provide an accessible set of essays devoted to 'the capabilities approach'. Finally, human suffering in sociology is given a strong introduction in Iain Wilkinson, *Suffering: A Sociological Introduction* (2005)

On specific inequalities, see: Hilary Graham, *Unequal Lives: Health and Socioeconomic Inequalities* (2007); Peter Iadicola and Anthony Shupe, *Violence, Inequality and Freedom* (2004); Tony Bennett *et al., Culture, Class, Distinction* (2009).

# 8

# WHY SOCIOLOGY?

The philosophers have only *interpreted* the world, in various ways.
The point, however, is to *change* it.

Karl Marx, *Theses on Feuerbach,* 1845,
Thesis 11 and engraved upon his tomb

To make our garden grow.

Voltaire, Leonard Bernstein, Stephen Sondheim, *Candide,*
1759, 1955, 1974

Sociology may have been born of eighteenth-century revolutions, but it now dwells in a world of constant transformations. As recent centuries have unfolded, our understanding of society has not become any easier. The mass slaughtering of the twentieth century in two major world wars and holocaust genocides – justified by the ideologies of communism and fascism – generated a very dark view of twentieth-century life and its appalling possibilities. And now a multitude of public social problems – environmental crisis, the AIDS pandemic, drugs wars and more – seem unremitting. Indeed, the proliferation of media has shifted our awareness of both ourselves and these problems whilst sociology itself provides an ongoing commentary. As more go to university, many people come to be lay sociologists, commenting and critiquing upon their society. Indeed, as world societies foster and claim versions of democracy, then a thinking sociology becomes a key issue for more and more of its members.

Critical sociology cannot function well in totalitarian societies – you cannot have groups of people thinking critically about society, if that society is unchallengeable. In such cultures sociology has to go underground. So academic sociology is certainly growing and important. The modern world needs the sustained and serious analysis of the workings of the massive and complex worlds we live in. That is sociology's mission. In this chapter I will look a little at this task – the value of sociology, its calling – in the twenty-first century. Contemporary societies, with all their change and 'problems', need sociology continuously to review and appraise what is going on. At its best, I believe it seeks to secure a world for the future which will be better for each generation. It is not utopian – in the sense that it believes an ideal state of human life could ever be achieved or that we should be absolutist about its pursuit. But it does have utopian strivings – gentle dreams of benevolence, a hoped for improvement in humanity's lot. Sociologists surely want to understand the social world so that the errors of its ways may be reduced as we move along and the world just might become a better place, even in our own life time.

A caution is needed. In this chapter, I will not be talking simply about the long (and sometimes pretentious and self-serving) meditations by the academically and university trained in recent times. I am also concerned with the oh-so-much more mundane activity that most people just routinely do at some points in their life. Most people think at least a little about the nature of the world around them: of the gods in the air, the land they live on, the animals and nature around them, what other people are like. It is important to recognise that part of sociological thinking has this personal character. In one small sense all people are sociologists; we develop common sense or folk accounts of everyday society; and we have done this throughout history. We are *reflective* – people try to make sense of the world they live in. And this in turn is *reflexive* – what we think about the world becomes social and actually plays a role reflecting back on our societies. And indeed in these very acts of thinking, we sometimes change our societies a little. Societies – groups, tribes, civilisations, 'other people' – are always on the move through what people (you and me) think and do, and thinking about society actually helps move it on. In this final chapter I also want to consider this linkage between everyday life practice and sociology.

## REVIEW OF THIS BOOK: MULTIPLE SOCIOLOGIES ALWAYS ON THE MOVE

There is most surely no one way of doing any of this. Sociology is a wide open, humanistic, hybridic and ever changing intellectual practice which aims to understand the human social worlds we live in. If there is a message that should have jumped at you in almost every chapter of this book, it must be *the multiplicities of sociologies*. Chapter 1 suggested that sociology can study anything under the sun. Chapter 2 suggested the very notion of social is multiple; that even a seemingly simple thing like the body has multiple social uses; and that the ways of thinking about the social are also many. Chapter 3 looked at a world of some seven billion people and the enormous varieties of religions, economies, governance – and change – in the drift from multiple modernities that this brings. Chapter 4 tried to provide a short history of (mainly Western) sociology – only indicating further how it is stuffed full of different positions (a **multi-paradigm discipline**). Sociology itself is a contested discipline. Chapters 5 and 6 took us into the heart of the sociological discipline – its imaginations, methods and theories – and once again demonstrated how it brings into play almost all other disciplines in study from the arts and the sciences – and all the 'isms' too: feminism, postmodernism, post-colonialism and the rest. Finally, Chapter 7 hurled us into the vast array of differences which congeal into dreadful patterns of social sufferings and inequalities, themselves being organised at the intersections of class, race, gender, disability, nation, sexuality and age. Complexity is the name of society – and the sociology which studies it.

Some sociologists might not agree with my view here. They may claim that their way of doing sociology – as a scientific methodologist, as an analytic theorist, as a feminist, as a 'professional sociologist' is the one 'true way'. So be it. My own view again is that in a world of such human multiplicities and complexities, many of them passionately and politically experienced, sociology can *never*

## THINK ON: THE SOCIOLOGIST AS DIALOGIST

[There is] a crucial feature of the human condition that has been rendered almost invisible by the overwhelmingly monological bent of mainstream modern philosophy ... This crucial feature of human life is its fundamentally dialogical character. ... The monological ideal seriously underestimates the place of the dialogical in human life

Charles Taylor, *The Politics of Recognition*, 1994: 32–33

Part of what sociologists invariably study is the contested relations between peoples across all spheres of social life. We examine the conflicts between countries, across groups, between and within social movements. The sociologist is regularly challenged to clarify debates, to sort out the relations across different voices – ordering them, classifying them, searching for agreements and disagreements, finding 'common grounds' (or not). This is a crucial task for sociology: its dialogic mission. So sociologists need the capacity to discuss reasonably, to talk with opposing others, and to dialogue. Sociologists have to ask how to:

1  Recognise the wide range of lives lived and stories to be told on any issue? Can we listen to the range of these lived stories and avoid dehumanising or silencing 'the other'?
2  Appreciate the social contexts of arguments? Sociologists above all must know that arguments are always bound up with particular social worlds or habitus: they do not float freely in the air. All ideas are local and grounded and we must hence ask: where are the arguments situated. Where are the arguments coming from?
3  Develop an awareness of the inequalities and the differences of power between speakers? How do voices without power get heard – indeed who is not being heard?
4  Reflect on our own location in all this. Sociologists do not dangle above it all in some superhuman place. We always

need to ask: just where do we stand as sociologists in all of this?

5 Weaken 'the argument culture'. This is a nice phrase coined by the psychologist Deborah Tannen to suggest that our culture always seems to want to make us take sides on everything. Life is turned into a polarity, a binary, a dichotomy, a split, a struggle between good and evil. Might not life be more like a continuum of differences – more subtle and complex than brute divides?

6 Understand the emotional and embodied basis (and history) of much life and talk? Often to hear people argue their positions is to sense immediately that something much grander than reason is at stake: it is often as if these people are literally fighting for their lives.

7 Find common ground? Never mind all the disagreement: surely there are many things that we can agree upon? Can we sort these out?

(I discuss these ideas and others a little more in my book: *Intimate Citizenship* (2003) Chapter 6: Dialogic Citizenship).

be a fully unified discipline. It needs its many practitioners doing its many different things, bringing different angles and perspectives on a moving whole that can never in principle ever be fully or wholly grasped. And often sociological stances will be radically at odds with each other. There is no fixed object awaiting study in sociology and there can be no fixed discipline. Indeed what we find – and need – are many divisions of sociological labours each of which will bring their own findings, insights and imaginations to a grasping of human social life in all its horrors and delights – each adapting and responding to its times and place. At the same time, it is not without many unifying themes and concerns; which indeed it has been a key task of this book to outline.

## SOCIOLOGY'S MULTIPLE MISSION: THE SOCIAL ROLES OF THE SOCIOLOGIST

Let me summarise here a number of simple roles for sociologists to adopt in the modern world. No one person can adopt them all – sociology, like everything else here, is open to massive divisions of labour. Sociologists do many things: we teach; we work in think-tanks and large (and small) research centres; we are activists; we work in both government and non-governmental agencies; we are social workers, police officers, lawyers, court workers; we work in human resources and social welfare; we work in media – and as website managers, journalists, film makers, artists. We work in international agencies and local ones. And above all we live in everyday worlds, leading everyday lives and doing everyday things – enhanced by sociological imaginations. There are many tasks to be done, something for everyone to do, and many standpoints to work from: the hope is that sociologists will share different roles with each other and ultimately work together.

### THE SOCIAL ROLES OF THE SOCIOLOGIST

A most basic function of the sociologist is that of the researcher, the gatherer (and hence creator) of social information. *We research and document the nature of the social times we live in.* Sociological information is always needed to take stock of the human world – otherwise we would be living in the dark. In the 1920s, the Chicago sociologist Robert Park advised his students to become super-journalists; his own background was that of a journalist before he became a sociologist. Thus, at the simplest levels, and as Chapter 3 has shown, sociology maps information on such things as population size, economic functioning, the shifts in religious belief, the move to the cities, the functioning state of whole countries and regions – along with concerns over crime, migration patterns, family life, the nature of social class. World societies cannot function these days without information on a myriad of things, and this is what social science has to help provide. Just imagine living in a social world where we knew nothing about it – it is a nightmare scenario. These days a lot of such data is but a click away.

But sociologists also know that data on its own is worthless – data does not present itself automatically and it certainly does not speak for itself. It is gathered by humans making decisions about what is significant, and it is then interpreted by multiple readers – each using it for their own ends. Ultimately much of this will be political in nature. We need to watch the move here from *mere information* to *knowledge* to *wisdom* and the imported politics and ethics that come with it.

Thus, the second task of the sociologist is that of the thinker, the theorist – the philosopher, even – of human social life and living. As this book has tried to show throughout, *more than information and data are needed in social life: we need wider understanding and the capacity to make connections, sense links with the rich heritage of thinkers from the past, shun seeing facts in isolation and out of context.* Sociologists – however falteringly – facilitate theoretical and general thinking about society. Theory work can be difficult and can sometimes be obscure but its aim is to foster deeper understanding of what is going on, and hopefully help to provide a way for sociological knowledge to become cumulative – wisdoms can be passed on and developed from generation to generation and may help more of us to understand social life a little better in each generation. Random facts and information are of little value.

This thinking is usually critical and so it is but a short step for the sociologist to also become and act as critic, radical and the agent for change. *Sociology fosters a critical attitude to social life*, seeing that things are never quite what they seem, and common sense never quite that common. Sociologists question and interrogate the taken for granted society, and connect it to alternative other possible worlds. They subvert the thinking as usual. In this sense sociologists can often become idealists – seeking advance and a 'better' world. Critical theory emerged in the early twentieth century as a tool for critiquing the Enlightenment claims of a developing rationality, science and new technological world. For them science was never neutral and positive thinking was never so positive. They argued for an emancipatory knowledge, one based on negative thinking and critique. This position has worked its way into sociological practice and there is an undeniable radical leaning to much of its work.

Next comes the sociologist as educator, teacher, and these days the media disseminator and the web coordinator of social knowledge. *We can facilitate both basic information and ways of thinking about social life* through which members of a society can try to take stock of where society has come from and where it is heading. Amongst the many things that we can do in this applied role is writing and teaching. But we can provide governments (and world organisations and NGOs) with information that help in planning future pathways for society, and we can work in media of all kinds (from journalism to websites) so that society can find its way around social knowledge. Nowadays we are in need of a sociological Wikipedia.

There are many other roles for sociologists. We can be subterranean story-tellers. *Here we reveal voices, ideas and social worlds that are subterranean in a society – subjugated knowledge, subaltern visions* that live underground and may not easily be heard. We can puncture the snoring and the sleeping in the wake of suffering. Sociologists can also be artists. *Here we generate ideas that can inform and enhance human creativity.* Sociological ideas feed into worlds of art, literature, music, poetry, film. The sociologists can be the policy shapers. Here we *advise governments and groups* on the nature of the social world. The sociologist can be the commentator and public intellectual. Here we *provide a social diagnosis of the ills of our time*, and make a contributions to the human world by clarifying options, sensing alternatives, and signposting directions for the future.

We might also be the dialogists. Here *we create organised dialogues across the multiple different voices to be heard in a society.* Sociologists must always sooner or later discover in both their research and theories that human life is always bound up with different social worlds that pose potentials for massive human conflict. As we have seen, contradiction, and ubiquitous conflict has to be lived with everywhere. It is lived at every level of social life: global (e.g. wars between nation states, conflicts between men and women), national (e.g. ethnic, religious), local (e.g. community politics, splits between social movements), personal (e.g. domestic violence, breakdown of trust between friends).

There is nothing new about such conflicts (and nor do I think they will ever end). Throughout history, wars may have always been simply the stuff of everybody's everyday life. Maybe what has happened in effect is a world where disagreements have now become more visible and more open to 'management'. It may be that democratising societies generate more public spaces for a wider range of people to engage in deliberative talk about these issues than has often been known before. It may be that sociologists can *facilitate organising principles of this deliberative talk and dialogue*. They can enable the capacity to discuss reasonably, to talk with opposing others, and to dialogue. They can *foster what might be called dialogic citizenship*. It is very hard in this culture not to engage with polarised debates since this is more or less our routine way of doing things. Yet too often arguments get needlessly polarised. Because arguments become firmly attached to individual people; they actually become part of them, are identified with them, belong to them. The very person then becomes what is at stake in the argument as they engage in their own private monologue.

Finally, then, sociology has a wide and generic role in society: the sociologist becomes the critical citizen in society. Anyone can do this. *We can all help create a widespread social awareness and what might be called social thinking*, which is often in contradistinction to common sense which usually sees the world in more individualising and 'natural' terms. Sociology has to start with trying to understand the complicated nature of 'common sense', but it can also help people to challenge what is taken for granted, to look at their social world creatively, and help them to make the link between the private problems of individuals with the public problems of cultures. Sociologists can help people make social connections and help foster aware citizens who know what is going on around them. Sociology *can help create good critical socially aware citizens*, who can make informed and knowledgeable decisions.

## AND THE WORLD GOES ROUND: THE CIRCLE OF SOCIOLOGICAL LIFE

Studying and thinking about society is itself a part of a society (in the jargon, it is 'recursive'). There is a loop which connects everyday practical thinking to the sociological knowledge; and a loop between this and all the public and popular discussions we have about social issues. All this in turn feeds into wider issues of

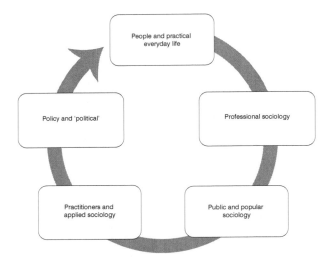

*Figure 8.1* The circle of sociological life

change and government and social movement change – which in turn feeds back into everyday practical life. And the world goes round …

Put simply and diagrammatically it can be depicted as a never ending revolving wheel or circle with phases. The first phase of the circle suggests that sociological life starts with people: with the everyday experience, common sense and practical knowledge used by everyone in daily life. We ground sociology in these concerns and questions that people have about living in society, and we always need to return to this, however far we move in the circle. As the Canadian feminist sociologist Dorothy E. Smith once remarked: We need a sociology 'of the people, by the people, and for the people'. Sociology always needs grounding in real everyday life and the people who live it.

A second phase is the 'professional sociology' we outlined in Chapter 5. This is the sociology that is taught in universities, and is organised through professional bodies like the International Sociological Association. Much of this book has been outlining the key features of this. It is a systematic, organised, sceptical and critical view of the world which does not take social things for granted but questions them. Sadly, much of it is esoteric, cult like and published in specialised journals in unreadable language.

Moving beyond this, we find what is now coming to be known as a **public** (or even popular) **sociology** – one which takes professional sociology and makes it very accessible to the wide public. Here sociologists move into the public sphere and speak in plain language. They become the PowerPoint lecturers with good visual imagery, the artists, the story-tellers, the film-makers, the website managers and the teachers. The idea of a public sociology was called for in a quite famous debate in 2004 with the then president of the American Sociological Association, Michael Burawoy (you can find his work online and also on the YouTube). At its best, this public sociology actually reaches to the wider population and becomes 'popular' (some professional sociologists want nothing to do with this!). The Box on p. 195 gives some instances of this.

Next there is a sociology for practitioners – those who work, for example, in teaching, sports, social work, criminology and the health professions. There are many groups who need to study sociology and apply it in their work. Typically, they will need to understand how face to face interactions work (micro-sociology); how organisations structure their work (meso-sociology); and ultimately how their work links to the wider even global world (macro-sociology) – studying the institutions and inequalities of health or education or crime or sport. Studying sociology in professional courses will bring its own text books like Elaine Denny and Sarah Earle's *Sociology for Nurses* (2008) or Vivienne Cree's *Sociology for Social Workers and Probation Officers* (2010).

Finally, there is a vast area where sociology is applied to significant decision making about the way our society should work. Here we enter the fields of public policy, social policy and of course politics and governance. Public policy studies is mainly concerned with the ways in which politics shapes the organisation of our laws and policy programmes; but social policy draws explicitly from sociological research and theories to help foster adequate responses to problems in such areas as health, crime, deprivation, poverty, city planning or the environment. At the same time, the sociological study of social policies makes it clear that the bridge from theory to practice is paved with good intentions yet littered with disasters. Much policy becomes its own form of fatal remedy, its own pyrrhic victory. In short, it often does not work at all well and can even make situations worse. Sociology has to advise caution. At the same time, there are many sociologists who have become prominent in the political debates of their countries: Jürgen Habermas in Germany, Amitai Etzioni in the USA, Pierre Bourdieu in France, Anthony Giddens in the UK, Fernando Henriques Cardoso in Brazil – amongst many others.

## THE MYTH OF PURE OBJECTIVITY: POLITICS AND THE MORAL IMAGINATION

> The social sciences are normative disciplines, always already embedded in issues of value, ideology, power, desire, sexism, racism, domination, repression and control. We want a social science that is committed up front to issues of social justice, equity, non-violence and peace, and universal human rights. We do not want a social science that says it can address these issues if it wants to. For us, that is no longer an option.
>
> (Norman Denzin and Yvonne Lincoln, *Handbook of Qualitative Research*, p.13)

There is a cliché of sociology that it is a scientific and objective study of society, but I hope that this book has shown you this to be a far too simple-minded view. As we have seen throughout this book, one of the continuing tensions of the sociologist is that of the seeming divide between being a neutral, dispassionate, objective – scientific – analyst of social life; and that of sociologist as partisan, a committed, passionate person who cares about change in the world. At the very least we might distinguish an empirical sociology which shows how people actually *are*, and a normative sociology which shows what people think we *should* do. In any event, this is a problem that has haunted sociology since its inception.

The great sociologists, of course, wanted to obtain a certain objectivity and truth – none were (or are today) simple relativists holding the view that anything goes. They do not adopt simple partisan and political views from their academic pulpits and we

## THINK ON: POP SOCIOLOGY

Although professional sociology discusses major issues in society, it is frequently not very accessible to wider audiences. Below are some instances where you can find sociological ideas at work in more popular and lively ways. Here are few examples.

*Documentaries*
For example, Nick Broomfield's *Ghosts* (2007); Andrew Jarecki's *Capturing the Friedmans* (2004)

*TV Drama*
For example, Jimmy McGovern's *The Street* (3 series from BBC 2007–2009)

*TV Series*
For example, former police reporter David Simon's *The Wire* (5 series from 2002) on the city, drugs, crime and politics.

*Popular best selling sociology* (rare in the UK)
For example, Malcolm Gladwell's *The Tipping Point;* Barbara Ehrenreich's *Nickel and Dimed;* Barry Glassner's *Culture of Fear;* Richard Wilkinson and Kate Pickett's *The Spirit Level* (UK 2009)

*Radio*
For example, BBC 4 Laurie Taylor's *Thinking Allowed* (weekly: see BBC web site)

*Reality Media*
For example, *Big Brother; Airport; Family; The Choir*

*Blogs*
Some leading sociologists have blogs. Amitai Etzioni – author of *The Monochrome Society* – has a blog where he encourages active debate. See also *Contexts:* it has a 'crawler' – 'the crawler scans the internet for media reports and other insights offered by sociologists and serves them up in a concise, snappy style'.

should indeed be very wary of those who do. They struggle for objectivity and are against pure relativist subjectivity. If we are to advance in the world we need the best – or at least 'adequately objective' – knowledge we can get. But this is hard because the very subject matter of sociology is bound up with meanings, subjectivities and values – that is what human lives live with. Likewise, human life is organised through power relations – some groups (and people) have authority and status over others (indeed congeal into massive systems of stratification which we saw in Chapter 7), and it would be naïve to think that sociologists are outside of this political process. Sociology also finds itself in a rapidly changing world and is part of that very change. So the task of sociology is to grasp this power, meaning and change through what might best be called an 'adequate objectivity' – a struggle to get at the truth of society, against the odds. We have looked at some of these strategies in Chapter 6.

There is a long history of discussing the role of values and ideologies in sociology – and they usually start with our old friend Max Weber who made key distinctions between value-free and value-relevant sociology. (You can note how often Weber has appeared in this book and sense therefore how important he is). Without detailing his work here, I find his arguments lead me to think of three key ideas linked to three phases of research. These can be summarised as:

1   *Value Relevance*: *be aware of your value and political baseline*. In the earliest stages of research, values become crucial in making selections and phrasing problems. Don't waste your time on worthless projects, think about what the value of your research should be and choose your area carefully. Often you will choose a topic on political and moral grounds.

2   *Value neutrality but ethical responsibility*: *be aware of the ethics of doing sociology*. Whilst doing your research, you will need to strive for adequate objectivity. Keep your eye on different perspectives, multiple representations, intimate familiarity, the balance of subjectivity and objectivity, good representativeness, sufficient contextualisation, and be aware of issues of reflexivity (see Chapter 6 on all this). At the same time, sociology always

deals with human life and people, and you will be need to think about your responsibilities towards the people you are studying. Doing sociology in the field is riddled with ethical dilemmas.

3 *Value Implications: be aware of the politics of how your research is used.* Once research conclusions are arrived at, think carefully about the implications of who this will impact and how? Do you have responsibilities to follow the idea and findings through to a wider audience and wider political actions? Will there be political fallout because of your findings?

Values, then, are everywhere. Sociologists often feel really *subjectively passionate* about social issues – world poverty, the fate of the environment, the clash of religions, violence against women, the rising crime rate – but then find that to study them seriously they have to do this in *an objectively detached way*. There is no point in a sociology which just adds yet another personal (even hysterical) viewpoint: some calm reflection and close observation of what is going on is needed. How can sociologists adopt *scientific attitudes* on things that harbour so much *personal involvement*? The sociologist's problem is simply put: how to be *objective* about the *subjective*, *passionate* while being *detached*, *scientific* yet *personal*, and *value free* while being *value relevant*. Sociologists walk moral and political high wires all the time.

There are some who will suggest that values should be kept strictly out of sociology. But if we look at the great sociologists of the past – and indeed many prominent sociologists today – you will soon find those who have been committed to major social change. Remember it was Marx who was personally outraged at the exploitation and damaged lives he saw created by capitalistic industrialisation; he inspired major world revolution for equality (which seriously and damagingly failed). It was Weber who said we are living in an iron cage and bemoaned – through his various depressions – the 'disenchantment of the world'. Every past sociologist has their personal and political, if often hidden, face. Many were much less radical.

Contemporary sociology is often quite explicit about its moral and political imagination. Thus feminist sociology declares the need to remove women's inequalities; anti-racism sociology critiques racism; queer sociology destabilises gender and sexual categories; and post-colonial sociologies critique the supremacy of the European/American model that dominates thinking. Today, the briefest excursions into contemporary social thinkers such as Zygmunt Bauman, Ulrich Beck, Seyela Benhabib, Judith Butler, Stanley Cohen, Patricia Hill Collins, Raewyn Connell, Norman Denzin, Amitai Etzioni, Anthony Giddens, Paul Gilroy, Jürgen Habermas, Stuart Hall, Donna Haraway, Chandra Mohanty, Martha Nussbaum, Stephen Seidman, Gayatri Spivak, Alan Tourraine, Jeffrey Weeks, and the rest – will soon lead you into social science worlds that are deeply partisan and explicitly political. Amongst these, there is no pretence at all of value neutrality. We live in a land of *Contested Knowledge* which asks: whose side are you on?

All sociologists have to live with this balancing act. How to juggle their science with their politics, their ethics, their passions? Some solve it by siding with science – they may well retreat to the academy to do their studies as neutrally as they can. Some solve it by leaving sociology and joining activism of one kind or other. And some – many – become marginal, living on the borders of objectivity and subjectivity, neutrality and passion, science and art, disenchantment with the world and a hope for a better one. My view is that it is *not* a sociologist's function to tell other people what to do in social life – that would be moralistic and moralising. But it is a challenge for sociologists to always keep in mind their own values and politics. So it is ultimately important for sociologists to spend some time considering their own moral and political baselines. To ask: *what is to be done and how should we live our lives?*

## COMMON GROUNDS? VALUES AND VIRTUES IN SOCIOLOGY

Values appear then in at least three ways in sociology. As baseline assumptions of research, as guidelines in the practices of doing sociological theory and research (research ethics), and as areas of research in their own right (the sociology of morality). So what kind of values are at stake? There are many values that interest sociology but here are some prominent ones worth exploring.

- *Care and love*: sociologists know that a recurring key feature of social life is the ways in which people look after each other in families, friendships and communities. There is even the kindness of strangers. Here sociologists can investigate caring relations, and they can also make sure their research relationships are grounded in care for the other.
- *Freedom and equality*: sociologists know that these are often seen as in competition with each other in the modern world but know they need not be. There is a democratic impulse – for freedom and equality – in much of sociology. Yet sociologists clearly know the paradox: total freedom or total equality are both total nonsense. The social always constrains the free and inequality is always shaped by the social. But there are many whose lives are damaged by a lack of freedom and huge inequality, and much sociological work is hence concerned with enhancing freedom and opportunities of equality. In this sense much sociology is emancipatory.
- *Human capabilities and human rights*: sociologists are concerned with what it means to function well in a society – and hence draw up conceptions of human needs and their potentials, thwarting and flourishing. Meeting human needs and developing human capabilities often connects to the development of human rights. In research, sociologists think about the rights of their human subjects; more widely there is a well developed sociology of human rights. We have explored this a little in Chapter 7.
- *Tolerance and cosmopolitanism*: built into the heart of sociology is an awareness of the multiplicities of ways in which human social lives are different – across people, groups, cultures and nations. Ethnocentrism is a cardinal sin for sociologists and a wide-awake openness to the values of others is central. Likewise, fundamentalisms of all kinds go against the grain of human diversity. There is also a growing sociology of cosmopolitanism which looks at the jostling diversities of living together.
- *Harm reduction:* sociologists are interested in researching the ways in which human social enterprises often damage other people (fatal remedies). Just as their interest in care suggests

ways in which people look after each after, so their interest in human damage asks questions about the ways in which certain social actions damage other people. At the simplest level, the human cost of war, the failure of massive imprisonment whilst crime still rages, and the failure of states to protect their peoples from environmental damage are all grounds of concern.

• *Hope:* sociology looks at both the good and bad things in life (see Chapter 1). It facilitates both positive thinking (looking for how things in the social world can be made better) whilst regularly engaging in critique (see Chapter 7). Keeping this balance and not drowning in the empirically observable 'misery of the world' is a perpetual challenge.

## CRITICAL CITIZENSHIP AND THE MORAL IMAGINATION

We have seen in this book over and over again how human social worlds are hugely complex and are stuffed full of problems. More and more people face the growing problems of living together. From abject poverty and inequality for much of the world to religious tribalism and environmental degradation, many people are very concerned about the state of the world. Just how can we live together and work to make the world a better place for all becomes a major and pressing problem.

One pathway into all this is through the notion of critical **citizenship**. How can and should people act in a civic culture that advances the needs and situations of all? A very influential – indeed classic – statement of citizenship is to be found in the work of Thomas Humphrey Marshall (1893–1981), probably the most influential sociologist in the UK after the Second World War. He defines citizenship (1963, p. 74) as

> a status bestowed on those who are full members of a community. All who possess the status are equal with respect to the rights and duties with which the status is endowed.

From this rather formal view of belonging and status, he distinguishes three clusters of citizen rights emerging chronologically during the past two centuries to deal with concerns over civil, political and social rights – to justice under the law, to political representation, and to basic welfare. Each can then be linked to key institutions: the civil and criminal courts, the Parliament and local elective bodies, and to the educational and welfare services. What we can thus see is the broadest emergence of communities which – to borrow from Marshall himself – establish the 'rights necessary for individual freedom: liberty of the person, speech, thought and faith, the right to their own property and the right to justice'; the 'right to participate in an exercise of political power'; and the 'right to a modicum of economic welfare and security, the right to share to the full in the social heritage and to live the life of a civilised being according to the standards prevailing in the society'.

This is an elegant and influential – if criticised – model which senses a general and slow expansion of the idea of the citizen in modern societies: people are gaining certain rights and the status of belonging as long as they also live up to the expectations of their society (for example to work, or to vote, or to live as a law-abiding citizen). In the latter part of the twentieth century, social scientists picked up on his ideas and developed them in many directions. Probably upwards of several hundred books were published which raised issues of citizenship. To name a few will give a sense of the range of what they covered: Nicholas Stephenson's *Cultural Citizenship* (2003), Gerard Delanty's *Citizenship in a Global Age* (2000), Chris Hable Gray's *Cyborg Citizen* (2002), Will Kymlicka's *Multicultural Citizenship* (1996) Aihwa Ong's *Flexible Citizenship* (1999) Ken Plummer's *Intimate Citizenship* (2003) David Evans *Sexual Citizenship* (1993), along with Engin Isin and Patricia Wood's *Radical Citizenship*, Ruth Lister's *Feminist Citizenship* and Ulrich Beck's *Cosmopolitan Citizenship*. The list seems endless.

These books develop many new areas of citizenship beyond the traditional ones of law, politics and welfare and highlight a plurality of rights, responsibilities, recognition and participation for living in the contemporary, global world. They raise in particular the huge problem of universalism – can there be one universal standard for citizenship in a world where there is so much conflict and difference? And they explore the idea of a 'differentiated universalism', one where differences across the world and groups are recognised and taken on board in discussions about human rights and responsibilities. Citizenship now becomes contingent upon the building of recognised identities around which different rights and responsibilities get developed, and of course in order for these to develop we will need dialogues across our differences.

## THE COMMON GROUND OF SOCIOLOGY: TOWARDS A BETTER WORLD?

> What we can do is ... make life a little less terrible and a little less unjust in every generation. A good deal can be achieved in this way.
>
> (Karl Popper, 1948)

Ultimately sociology hurls us towards some of the really big questions of life – and many of the smaller ones. Are societies making progress and getting better – or are we heading for Armageddon? (And what does 'better' mean?). Is inequality growing when compared with earlier societies – and is it inevitable? Do all societies have crime – and do we need scapegoats and outsiders in all societies? How does our social life corrupt the environment we live in? What are the social factors that organise AIDS and can we use this understanding to alleviate the problems it is causing across the world? Why do religions generate hatred and war – as well as benevolence and kindness? And in all cases, what could we – should we – do about it? How *should* we work to prevent world problems and how indeed might we make the world a better place? Is justice possible in society? Once we have entered these kinds of issues, we are a very long way indeed from the simple facts. But then, *there are no simple facts in sociology*. And this suggests that sociology – like it or not – will sooner or later become embroiled in political and moral life.

Studying sociology inevitably deepens the understanding of how human social worlds work, and in doing this it helps provide a basis for thinking of how social life can function better. Sociology fosters thinking about what it means to be a good citizen in the current world. Sociology is at it best when it starts with researching and trying to understand – as objectively as it can – the everyday sufferings and troubles of everyday people in their multiplicities of worlds and asks how our social doings have helped generate 'problems' – how our social structures and actions, our cultures and material worlds, our biographies, histories and spaces have worked to bring these sufferings about. Sociology's ultimate mission – like all of science and art in the end – is surely a mission for a better world. It does not do all this serious thinking and pioneering of ideas for mere fun (though hopefully this may happen along the way). It is, rather, driven by a sense of a better world for all that could be ours. It is hence ultimately charged with a moral, political and critical responsibility. It is an emancipatory discipline which can increase the spaces for democracy and justice.

In the end, it needs to show that human social worlds are ultimately the consequence of human social actions, even as we lose control over them. And so we had better be careful what these actions are – of how we act in the social world – and remain vigilantly aware of our past and futures. We dwell in the social, living with others of the present, alongside the dead and the about to be born. Like it or not, we are always haunted by the social whilst we shape the social world to come.

## SUMMARY

Sociology lives in human social worlds, studies them and has to take very seriously the values and politics that help shape them into the future. It can never be easily value-free. The chapter looked at some of the social roles that sociologists can perform – researcher, thinker, critic, educator, dialogist, critical citizen, enhancer of art and creativity, and facilitator of unheard voices being heard. Sociology should be grounded in the people it serves, and Figure 8.1 suggests a wheel of sociological life which flows from everyday life to professional, popular, practical and policy-oriented sociology. The overall goal of sociology is to help us all act as critical citizens in a world we never made but every day help to re-create. It does its work with a firm eye on making the world a better place *for all* in a hugely unequal world. The challenge is on for each generation to leave behind a better place for subsequent generations.

## CODA: SOCIOLOGICAL EYES

We are the thinkers who puzzle and ponder.
Social critics with our eyes on the world.
Scientific artists, passionately objective.
Patchwork quilters with an eye for the queer.
Sympathetic tellers of lives damaged and draining.
Outsiders looking on margins, drowning in hope.
Wounded reformers for a better world to come.
Utopian dreamers disappointedly cheerful.
Thwarted radicals angered in worlds of injustice.
Time travellers in cyborged lands.
Critical citizens with an eye for the future.

## EXPLORING FURTHER

### MORE THINKING

Although it is a ridiculously grand way to end reading a small introductory book, you might like now to set aside some time to ponder the meaning of your life and its values. Yes, do laugh at me, as this is in effect a life project. Make it a bit simpler – how might your life connect practically to the circle of sociological life and ponder what it might mean to be a good critical sociological citizen.

### FURTHER READING

C. Wright Mills, *The Sociological Imagination* (1959) is the classic text to inspire students to bring together the personal and the political in their work. More recent books to do this well include Charles Lemert's *Social Things* (2008), Steven Dandaneau's *Taking it Big: Developing Sociological Consciousness in Postmodern Times* (2001) and Ben Agger's *The Virtual Self* (2004) – all of which also serve as lively introductions. More advanced arguments for the connections between the personal and the sociological can be found in Pierre Bourdieu, *In Other Words: Essays Towards a Reflexive Sociology* (1990) and Dorothy E. Smith, *Writing the Social: Critique, Theory and Investigations* (1998). A recent challenge to the sociological enterprise in its traditional form comes from Avery Gordon, *Ghostly Matters:*

*Haunting and the Sociological Imagination* (2008). I think the collection of writings gathered and edited regularly by Norman Denzin and Yvonne Lincoln, *Handbook of Qualitative Research* (several editions, and published as one major volume as well as three paperback parts) is a helpful guide to new ways of doing sociology.

Entering philosophy, I found Zygmunt Bauman's *Postmodern Ethics* (1993) fascinating.

Oyvind Ihlen, Magnus Fredrickson and Betteke van Ruler, in *Social Theory for Public Relations: Key Figures and Concepts* (2009), have gathered a very interesting collection of reviews of major sociologists (including Giddens, Foucault, Habermas and Weber) and their impacts on society. Alan Sica and Stephen Turner, *The Disobedient Generation: Social Theories in the Sixties* (2005) contains essays by established sociologists on their politics in their student days. Alan Wolfe's *Marginalized in the Middle* (1996) debates the problems from a liberal sociologist's viewpoint and Chandra Talpade Mohanty, *Feminism Without Borders: Decolonizing Theory, Practicing Solidarity* (2003) provides a rallying cry for change.

The recent debate on public sociology was initiated by Michael Burawoy 'For Public Sociology' (2005). A lively series of debates on it can be found in Dan Clawson *et al., Public Sociology: Fifteen Eminent Sociologists Debate Politics and the Profession in the Twenty-First Century* (2007). Amitai Etzioni's writings and website is a good example of a passionate sociologist committed to a communitarian change.

# CONCLUSION

## THE SOCIOLOGICAL IMAGINATION: TWENTY THESES

> Caution! Danger! Beware! Sociology will change your life
> (Opening slide to Ken Plummer's introductory first-year lecture at
> Essex University, 1987–2004)

Sociology is passionate about the social. It brings a distinctive consciousness and an imagination to think outside of that limiting frame whereby everything can be explained through 'individuals' or the 'natural'. Sociology questions the 'certain blindness' of human beings' which takes the world for granted. Everywhere it looks at the hauntings of social life. Here, as summary and challenge, are twenty of its key features to argue about.

1   Sociology is the systematic, sceptical and critical study of the *social*, investigating the human construction of *social* worlds.
2   'The social' captures the idea that we live with others but it also constitutes a level or layer of reality which is quite distinctive and which exists ontologically *sui generis* to constrain and coerce us in our everyday life..
3   Social life is awesome, amazing and often horrendous, sometimes to be celebrated and sometimes to lead to disenchantment. The air we breathe is social. We can't stop 'experiencing the social' and seeing 'the social' everywhere.

4  Sociology is a way of thinking – an imagination, a form of consciousness – that can/will change your life. It defamiliarises the familiar, questions the taken for granted, treats social facts as things, and destroys the myths we choose to live by. It is a haunting.

5  Sociologists always look for the social patterns, prisons, predictabilities in human social life – the social structures in which we dwell.

6  Sociologists see human beings as acting in social worlds *with others* – they create daily life in a search for meaning. Human beings live in worlds of complex symbolisation, living with others through social actions. All of human social life is inherently about meanings and social actions.

7  Human beings weave webs of cultures – life designs, toolkits for life and ways of living which are composed of complex, multi-layered, negotiable and ever emergent symbolic actions. Cultures are never tight, fixed or agreed upon but are multilayered 'mosaics of social worlds'.

8  Human beings live in material worlds of brute reality: environments, economies, bodies. We are both animals and cultural creatures – we are intrinsically dual – living simultaneously in material and symbolic worlds. We are the little gods who shit.

9  We live with the tensions of constraining structures and creative meanings: sociology sees this tension everywhere.

10  All social worlds are 'incorrigibly plural' and we dwell in social tensions and contradiction. Everything in social life – including sociological thinking – brings tensions, conflicts, contradictions.

11  We live in a deep swirling matrix of differences and inequalities. Human capabilities are structured through divisive processes into structured inequalities which have damaging effects on our lives. Our opportunities for human flourishing can be thwarted by our class, gender, ethnicity, age, health, sexuality and nationhood.

12  Social life is always shaped by time and space. Change and contingency are ubiquitous.

13   Social life is structured by power relations: we ask who and what can shape our lives?

14   Sociology was born of radical social change and continues to dwell in major social change. Social worlds are always changing – and every social thing has a constantly changing history.

15   All of social life is dialogical not monological. Human beings are narrators and are in a constant round of telling tales of lives and societies to each other. And all knowledge – whatever else it may be – is within this social dialogue: it is always local, contested, relational knowledge.

16   Sociologists describe, understand, and explain the social world using the best 'tricks of the trade' they can muster. They must straddle art, science and history. They think hard, conduct rigorous empirical research, and skilfully make sense of data

17   The new information technologies are radically reforming this sociological project – providing new tools for research and new source of data and even new ways of thinking about social life.

18   Sociologists are researchers, thinkers, critics, educators, dialogists, critical citizens, enhancers of art and creativity, and facilitators of unheard voices being heard. Above all, sociology fosters critical citizens alive and changing their own social worlds. They dwell in a flowing circle of sociological life

19   Sociologists put their tools to work in envisaging a better world. Sociology lives in human social worlds, studies them and takes very seriously the values and politics that help shape them into the future.

20   Sociology helps us all to act as critical citizens in a world we never made but which every day we have to help to re-create. The challenge is on for each generation to leave behind a better place for subsequent generations. There is a social dream of a better world which haunts sociology. Maybe there could be a flourishing for all?

# APPENDIX

## EPIGRAMMATIC SOCIOLOGY: TWENTY-FIVE LITTLE WISDOMS TO PONDER

Here are twenty-five little sayings that thinkers about society have bequeathed us. There are many more on the web site for the book. They are worth puzzling a little.

1 Dare to think. (Immanuel Kant's Enlightenment challenge, 1784.)
2 How is society possible? (A disturbing little question posed by Georg Simmel in an essay with that title, 1910.)
3 Man was born, free but everywhere he is in chains. (Jean-Jacques Rousseau's challenge in *The Social Contract,* 1762.)
4 Society is a contract, a partnership between those who are living, those who are dead and those who are to be born. (Edmund Burke's conservative attack on the French Revolution in *Reflections on the Revolution in France* (a best-seller in 1790; Oxford edition, 1993.)
5 Things are not what they seem. (Peter Berger, *Invitation to Sociology,*1966.)
6 Things are what they seem. (Zen saying.)
7 The sociologist is a destroyer of myths. (Norbert Elias, *What is Sociology?,* 1978.)
8 Defamiliarise the familiar. (Zygmunt Baumann. *Thinking Sociologically*, 1990.)

9    Treat social facts as things. (Émile Durkheim, *The Rules of Sociological Method*, 1982.)

10   We are mere bundles of habits. (William James, *Principles of Psychology*, 1890.)

11   Consciousness does not determine life, but life determines consciousness. (Marx, *German Ideology*, 1845.)

12   We live in the minds of others without knowing it. (Charles H. Cooley, *Human Nature and Social Order*, 1902.)

13   All science would be superfluous if the outward appearance and essences of things directly coincided. (Marx: *Capital*, III.)

14   Human beings cannot live together without acknowledging and, consequently, making mutual sacrifices … Every society is a moral society. (Émile Durkheim, *Division of Labour*, 1893.)

15   Be a good craftsman: Avoid any rigid set of procedures … Avoid the fetishism of method and technique. Let every person be their own methodologist; let every person be their own theorist. (C.Wright Mills, *The Sociological Imagination*, 1959.)

16   The sociological imagination enables us to grasp history and biography and the relations between the two within society. That is its task and its promise. (C. Wright Mills, *The Sociological Imagination*, 1959.)

17   Objectivity is the term that men have given their own subjectivity. (Liz Stanley and Sue Wise, *Breaking Out*, 1983.)

18   There is no best way to tell a story about society. Many genres, many methods, many formats – they can all do the trick. Instead of ideal ways to do it, the world gives us possibilities among which we choose. Every way of telling the story of a society does some of the job superbly but other parts not so well. (Howard S Becker, *Telling About Society*, 2007.)

19   Every human is in certain respects
     a. like all other humans.
     b. like some other humans.
     c. like no other human.
     (The Kluckhohn–Murray aphorism from Clyde Kluckhohn and Henry Murray, *Personality in Nature, Culture and Society*, 1953.)

20   When people define situations as real they are real in their consequences. (W. I. Thomas, *The Unadjusted Girl*, 1925.)

21   There is no way out of the game of culture. (Pierre Bourdieu, *Distinction*, 1986.)

22   From now on nothing that happens on our planet is only a limited local event. (Ulrich Beck, *What is Globalization*, 2000.)

23   Civil society is a project. It inspires hope for democracy. (Jeffrey Alexander, *The Civil Sphere*, 2006.)

24   I define postmodernism as incredulity towards metanarratives. (Jean-François Lyotard, *The Post-Modern Condition*, 1979.)

25   We only become what we are by the radical deep-seated refusal of that which others have made of us. (Jean-Paul Sartre, Preface to Frantz Fanon's *The Wretched of the Earth*, 1968.)

# GLOSSARY

All disciplines – from photography to physics – develop their own complicated but necessary languages. As the world is seen more complexly, so words are often needed to capture this complexity. There are many dictionaries, encyclopaedias, websites and glossaries which can help you in sociological language. See John Scott and Gordon Marshall, *Oxford Dictionary of Sociology* (2009). Longer entries can be found in Bryan S. Turner' *Dictionary of Sociology* (2006). John Scott's series of books – *Fifty Key Concepts* (2006), and *Fifty Key Sociologists* (2007) are worth a good look too. Good libraries will have encyclopedias like George Ritzer's *Encyclopaedia of Sociology* (2007) (which also has web links).

Below is a short 'starter' list of some key words found in this book. They are in bold in the text. The bracket indicates pages in this book where they are raised; an author is sometimes named where more details will be found in the references.

**action:** theories which highlight people's conduct being oriented to subjective meanings of others (pp. 101–3; Stones, 2008).

**action-structure debate:** a longstanding and contentious debate among sociologists on the relative importance of individuals' localised creative actions respectively large-scale social patterns and forces have in shaping society and everyday life (pp. 104-5; Giddens, 1986).

**anomie:** lack of norms (more technically a tension between cultural goals and social structures) (p. 31; Durkheim, 1984).

**capabilities:** opportunities for functioning in various areas of life (pp. 178–9; Deneulin and Shahani, 2009).

**capitalism:** diverse economic systems all of which stress private ownership, profit and usually competition (pp 51–3; Fulcher, 2004).

**caste:** stratification system based on inherited status (p. 155).

**Chicago School:** first major school of US sociology (1915–1935) with a focus on the city and its problems. (Not to be confused with the Chicago School of neo-liberal economics.) (p. 81; Plummer, 2001).

**citizenship:** formal status as recognised member of a particular social group, such as a nation or state, which usually brings both rights and responsibilities (pp. 201–2; Marshall 1950).

**class:** stratification based on economic and social position (Chapter 8; Marx, 2000; Weber 1978).

**colonialism:** process by which some nations enrich themselves at expense of others (p. 91; Said, 2003; Young, 2003).

**comparative method:** many meanings but tends to suggest a contrast between social things – like comparing different cultures, different histories or different situations (p. 146).

**cosmopolitanism:** differences, tolerance, showing common humanity (p. 62; Fine, 2007).

**critical theory:** knowledge masks interests behind it, and critical theory unmasks these interests. A Marxist inspired theory which gives emphasis to the way popular culture shapes people's lives (pp. 82–3).

**culture:** the ideas, customs and ways of life of a group, including language, values (pp. 38–40; Williams, 1989).

**deductive logic:** method which conclusions from testing general hypotheses (see also inductive method) (p. 134).

**diachronic:** technical term, to analyse phenomena in terms of their development over time. Contrasts with synchronic. (p. 123)

**dialogue/dialogic:** a recognition of multiple voices, not a single united one (p. 186–7; Bahktin, 1982).

**diaspora:** the movement and dispersals of people around the world, as in the slave trade (p. 169).

**difference:** a relational idea – showing how one thing connects to another, often in binaries, (oppositions like black/white; gay/straight) (p. 153; Fraser and Greco, 2004; Taylor, 1994).

**digitalisation:** digitalisation, in contrast to mediatisation, is the social process through which much of social life becomes organised through the new information technologies. Digitisation refers to the process by which electrical signals in the traditional analogue system get converted to digital (p. 63).

**discourse:** written or spoken communications (and often the power relations contained) (p. 36–7; Foucault, 1991).

**dramaturgy:** society analysed as if it was a theatre and viewed through its theatrical properties (p. 36, 108; Goffman, 1956).

**empirical:** based on evidence and experience, not theory or speculation (p. 132).

**Enlightenment:** major seventeenth–eighteenth century movement of thought based on belief in rationality, progress, individualism and critique of main religions, monarchy and traditions (p. 74; Hyland, Gomoez and Greensides, 2003).

**epistemology:** branch of philosophy that deals with what is knowledge and truth (pp. 127–8).

**ethnicity:** people sharing common histories, beliefs and lives based on common national or cultural tradition (p. 168; Fenton, 2003).

**ethnocentrism:** appraising cultures through the eyes and prejudices of your own culture (pp. 15, 17, 45, 161).

**ethnography:** research tool that involves describing closely culture and its ways of life (p. 107; Lofland *et al.*, 2004).

**ethnomethodology:** study of the ways and logics in which we make sense of everyday life (p. 30).

**feminism:** diverse positions which are in opposition to sexism and patriarchy and usually advocate equality of sexes (pp. 89–90; Collins, 1990; Delamont, 2003; Lengermann and Niebrugge-Brantley, 1988).

**form:** see social form

**function:** the intended and unintended consequences of any social thing or pattern for the operation of society. Functions can be negative, positive or neutral. (p. 30; Swingewood, 2000)

**functionalism:** examines social life and institutions in terms of their consequences and purposes. Some are direct and manifest; many are hidden or latent. Some consequences may be dysfunctional. Updated it is often called neo-functionalism (pp. 30, 83).

**fundamentalism:** conservative doctrine opposing modern world in favour of traditionalism based on absolute authority, usually religious (p. 63; Bruce, 2007).

**Gemeinschaft:** strong social ties: see also Gesellschaft (p. 77; Tönnies, 2003; DeLanty, 2005).

**gender:** social attributes of men, women and others; not biological (p. 166).

**Gesellschaft:** linked to Gemeinschaft; here bonds are weaker. (p. 77; Tönnies 2003).

**Gini coefficient:** A commonly used measure of inequality which examines the distribution of wealth within a country and how it differs from an imagined perfectly equal distribution. The higher the index, the greater the inequality (p. 159).

**globalisation:** the increasing interconnectedness of the world's countries (p. 64; Beck, 200; Pieterse, 2004).

**habits:** social behaviour that is regularly enacted and taken for granted by individuals over a prolonged period of time. A term introduced by William James; a precursor of habitus (pp. 98–9).

**habitus:** the habits we acquire in social life and that we carry around with us, 'transposable and durable dispositions through which people perceive, think, appreciate, act and judge in the world' (p. 103; Bourdieu, 1986).

**hegemony:** the ability of a dominant (class) group to win over a subordinate (mass) group to their ideas and values (p. 118; Gramsci, 1998).

**hermeneutics:** philosophical perspective which inspects the ways and processes in which the world is interpreted. (p. 146; Ricoeur, 1981).

**heteronormative:** the privileging of heterosexual relations (p. 170; Sullivan, 2003; Weeks, 2009).

**homophobia:** fear of same-sex relationships (p. 170; Sullivan, 2003; Weeks, 2009).

**hybridic:** diversification, as old elements are merged into a mélange with new ones (pp. 168).

**ideal type:** extracting key features (not perfect ones) for comparing with real life examples (p. 146; Weber, 1978).

**idealism:** contrasts with materialism, and ultimately locates reality in mind and ideas (p. 110).

**identity:** the recognition of who one is and how one is recognised by others (p. 172; Mead, 1967).

**imagined communities:** not based on actual face-to-face relations but on a mental image of an affinity between people (p. 57; Anderson, 1983).

**inductive method:** method which draws conclusions from observation and experience; see also deductive (p. 134).

**interpretivism:** understanding of behaviour that includes the meaning of people (p. 128).

**inter-subjectivity:** (which links to empathy, sympathy, dialogue, role-taking and self) a condition which allows people to share meanings and understandings (p. 20).

**institutions:** established social patterns or habits (p. 98).

**life narrative:** the organisation and meanings coded into a telling of a life (p. 116; Plummer, 2001).

**materialism:** the philosophy which claims all aspects of social life flows from matter. (p. 109)

**mediatisation:** the increasing constitution of everyday social relationships and interaction through technologically based media, both for individual use (e.g. mobile phones; social networking websites) and mass consumption (e.g. radio; television). It is a new concept and is sometimes also called mediasation, or even mediatation (p. 64).

**methodology:** general approach to studying how we do research (Chapter 6).

**mode of production:** Marxist term for a specific form and organisation of material production, which involves both the forces of production such as tools and machinery, and the relations of production (such as serf/peasant or capitalist) (p. 79).

**modernity:** stage of society development in the West from the Enlightenment /eighteenth century to at least the end of the twentieth century (p. 61).

**multiculturalism:** recognition of difference and diversity in a society, usually ethnic; often linked to educational programmes (p. 62; Taylor, 1994).

**multi-paradigmatic:** the existence of many different schools and traditions of thought (p. 185).

**multiple modernities:** the denial of one route or kind of modernity and the view that there are a multiplicity of pathways in the creation of 'modernities' (pp. 44, 61; Eisenstadt, 2000).

**narrative:** a basic way of apprehending the word usually connected to the stories we tell of our lives (ppp. 116, 143; Plummer, 2001).

**nation:** group of people sharing same culture; nation-state is a political unit (p. 62; Smith, 2009).

**neo-liberalism:** term which has come to be used to designate new right policies and politics and is based on the philosophy of Hayek; not to be confused with liberalism itself, which is often radical and critical (p. 51; Harvey, 2007).

**norms:** shared expectations of behaviour (p. 31).

**ontology:** a philosophical perspective on the nature of social reality; it tells us how the world is made up, what human nature is like, what the nature of things are. (p. 127; Delanty, 2005).

**perspective:** a specific point of view of the social world (p. 143).

**pluralism:** can mean two, but usually means multiple sources, rather than one (p. 61).

**positivism:** philosophy of science which stresses logical or empirical proof (pp. 77; Delanty, 2005).

**post-colonialism:** positions that recognise that many cultures have been built out of oppressors who have shaped the worlds and realities of those colonised (p. 91; Young, 2003).

**postmodernism:** death of any one grand or absolute truth and the recognition of multiplicities (pp. 62, 88; Seidman 2008).

**power:** ability to achieve one own aims against opposition (pp. 117–19).

**practical reason:** the everyday ability of people to make sense of their world, make themselves understood and carry out daily project (p. 179).

**public sociology:** sociology which is made more relevant and accessible to the wider population outside professional sociology (p. 193; Burawoy, 2005).

**racial formation:** linkage between racial structures and economies and meanings and cultures (p. 168; Winant, 2004).

**racialisation:** process of ranking people on the basis of their presumed race (p. 169; Back and Solomos, 2007).

**realism:** epistemology which stresses social phenomena have an existence beyond lives of individuals (p. 128; Delanty and Strydom, 2003).

**reflexivity:** reflecting on own actions and knowledge (pp. 127, 148).

**risk society:** society where technology and globalisation shift the nature of risks (p. 54; Beck, 1992).

**self:** in common sense terms this often means a person's being; in sociology it always implies others. The self is constituted through the way we see ourselves and how others see us (p. 21; Cooley, 1998; Mead, 1967).

**semiotics:** study of signs and symbols (p. 22).

**social capital:** friendships, networks, connections over time which create links and bonds; they often shape the quality of a life (p. 32; Field, 2008).

**social constructionism:** theory which suggests that the social is made by human actors giving meaning to the world (p. 30; Berger and Luckman, 1967).

**social facts:**   phenomena external to the individual but which acts to constrain the person (p. 19; Durkheim, 1982).

**social forms:**   underlying patterns and principles through which social life and social relations are organised (p. 19; Simmel 1971/1908).

**social structure:**   enduring social arrangements that influence individuals and selves; one of the most used of sociological concepts with a long history and multiple uses: recurrent and relatively stable patterns of social conduct (pp. 35, 98).

**socialisation:**   multiple processes across the life cycle through which people acquire social competence (p. 20).

**society:**   a group of people who share a common culture and usually interact in a defined territory (p. 24).

**standpoint:**   an epistemological position which examines the social conditions (often of oppression) which generate a version of truth grounded in a social position (like gender or race) (p. 128; Collins 1990; Harding, 1998).

**state:**   institution which holds the monopoly of force (p. 58) Weber, 2001).

**structuration:**   process by which social structures are reproduced in social actions (p. 105; Giddens, 1986).

**structure:**   see social structure.

**subaltern:**   subordinate and outside the power structure; often used in debates on post-colonialism (p. 91).

**symbolic interaction:**   theory which highlights how meanings emerge through interaction. Core idea is the self (p. 21; Mead, 1967; Plummer in Stones, 2008).

**theory:**   abstract reasoning, logic and speculation, often turned into hypotheses and principles for empirical examination (Chapters 2 and 6).

**triangulation:**   the bringing of many methods, theories and perspectives to one theme or concern (p. 135).

**Verstehen:**   German for 'understanding', a key feature of Max Weber's sociology (pp. 108; Weber, 1978).

# WEBSITES
## A SHORT GUIDE

This is the time to think seriously about the saturation and overload found on the internet, as well as the reliability and representativeness of what you read. There is a lot 'out there' for sociologists – and equally, a lot to waste their time. Take time out to ponder the value of Wikpedia entries. Think about the dross found on the YouTube. Work on your own evaluative skills for approaching the internet and surfing.

There is a web site to accompany this book (http://www.routledge.com/books/details/9780415472067/). You will find quite a lot of links to web sites on this. For starters though, to get you going, here are five good sites:

- **The Internet Sociologist** at http://www.vts.intute.ac.uk/he/tutorial/sociologist is one of a national series of tutorials written by qualified tutors, lecturers and librarians from across the UK.
- **Sociology Central** at http://www.sociology.org.uk/ is UK based and has a host of useful links, and advice on different universities and their courses in sociology.

- **The Sociolog** at http://www.sociolog.com/ is US based, it is also good at detailing US universities, journals and organisations.
- **SocioSite** at http://www.sociosite.net Like the above, only this time based in Amsterdam,
- **The SocioWeb** at http://www.socioweb.com

It may also be useful to look at sociological associations:

- British Sociological Association (BSA) http://www.britsoc. co.uk
- American Sociological Association (ASA http://www.asanet. org

Both of these have sections which can assist students. See also:

- European Sociological Association (ESA) http://www. europeansociology.org
- International Sociological Association (ISA) http://www.isa-sociology.org

# REFERENCES

Agger, B. (2004) *The Virtual Self*, Oxford: Blackwell.

Alexander, J. C. (2006) *The Civil Sphere*, Oxford: Oxford University Press.

Althusser, L. (2008) *On Ideology*, London: Verso.

Anderson, B. (1983) *Imagined Communities* London: Verso.

Anderson, E. (1999) *Code of the Street: Decency, Violence and the Moral Life of the Inner City*, New York: Norton.

Babbie, E. (2009) *The Practice of Social Research*, Belmont, CA: Wadsworth.

Back, L. (2007) *The Art of Listening*: Oxford: Berg.

Back, L. and Solomos, J. (eds) (2007) *Theories of Race and Racism: A Reader*, London: Routledge

Bakhtin, M. (1982) *The Dialogic Imagination*, Austin, TX: University of Texas Press.

Bauman, Z. (1990) *Thinking Sociologically*. Oxford: Blackwell.

Bauman, Z. (1993) *Postmodern Ethics*. Oxford: Blackwell.

Bauman, Z. (1998) *Globalization: The Human Consequences.* Cambridge: Polity.

Bauman, Z. (2000) *Liquid Modernity*. Cambridge: Polity.

Bauman, Z. (2004) *Wasted Lives*. Cambridge: Polity.

Bauman, Z. and May, T. (2001) *Thinking Sociologically*, 2nd edn, Oxford: Wiley Blackwell.

Beck, U. (1992) *Risk Society*. London: Sage.

Beck, U. (2000) *What is Globalization?* Cambridge: Polity.

Beck, U. (2006) *Cosmopolitan Vision*, Cambridge: Polity.

Becker, H. S. (1998) *Tricks of the Trade: How to Think About Your Research While You're Doing It*, Chicago, IL: University of Chicago Press.

Becker, H. S. (2007) *Telling About Society*, Chicago, IL: University of Chicago Press.

Bell, D. (2006) *Cyberculture Theorists*, London: Routledge.

Bellah, R. N., Madsen, R., Sullivan, W., Swidler, A. and Tipton S. M. (2007) *Habits of the Heart: Individualism and Commitment in American Life*, 3rd edn, Berkeley, CA: University of California Press.

Bennett, T., Savage, M., Silva, E., Warde, A., Gayo-Cal, M. and Wright, D. (2009) *Culture, Class, Distinction*, London: Routledge.

Berger, P. (1966) *Invitation to Sociology*, Harmondsworth: Penguin.

Berger, P. and Luckmann, T. (1990) *The Social Construction of Reality*, 2nd edn, Harmondsworth: Penguin.

Best, J. (2001) *Damned Lies and Statistics.* Berkeley, CA: University of California Press.

Best, S. (2002) *A Beginner's Guide to Social Theory*, London: Sage.

Bhambra, G. K. (2007) *Rethinking Modernity: Postcolonialism and the Sociological Imagination*, Basingstoke: Palgrave Macmillan.

Booth, C. (2009) *Life and Labour of the People in London.* London: Bibliolife.

Bottero, W. (2005) *Stratification: Social Division and Inequality*, London: Routledge.

Bourdieu, P. (1990) *In Other Words: Essays Towards a Reflexive Sociology*, Cambridge: Polity Press.

Bourdieu, P. (1999 [1993]) *Weight of the World: Social Suffering in Contemporary Society*, Cambridge: Polity.

Bourdieu, P. (2010 [1986]) *Distinction*, London: Routledge Classics.

Bruce, S. (2007) *Fundamentalism*, 2nd edn, Cambridge: Polity.

Bryman, A. (2004) *The Disneyization of Society*, London: Sage.

Bryman, A. (2008) *Social Research Methods*, Oxford: Oxford University Press.

Burawoy. M. (2005) 'For Public Sociology', *American Sociological Review* Vol. 70, (February): 4-28.

Burke, E. (2009 [1790]) *Reflections on the Revolution in France*, Oxford: Oxford University Press.

Calaprice, A. (2005) *The New Quotable Einstein,* Princeton NJ: Princeton University Press.

Castells, M. (2002) *The Internet Galaxy*, Oxford: Oxford University Press.

Castells, M. (2009 [1996]) *The Information Age*, Oxford: Blackwell.

Castells, M. (2009) *The Rise of the Network Society,* 2nd edn, Oxford: Wiley Blackwell.

Clarke, A. E. (2005) *Situational Analysis: Grounded Theory After the Postmodern Turn*. London: Sage.

Clawson, D., *et al.* (2007) *Public Sociology: Fifteen Eminent Sociologists Debate Politics and the Profession in the Twenty-First Century*, Berkeley, CA: University of California Press.

Cohen, R. and Kennedy, P. (2007) *Global Sociology*, 2nd edn, Basingstoke: Palgrave.

Cohen, S. (2001) *States of Denial: Knowing about Atrocities and Sufferings*, Cambridge: Polity.

Collins, P. H. (1990) *Black Feminist Thought: Knowledge, Consciousness and the Politics of Empowerment*, New York: Routledge.

Collins, R (1998) *The Sociology of Philosophies: A Global Theory of Intellectual Change*, Cambridge, MA: Belknap Press of Harvard Press.

Connell, R. (2005) *Masculinities,* 2nd edn, Cambridge: Polity.

Connell, R. (2007) *Southern Theory: The Global Dynamics of Knowledge in Social Science*, Cambridge: Polity Press.

Cooley, C. H. (1998) *On Self and Social Organization*, edited by H. Schubert, Chicago, IL: University of Chicago Press.

Cree, V. (1999) *Sociology for Social Workers and Probation Officers*, London: Routledge.

Dahl, R. (2005) *Who Governs? Democracy and Power in the American City*, 2nd edn, New Haven, CT: Yale University Press.

Dandaneau, S. (2001) *Taking It Big: Developing Sociological Consciousness in Postmodern Times*, Thousand Oaks, CA: Pine Forge Press.

Davis, M. (2007) *Planet of Slums*, New York: Verso.

De Beauvoir, S. (2009) *The Second Sex*, new edn, London: Jonathan Cape.

DeLamont, S. (2003) *Feminist Sociology*, London: Sage.

Delanty, G. (2000) *Citizenship in a Global Age,* Milton Keynes: Open University Press.

Delanty, G. (2005) *Social Science: Philosophical and Methodological Foundations* Milton Keynes: Open University Press.

Delanty, G. and Strydom, P. (2003) *Philosophies of Social Science: The Classic and Contemporary Readings.* Milton Keynes: Open University Press.

Deneulin, S. and Shahani, L. (eds) (2009) *An Introduction to the Human Development and Capability Approach,* London: Earthscan.

Denny, E. and Earle, S. (2009) *Sociology for Nurses*, Cambridge: Polity Press.

Denzin, N. and Lincoln, Y. (eds) (2005) *Handbook of Qualitative Research*, 3rd edn, London: Sage.

du Bois, W. E. B. (2007 [1903]) *The Souls of Black Folk*, Oxford: Oxford University Press.

Dunier, M. (1992) *Slim's Table: Race, Respectability and Masculinity,* 2nd edn, Chicago, IL: University of Chicago Press.

Dunier, M. (2002) *Sidewalk,* New York: Farrar,Straus & Giroux.

Durkheim, E. (1982 [1895]) *The Rules of Sociological Method*, Glencoe, IL: Free Press.

Durkheim, E. (1984 [1893]) *The Division of Labour in Society*. London: Palgrave Macmillan.

Durkheim, E. (2002 [1897]) *Suicide*, 2nd edn, London: Routledge.

Durkheim, E. (2008 [1912]) *The Elementary Forms of Religious Life*, student edn, Oxford: Oxford University Press.

Ehrenreich, B. (2002) *Nickel and Dimed: Undercover in Low-Wage America*, London: Granta.

Einstein, A. (2006) *The Einstein Reader*, New York: Citadel Press.

Eisenstadt, S. N. (2000) 'Multiple Modernities', *Daedalus* 129(1) 1–29.

Elias, N. (1978) *What is Sociology?* London: Hutchinson.

Elias, N. (2000 [1939]) *The Civilizing Process*, 2nd edn, Oxford: Blackwell.

Etzioni, A. (2001) *The Monochrome Society*, Princeton, NJ: Princeton University Press.

Evans, D. (1993) *Sexual Citizenship*, London: Routledge.

Evans, M. (2006) *A Short History of Society*, Maidenhead: Open University Press.

Fenton, S. (2003) *Ethnicity*. Cambridge: Polity.

Field, J. (2008) *Social Capital*, 2nd edn, London: Routledge.

Fine, R. (2007) *Cosmopolitanism*, London: Routledge.

Foster, Robert J. (2008) *Coca-Globalization: Following Soft Drinks from New York to New Guinea.* Basingstoke: Palgrave.

Foucault, M. (1991) *Discipline and Punish: Birth of the Prison*, new edn, Harmondsworth: Penguin.

Foucault, M. (2001 [1969]) *The Order of Things*, London: Routledge.

Fox, K. (2005) *Watching the English: The Hidden Rules of English Behaviour*, London: Hodder and Stoughton.

Frank, A. W. (1997) *The Wounded Storyteller*, Chicago, IL: Chicago University Press.

Fraser, M. and Greco, M. (eds) (2004) *The Body: A Reader*, London: Routledge.

Freud, S. (2002 [1930]) *Civilization and Its Discontents*, London: Penguin.

Fukuyama, F. (1993) *The End of History and the Last Man*, London: Penguin.

Fulcher, J. (2004) *Capitalism: A Very Short Introduction*, Oxford: Oxford University Press.

Fulcher, J. and Scott, J. (2007) *Sociology*, 3rd edn, Oxford: Oxford University Press.

Giddens, A. (1973) *Capitalism and Modern Social Theory*, Cambridge: Cambridge University Press.

Giddens, A. (1986) *The Constitution of Society*, Cambridge: Polity Press.

Giddens, A. (1999) *Runaway World: How Globalisation is Shaping our Lives*, London: Profile.

Giddens, A. (2006) *Sociology*, 6th edn, Cambridge: Polity.

Giddens, A. (2009) *Politics of Climate Change*, Cambridge: Polity.

Gladwell, M. (2001) *The Tipping Point: How Little Things Can Make a Big Difference*, London: Abacus.

Glassner, B. (2000) *The Culture of Fear: Why Americans are Afraid of the Wrong Things*, New York: Basic Books.

Goffman, E. (1959 [1956]) *The Presentation of Self in Everyday Life*, Harmondsworth: Penguin.

Goffman, E. (1968) *Stigma: Notes on the Management of Spoiled Identity*, Harmondsworth: Pelican.

Goffman, E. (1991 [1961]) *Asylums*, London: Penguin.

Gordon, A. (2008) *Ghostly Matters: Haunting and the Sociological Imagination*, Minneapolis, MN: University of Minnesota Press.

Gouldner, A. (1970) *The Coming Crisis of Western Sociology*, London: Heinemann.

Graham, H. (2009) *Unequal Lives: Health and Socioeconomic Inequalities*, Maidenhead: Open University Press.

Gramsci, A. (1998) *Prison Notebooks: Selections*, London: Lawrence and Wishart.

Habermas, J. (1989 [1962]) *The Structural Transformation of the Public Sphere*, Cambridge: Polity.

Habermas, J. (2001) *The Postnational Constellation*, Cambridge: Polity.

Hable Gray, C. (2002) *Cyborg Citizen*, London: Routledge.

Halsey, A. H. (2004) *A History of Sociology in Britain*, Oxford: Oxford University Press.

Harding, S. (1998) *Is Science Multi-cultural? Postcolonialism, Feminism and Epistemologies*, Bloomington, IN: Indiana University Press.

Harvey, D. (2007) *A Brief History of Neo-liberalism*, Oxford: Oxford University Press.

Harvey, M., Quilley, S. and Benyon, H. (2002) *Exploring the Tomato: Transformations of Nature, Society and Economy*, Cheltenham: Edward Elgar.

Hobbes, T. (2008 [1651]) *Leviathan*, London: Penguin.

Hochschild, A. R. (1983) *The Managed Heart: Commercialization of Human Feeling*, Berkeley, CA: University of California Press.

Holman, R. J. (2009) *Cosmopolitanisms: New Thinking and New Directions*, Basingstoke: Palgrave.

Hughes, J., Sharrock, W. and Martin, P. J. (2003) *Understanding Classical Sociology*, 2nd edn, London: Sage.

Humphreys, L. (1975) *Tearoom Trade: Impersonal Sex in Public Places*, Edison, NJ: Aldine Transaction.

Hyland, P., Gomez, O. and Greensides, F. (eds) (2003) *The Enlightenment: A Sourcebook and Reader*, London: Routledge.

Ihlen, O., Fredrikson, M. and van Ruler, B. (2009) *Social Theory for Public Relations: Key Figures and Concepts*, London: Routledge.

Isin, E. F. and Wood, P. K. (1999) *Citizenship and Identity*, London: Sage.

James, W. (1977) *The Writings of William James*. Chicago, IL: University of Chicago Press.

Jenkins, R. (2002) *Foundations of Sociology: Towards a Better Understanding of the Human World*, Basingstoke: Palgrave Macmillan.

Jenks, C. (1998) *Core Sociological Dichotomies*, London: Sage.

Kallen, E. (2003) *Social Inequality and Social Injustice: A Human Rights Perspective*, London: Palgrave Macmillan.

Kluckhohn, C. (1948) *Personality in Nature, Society and Culture*, New York: Knopf.

Kumar, K. (1978) *Prophecy and Progress: Sociology of Industrial and Post-Industrial Society*, London: Viking.

Kymlicka, W. (1996) *Multicultural Citizenship*, Wotton-under-Edge: Clarendon Press.

Lemert, C. (2004) *Social Theory: The Multicultural and Classic Readings*, Boulder, CO: Westview Press.

Lemert, C. (2008) *Social Things: An Introduction to the Sociological Life*, 4th edn, New York: Rowman & Littlefield.

Lengermann, P. M. and Niebrugge-Brantley, J. (1998) *The Women Founders: Sociology and Social Theory 1830–1930*, London: McGraw-Hill.

Levine, D. (1995) *Visions of the Sociological Tradition*, Chicago, IL: Chicago University Press.

Lister, R. (2003) *Citizenship: Feminist Perspectives*, London: Palgrave Macmillan.

Lofland, J., Snow, D., Anderson, L. and Lofland, L. H. (2004) *Analyzing Social Settings: A Guide to Qualitative Observation and Analysis*, Belmont, CA: Wadsworth.

Lukes, S. (2004) *Power*, 2nd edn, Basingstoke:Palgrave.

Lyotard, F. (1984) *The Postmodern Condition*, Manchester: Manchester University Press.

Macchiavelli, N. (2004 [1513]) *The Prince*, London: Penguin.

Macionis, J. and Plummer, K. (2011) *Sociology: A Global Introduction*, 5th edn, Harlow: Pearson.

MacNeice, L. (2007) *Louis MacNeice: Collected Poems*, London: Faber and Faber.

Malthus, T. (2008) *An Essay on the Principles of Population*, Oxford: Oxford Classics.

Mann, M. (2004) *The Dark Side of Democracy: Explaining Ethnic Cleansing*, Cambridge: Cambridge University Press.

Marshall, T. H. (1950) *Citizenship and Social Class and Other Essays*, Cambridge: Cambridge University Press.

Marx, K. (2000) *Karl Marx: Selected Writings*, ed. D. McLellan, Oxford: Oxford University Press.

Mead, G. H. (1967 [1934]) *Mind, Self and Society*, Chicago, IL: University of Chicago Press.

Miliband, R. (1973) *The State in Capitalist Society*, London: Quartet Books.

Mills, C. W. (1956) *The Power Elite*, Oxford: Oxford University Press.

Mills, C. W. (1959) *The Sociological Imagination*, Oxford: Oxford University Press.

Mohanty, C. (2003) *Feminism Without Borders: Decolonizing Theory, Practicing Solidarity*, Durham, NC: Duke University Press.

Molotch, H. and Noren, L. (2010) *Toilet: Public Restrooms and the Politics of Sharing*, New York: New York University Press.

Narayan, D. (2000) *Can Anyone Hear Us? Voices of the Poor*, Oxford: Oxford University Press.

Nisbet, R. (1976) *Sociology as a Art Form*, Oxford: Oxford University Press.

Nisbet, R. (1993 [1966]) *The Sociological Tradition*, Edison, NJ: Transaction Publishers.

Nolan, P. and Lenski, G. (2008) *Human Societies: An Introduction to Macrosociology*, 11th edn, Boulder, CO: Paradigm.

Nussbaum, M. (2001) *Women and Human Development: The Capabilities Approach*, rev edn, Cambridge: Cambridge University Press.

Omi, M. and Winant, H. (1994) *Racial Formation in the United States*, London: Routledge.

Ong, A. (1999) *Flexible Citizenship*, Durham, NC: Duke University Press.

Orwell, G. (2004 [1940]) *Why I Write*, London: Penguin.

Park, R. E. and Burgess, E. (1921) *Introduction to the Science of Sociology*, (*The Green Bible*), Chicago, IL: University of Chicago Press.

Parsons, T. (1951) *The Social System*, London: Routledge.

Payne, G. (ed.) (2006) *Social Divisions*, Basingstoke: Palgrave.

Pieterse, J. N. (2004) *Globalization and Culture: Global Melange*, Lanham, MD: Rowman & Littlefield.

Pirandello, L. (1965 [1921]) *Six Characters in Search of an Author*. Harmondsworth: Penguin.

Plummer, K. (2001) *Documents of Life-2: An Invitation to a Critical Humanism*, London: Sage.

Plummer, K. (2003) *Intimate Citizenship*, Seattle, WA: University of Washington Press.

Plummer, K. and Nehring, D. (2011) *The Introductory Sociology Reader and Resource*, Harlow: Pearson.

Popper, K. (1948) 'Utopia and Violence', *Hibbert Journal* vol. 46, pp 109-16.

Popper, K. (2002 [1957]) *The Poverty of Historicism*, London: Routledge.

Putnam, D. R. (2000) *Bowling Alone: The Collapse and Revival of American Community*, New York: Simon and Schuster.

Ricoeur, P. (1981) *Hermeneutics and the Human Sciences*, Cambridge, Cambridge Univeriaty Ptres.

Riesman, D. (2001 [1950]) *The Lonely Crowd*, New Haven, CT: Yale University Press.

Rigney, D. (2001) *The Metaphorical Society: An Invitation to Social Theory*, Boulder, CO: Rowman & Littlefield.

Ritzer G. (2007) *Encyclopaedia of Sociology*, Oxford: Blackwell.

Ritzer, G. (2007) *The McDonaldization of Society*, 5th edn, Thousand Oaks, CA: Pine Forge Press.

Rousseau, J.-J. (2008 [1762]) *The Social Contract*, Oxford: Oxford University Press.

Rousseau, J.-J. (2009 [1754]) *Discourse on the Origin of Inequality*, Oxford: Oxford University Press.

Said, E. (2003 [1978]) *Orientalism,* Harmondsworth: Penguin Classics.

Sandel, M. J. (2009) *Justice: What's The Right Thing To Do?* London: Allen Lane.

Sassen, S. (2006) *Cities in a World Economy*, Thousand Oaks, CA: Pine Forge Press.

Sassen, S. (2006) *Territory, Authority, Rights: From Medieval to Global Assemblages*, Princeton, NJ: Princeton University Press.

Scott, J. (2006a) *Social Theory: Central Issues in Sociology*, London: Sage.

Scott, J. (2006b) *Sociology: The Key Concepts*, London: Routledge.

Scott, J. (2007) *Sociology: Fifty Key Sociologists*, London: Routledge.

Scott, J. and Marshall, G. (2009) *Oxford Dictionary of Sociology*, 4th edn, Oxford: Oxford University Press.

Seidman, S. (2008) *Contested Knowledge: Social Theory Today*, 3rd edn, Oxford: Blackwell.

Shakespeare, W. (2007) *Complete Works,* ed Jonathan Bate and Eric Rasmussen, Basingstoke: Macmillan.

Shaw, C. (1966 [1930]) *The Jack-Roller: A Delinquent Boy's Own Story*, Chicago, IL: The University of Chicago Press.

Sica, A. (2006) *The Disobedient Generation: Social Theorists in the Sixties*, Chicago, IL: University of Chicago Press.

Simmel, G. (1971 [1908]) 'How is Society Possible?', in D. Levine (ed.) *Georg Simmel on Individuality and Social Forms*, Chicago, IL: University of Chicago Press.

Skeggs, B. (1997) *Formations of Class and Gender*, London: Sage.

Smith, A. (2008 [1776]) *The Wealth of the Nations*, Oxford: Oxford University Press.

Smith, A. (2009) *The Cultural Foundations of Nations*, Oxford: Blackwell.

Smith, D. E. (1998) *Writing the Social: Critique, Theory and Investigations*, Toronto: University of Toronto

Smith, G. (2007) *Erving Goffman*, London: Routledge.

Stanley, L. and Wise, S. (1983) *Breaking Out Again: Feminist Ontology and Epistemology*, London: Routledge.

Stevenson, N. (2003) *Cultural Citizenship*: *Cosmpolitan Questions,* Milton Keynes: Open University Press.

Stones, R. (2008) *Key Sociological Thinkers,* 2nd edn, Basingstoke: Palgrave.

Sullivan, N. (2003) *A Critical Introduction to Queer Theory*, Edinburgh: University of Edinburgh Press.

Swingewood, A. (2000) *A Short History of Sociological Thought*, London: Macmillan.

Taleb, N. (2008) *The Black Swan: The Impact of the Highly Improbable*, London: Penguin.

Taylor, C. (1994) *Multiculturalism: Examining the Politics of Recognition*, Princeton, NJ: Princeton University Press.

Taylor, C. (2007) A *Secular Age*, Cambridge, MA: Harvard University Press.

Therborn, G. (2004) *Between Sex and Power: Family in the World 1900–2000*, London: Routledge.

Therborn, G. (2006) *Inequalities of the World: New Theoretical Frameworks, Multiple Empirical Approaches*, London: Verso.

Thomas. W. I. (1966) *Social Organization and Social Personality*. Chicago, IL: University of Chicago Press.

Tilley, C. (2004) *Social Movements: 1768-2004*, New York: Paradigm.

Tong, R. (2008) *Feminist Thought*, 3rd edn, Boulder, CO: Westview.

Tönnies, F. (2003 [1887]) *Community and Society*, London: Dover Publications.

Turnbull, C. (1984) *The Human Cycle*, New York: Simon and Schuster.

Turner, B. S. (2006) *Dictionary of Sociology,* Cambridge: Cambridge University Press.

Turner, B. S. (2008) *The Body and Society: Explorations in Social Theory*, London: Sage.

United Nations (2009) *Human Development Report 2009*, Basingtoke, Palgrave Macmillan (published annually).

Urry, J. (2000) *Sociology Beyond Societies: Mobilities for the Twenty-First Century*, London: Routledge.

Urry, J. (2007) *Mobilities*, Cambridge: Polity.

Wacquant, L. (2008) *Urban Outcasts: A Comparative Sociology of Advanced Marginality*, Cambridge: Polity.

Walby, S. (2009) *Globalization and Inequalities: Complexities and Contested Modernities*, London, Sage.

Wallerstein, I. (1999) *The End of the World as We Know it*, Minneapolis, MN: University of Minnesota Press.

Weber, M. (1978) *Economy and Society,* ed G. Roth and C. Wittich, Berkeley, CA: University of California Press.

Weber, M. (2001) *The Protestant Ethic and the Spirit of Capitalism,* London: Routledge.

Weeks, J. (2009) *Sexuality*, 3rd edn, London: Routledge.

Wilkinson, I. (2005) *Suffering: A Sociological Introduction*, Cambridge: Polity Press.

Wilkinson, R. and Pickett, K. (2009) *The Spirit Level: Why More Equal Societies Almost Always Do Better*, London: Allen Lane.

Williams, R. (1989) *Resources of Hope: Culture, Democracy, Socialism.* London: Verso.

Willis, P. (1978) *Learning to Labour,* Farnham: Ashgate.

Winant, H. (2004) *The New Politics of Race: Globalism, Justice, Difference*, Minneapolis, MN: University of Minnesota Press.

Winch, P. and Gaita, R. (2007) *The Idea of a Social Science and Its Relation to Philosophy*, London: Routledge.

Wolfe, A. (1998) *Marginalized in the Middle*, Chicago, IL: University of Chicago Press.

Young, I. M. (1990) *Justice and the Politics of Difference*, Princeton, NJ: Princeton University Press.

Young, R. J. C. (2003) *Postcolonialism*, Oxford: Oxford University.

Zuckerman, P. (2003) *Invitation to the Sociology of Religion,* New York: Routledge.

# INDEX